# TWO LITTLE BOYS

Dedicated to Edward O'Neill Snr and all the other people
murdered and injured on 17 May 1974
in what is known as
The Dublin & Monaghan Bombings.

# Two Little Boys

## An account of the Dublin & Monaghan Bombings and their Aftermath

Edward O'Neill
with Barry J. Whyte

CURRACH PRESS

First published in 2004 by
CURRACH PRESS
55A Spruce Avenue, Stillorgan Industrial Park, Blackrock, Co Dublin

www.currach.ie


Cover by Liam Furlong of Space Design
Origination by Currach Press
Printed in Ireland by Betaprint Ltd, Dublin


ISBN 1-85607-909-0

*Acknowledgements*

The authors and publisher gratefully acknowledge the permission of the following to use material in their copyright: the Oireachtas Joint Committee on Justice, Equality, Defence and Women's Rights for excerpts from the *Report of the Independent Commission of Inquiry into the Dublin and Monaghan Bombings*, and *The Irish Times* for excerpts from an article by Dr Garret FitzGerald on 20 December 2003.

Every effort has been made to trace copyright holders. If we have inadvertently used copyright material without permission we apologise and will put it right in future editions.

Edward O'Neill would like to thank: My wife, Sandra, and children, Edward Jnr and Evan; My family – Martha, Billy, Niall, Denise and Angela; The 'Dream Team': Desmond J Doherty, Michael Mansfield QC, Eoin McGonigal SC and Miriam Reilly BL.

Barry J. Whyte would like to thank: My family – Phil, Paddy, Sean and Jim; Gillian; and all my friends.

Edward and Barry would like to thank the following: Don Mullan; John and Bernie Bergin; Liam O'Sullivan; Brian Lynch; William B. Devine; Emer Ryan; Áine Grealy; Nora Comiskey; Glyn Middleton; Denis Lawlor; Margaret Urwin; Joe Murray of AFrI; and Donal Griffin.

# CONTENTS

Foreword 7

Prologue 9

Introduction 13

Day of the Bombings 33

Media Reaction 49

Dominick Street to Portland Court 66

Eddie O'Neill 76

Getting Started 96

Hidden Hand 114

Justice for the Forgotten 137

The Barron Inquiry 175

Aftermath of the Barron Report 204

List of Those Killed in the Bombings 216

Bibliography 218

Index 220

# FOREWORD

This is truly a chronicle of our time. A testament to how strength born out of adversity can provide hope and force change. Not the strength of super-humans, but of ordinary people propelled by a deep and abiding sense of injustice. Their struggle involves commitment, persistence, stamina and often bitter disappointment. It could happen to any one of us, and what they do is on behalf of us all. Without stories like this one, the human condition would be both poorer and weaker.

What is demonstrated in page after page of compelling writing is that the quality of life is underpinned in large measure by truth and justice. Wherever a disaster is suffered, inevitable questions are on everyone's lips. How? Who? Why? However unpalatable the answers, people must be convinced that they have reached the bottom of it. They must be reconciled with the past before the present and the future can be infused with meaning. Martin Luther King's motto was 'There can be no peace without justice.' In the context of these events, peace is not just the absence of violence, but peace of mind. Justice is not merely the potential prosecution of the perpetrators but the restoration of public confidence that those who exercise the power of justice are acting responsibly and equably. It was a recognition of all these needs that led to the establishment of the Truth and Reconciliation Commission at the birth of a new South Africa under Nelson Mandela. It was similar concerns in the wake of the Lawrence Inquiry in England that led myself and others to create a National Civil Rights Movement, principally for the benefit of victims and their families.

Unfortunately all families, all civilians, especially in urban areas, are now only too conscious on a daily basis of the risk that a seemingly normal day, an habitual or humdrum moment, can be shattered permanently in seconds by an explosion. No one reading these words can be unaware of the ramifications of 9/11, of Bali, of Basra and Baghdad, of Gaza, and of Madrid. The concept of the global village described by Marshall McLuhan ensures that we have the information instantaneously.

Yet the explosions described so graphically in this book, constituting as they do the single largest peacetime attack on a civilian population within the islands of Ireland and Great Britain, are barely remembered and barely referred to. Unlike 9/11 and Madrid there was no national day of mourning, attended by the great and the good from all over the world. Unlike Bloody Sunday, as stated by Bishop Edward Daly, not even a Widgery. It was 25 years before the Taoiseach would even agree to meet the families and survivors in 1999.

The authors expose why – and it is a blot on the landscape of British and Irish democracy. They do so not through words of rhetoric but through the prism of personal experience. This is vital. The impact of current information technology, of continuous news channels, of a sound-byte culture, is to dehumanise, to anaesthetise our senses and retard our responses. As the authors put it at the beginning of Chapter 4, colour must be put back into an anonymous gray world in the way Spielberg employs the colour red in *Schindler's List* to bring home individuality.

Ed O'Neill was only four when he witnessed the murder of his father. He was blown across the road, and was lucky to survive. The scars, the shrapnel have been carried by him ever since. His mother was pregnant at the time. The baby was stillborn – the thirty-fifth death from the bombings – together with the hundreds of injured. It is not surprising, and certainly refreshing, to read a narrative imbued with passion, anguish, sorrow and anger but most of all a tinge of humour.

The result is perhaps the most important achievement to date won by the families in the face of flawed investigation, obstruction, delays, obfuscation and hostility – recognition by the authorities, at long last, that justice in this instance can only be satisfied by a properly constituted public inquiry under the Tribunal of Inquiries Act 1921 [Oireachtas Joint Committee on Justice – Final Report p.76] March 2004.

Michael Mansfield QC
London, April 2004

# PROLOGUE

*'The true cost of these atrocities in human terms is incalculable. In addition to the loss of innocent lives, hundreds more were scarred by physical and emotional injuries. The full story of suffering will never be known, and it is ongoing in many cases. There are those who, to this day, are marked by injuries and illnesses caused by the bombings.'*

Mr Justice Henry Barron

On 10 December 1999 the government established an inquiry under Chief Justice Liam Hamilton (later replaced by Mr Justice Henry Barron) to 'undertake a thorough examination, involving fact finding and assessment of all aspects of the Dublin, Monaghan and Dundalk bombings in 1974.'

The report of that inquiry was to be given to a Joint Oireachtas Committee on Justice, Equality, Defence and Women's Rights.

The Committee would, according to its remit:

consider the Report of the Independent Commission of Inquiry into the Dublin and Monaghan bombings, and to report back to Dáil Éireann within three months concerning:

whether the Report of the Independent Commission of Inquiry into the Dublin and Monaghan bombings of 1974 addresses all of the issues covered in terms of:

- the lessons to be drawn and any actions to be taken in the

light of the Report, its findings and conclusions
- whether, having regard to the Report's findings, and following considerations with the Inquiry, a further public inquiry into any aspect of the Report would be required or fruitful.

Four years later, and more than three years overdue, the Report was issued and the Joint Oireachtas Committee was established.

The families could be excused for not being hopeful. Thirty years had elapsed since their loved ones had been killed and maimed. It had been more than a decade since the first stirrings of a campaign to see justice done for the murdered, injured and bereaved. Since then, successive governments had failed to provide those people with the one thing they wanted: justice.

They had been disappointed on many occasions in the past; it seemed to be an integral part of being involved in the Dublin and Monaghan bombings.

And when the Barron Report was issued, they were disappointed again. The judge had, in the words of many commentators, pulled his punch. Thirty years of precedent indicated that the next phase would provide the same result. But the disappointment was tempered by the hope, however faint, that when the Oireachtas Joint Committee on Justice, Equality, Defence and Women's Rights deliberated on the Barron Report they would live up to its name and finally put in place the means by which the families and injured would see justice done.

Needless to say, they were to be disappointed once more.

When, on 30 March 2004, the Joint Committee published its report, the families yet again saw an administration shirk its responsibility towards its citizens. The Joint Committee announced that it would be recommending that the government establish two statutory inquiries; one would investigate why the Garda investigation was wound down in 1974; the other would look into the loss of the Garda security files on the case.

With regard to the matter of the inquiry into the bombings themselves, the Joint Committee had recommended that, rather than urging the Irish government to establish a public inquiry and finally uncover what had lain covered for thirty years, they recommended that the Irish government should instead press the British government to do it in the UK.

Edward O'Neill had been seriously injured in the Parnell Street explosion. His brother Billy was also seriously injured and their father was killed. When the Joint Committee made its recommendations, Ed was stoical. Thirty years of disappointment had conditioned him to expect nothing from his government.

'The Oireachtas Committee report was deeply disappointing, but not altogether unexpected.'

'They just obfuscated and tried to shift the blame from them to the British [government]. What was the point in recommending a public inquiry in the UK or Northern Ireland when it is plain that [the British government] will never agree to an inquiry? I'm not angry about it, I'm just very disappointed in the people that we elected as our leaders.'

However, while they had failed to satisfy Ed O'Neill and the other families bereaved on 17 May 1974, they had inadvertently indicated one very important thing. They had shown that a fully constituted public inquiry into the bombings with cross-jurisdictional powers and the ability to compel witnesses to appear before it, 'the only manner in which the truth about the bombings could be properly investigated', was necessary.

In its remit it had been instructed to examine whether 'a further public inquiry into any aspect of the Report would be required or fruitful'. Clearly, since they had instructed that not one but three inquiries into matters relating to the bombings be established, they felt that a public inquiry into the bombings was indeed required or would in fact prove fruitful.

In recommending any action at all, they had indicated that, as per the terms of their remit, a public inquiry was required. By not recommending that the Irish government establish even one public inquiry, they had failed to take responsibility for a proper investigation into the bombings and had failed to fulfil their duty to the citizens of Ireland and the bereaved and injured of the Dublin and Monaghan bombings.

The two inquiries they had recommended to be held in this jurisdiction, 'the inquiry into the Garda investigation and the loss of Garda files relating to the investigation' would not be public inquiries but private ones. And the inquiry into the bombings themselves, according to the Joint Committee, was the responsibility of the British government to carry out within the UK. It was an infuriating decision but, as Edward O'Neill said, not completely unexpected.

Whether the British government is willing to set up an inquiry into the Dublin and Monaghan bombings or not is a matter for the future. All that can be said now is that the Irish government, once again, has let its citizens down.

# INTRODUCTION

*Background*

Since Queen Elizabeth I's concerted efforts to subdue the island of Ireland, followed by the Plantation of Ulster in 1609, under her successor, James I, there has been serious internecine conflict between Protestants and Catholics, and their various subdivisions, on the island. Ulster, the most difficult of provinces from a British perspective, was quite effectively broken, and the loose amalgam of clan leaders who came together to defend their homeland fled to the continent. With no opposition, the Crown divided up the land and parcelled it out to loyal colonists from Britain.

For most of the following two centuries, Ulster was docile and loyal, while the rest of the country revolted spasmodically. Every insurrection failed, and many were hardly worthy of the name. However, around 1880, a movement arose which sought Home Rule for Ireland. This would afford the island a limited form of self-government. The movement had been started in a parliamentary setting, with Isaac Butt being its first champion. Previous independence campaigns had not been as split along religious lines as we now suppose they would be. The movement for Home Rule was the first in which Ulster Protestants and others disagreed. So, in 1880, Ulster Protestants in particular began to prepare to resist this new and, to them, frightening move to weaken Ireland's union with Britain (enshrined in the 1800 Act of Union). The conflict as we now know it began in earnest.

The Home Rule movement provided no actual violence and no battle was fought, but it was the first time either side got a chance to rattle sabres. The Home Rule Bill was a long time in gestation. Many other important events were taking place at the same time, most significantly the settling of the age-old issue of land and land ownership in Ireland. It was more than thirty years after the establishment of the Home Rule movement before a Home Rule Bill was even drawn up, and many careers had been ruined along the way. William Ewart Gladstone's support for Home Rule brought down his government and forever destroyed his party. Charles Stewart Parnell, who picked up where Isaac Butt had left off, went from holding the balance of power in the House of Commons and being considered by his many supporters as the Uncrowned King of Ireland, to dying a wretched and broken man. The only person left to fight for Home Rule was the leader of the Nationalist Party, John Redmond, who had little stomach for the fight that Parnell had begun.

The decisive moment in the campaign was the First World War. The British government had promised to introduce Home Rule and had even written up a Home Rule Bill, but with the outbreak of war, the idea was shelved. By the time the war had ended, things had changed utterly.

In 1916, a group of revolutionaries staged an uprising centred mainly in Dublin and its environs. The planning of the uprising had been dogged by difficulties from the start, not least the seeming desire of one of its principle organisers, Pádraig Pearse, to follow in the footsteps of generations of Irish revolutionaries who had died for their country in a glorious blood sacrifice — as opposed to staging a successful attempt to overthrow British rule in Ireland.

The Irish people seemed either to have forgotten about Home Rule or to have put complete faith in the British government to deliver it as soon as the war was over. In any case, the 1916 Rising, as it became known, was not a success. The people of Dublin were outraged at the destruction wreaked on their city, and the British army easily defeated the badly organised and badly positioned insurrectionists. It wasn't until the British executed the leaders of the insurrection that public opinion in Ireland changed. The executions were heavy handed, particularly the killing of trade union leader James Connolly whose injuries were so bad that he couldn't stand and was instead tied to a chair and shot. It was this that re-ignited in Ireland the debate over independence.

Those who had taken part in the Rising, among them Eamon de Valera and Michael Collins, began to organise a new movement towards independence. Meanwhile in Ulster, unionists William Carson and James Craig began to organise their supporters in opposition to any move towards Irish independence. An Anglo-Irish war, organised mainly by Collins, ensued, and the nationalist Irish forced the British government to come up with an answer to the so-called Irish Question. It would not be possible to satisfy everyone on the island. The only answer seemed to be, like that proposed by Solomon, to cut the country in two.

The treaty which followed the negotiations between the Irish and the British gave rise to the Government of Ireland Act, 1920. From six of the eight counties in Ulster would be created the statelet of Northern Ireland, and from the rest of the island would be created the Irish Free State. This partition of the country still affects party politics on both sides of the border.

Both statelets were to have a certain degree of independence on domestic issues within the union, but under Eamon de Valera's Fianna Fáil party, the Free State began to sever its ties with Britain and eventually (under a Fine Gael government in 1949) was declared a republic.

While the Irish Free State metamorphosed into Éire and took on a definite Roman Catholic aspect, Northern Catholics were a powerless minority. Northern Ireland was a segregated society, with the Protestant Ulster Unionist Party permanently in government.

As time passed, the will to erase the border and reunite the country waned. Only a very few dedicated to the cause of unity continued to talk about, and ask for, a thirty-two county republic. No one acted upon that desire until in 1956 the IRA, which had fought the Anglo-Irish war but had been split by the treaty talks afterwards, began a border campaign, with the intention of ending partition and uniting Ireland once more. The campaign led only to the introduction of internment and the further maltreatment of Catholics in Northern Ireland. In 1962, with its reputation in tatters, the IRA was forced to abandon the campaign.

In 1963, Terence O'Neill was elected Prime Minister of Northern Ireland and began a series of conciliatory meetings with Irish Taoiseach Sean Lemass. O'Neill was widely criticised by unionists for betraying them and putting the union with Britain in danger.

Instead of improving relations between the Republic and Northern Ireland, these talks incensed unionists, and political and religious conflict continued to smoulder. The spark that would ignite the incipient civil war would be the issue of housing. Housing lists (the means by which council housing was allocated in Northern Ireland) had always been weighted in favour of Protestant families, with Catholic families, although traditionally larger, being forced to live together in small houses with many generations under the same roof.

In 1967, the Northern Ireland Civil Rights Association (NICRA) was founded, with the aim of making Northern Ireland a more equitable place for Catholics. Its aims were the removal of discrimination in jobs, the removal of permanent emergency legislation (the legislation which allowed for internment), the ending of electoral abuses (such as gerrymandering, a process by which electoral borders would be redrawn in order to ensure a unionist majority, thereby securing a seat for the unionist politician in that area), and equality in housing.

In 1968, Austin Currie, a nationalist politician, held a sit-in at a house in Dungannon where a Catholic family was being evicted to make way for a young Protestant woman who worked for the local unionist MP. The NICRA organised the first civil rights march in Northern Ireland, from Coalisland to Dungannon, to protest at the treatment of the Catholic family that was being evicted. Civil rights marches were soon being organised all over Northern Ireland, and the Royal Ulster Constabulary (RUC) was beginning to take a more violent approach to them. In Derry, a march was broken up by baton charges, and riots ensued.

Tension was mounting in Northern Ireland. Nationalist Party members, who had resigned their positions in the Stormont Assembly (Northern Ireland parliament) over the violent treatment of peaceful protesters, began a policy of civil disobedience. O'Neill's hand had been forced and he introduced a five-point plan, consisting of housing reform, an end to company votes in council elections, the introduction of an Ombudsman, a review of the Special Powers Act, and a Londonderry Development Commission. It was quickly followed by a vote of confidence as many in the Unionist Party believed that he was conceding too much to nationalists, and would eventually condone a united Ireland. He won the vote, but only just.

In January 1969, with civil violence and police brutality spiralling out of control all over the statelet, and Derry almost a no-go area, British Prime Minister Harold Wilson, of the Labour Party, began to suggest that the British would have to take a direct hand in Northern Ireland. By this stage, O'Neill's leadership was being continually questioned, and a group of twelve unionist MPs had signed a document calling for a change of leadership.

In the general election of that year, unionists increased their majority, and O'Neill managed to hold onto power. However, on the streets, things were taking an even more violent turn. Loyalist extremists began to bomb electricity sub-stations and water installation plants, and civil rights marches continued to end in serious rioting. On 25 April, after more bombings by extremists, 500 British troops were sent to aid the RUC. Members of the police force were now being allowed to carry firearms — the first time since the IRA border campaign had ended in 1965. Three days later, Terence O'Neill resigned and was replaced by Major James Chichester-Clarke.

In November 1969, the Electoral Law Act was introduced and, in early 1970, the nationalist and republican Sinn Féin party split over the issue of abstention. The split, into the Officials and the Provisionals, mirrored the IRA split months earlier. Official Sinn Féin would eventually go back into parliament, while Provisional Sinn Féin continued its policy of refusing to acknowledge the legitimacy of the Stormont government.

In June 1971, TDs Neil Blaney and Charles Haughey were sacked from government in the Republic of Ireland, by Taoiseach Jack Lynch, over allegations that they had sent arms to help Republican paramilitaries in Northern Ireland.

In August of the same year, only a month after all marches in Northern Ireland had been banned, the Social and Democratic Labour Party (SDLP) was formed under the leadership of Gerry Fitt. At the same time, volunteer reservists, known as the B-Specials, were coming into more conflict with the Catholic population, and Chichester-Clarke was forced to call in British troops to patrol the streets.

In an early example of what would later become known as 'ethnic cleansing', an estimated 7,000 Catholics were said to have moved to the Republic of Ireland. However, gun running by members of the government aside, the Republic seemed to have no official interest in the troubles in Northern Ireland.

In January 1972, thirteen men were shot dead by the British army during a civil rights march in Derry. Bloody Sunday, as it became known, was the catalyst for the IRA to escalate its activities, as hundreds of new recruits clamoured to join. In July, nine people were killed in a highly organised bombing campaign in Belfast, in which thirty devices were exploded by the Provisional IRA.

The following year, a British government White Paper proposed a proportionally elected assembly for domestic affairs in Northern Ireland. London, meanwhile, would retain control of external affairs. Essentially it was a form of Home Rule, more than half a century after the original Bill had been shelved. The White Paper, 'Northern Ireland Constitutional Proposals', proposed a number of measures, the aim of which was to bring about a fair distribution of power in Northern Ireland and to end the burgeoning Troubles. It proposed, among other things, a new government for Northern Ireland, under the control of the British Secretary of State. This government would be elected by proportional representation and would have a power-sharing executive. The White Paper also proposed a Council of Ireland, in which politicians from the Republic and politicians from Northern Ireland would consult on issues of mutual and collective interest. This Council would be set up on the understanding that the Irish government would finally recognise the status of Northern Ireland within the UK. Since the inception of the six-county statelet in 1921, the government of the Irish Free State followed by that of the Republic of Ireland had refused to recognise its legitimacy. The Irish constitution, drawn up by Eamon de Valera, laid territorial claim to the six counties of Northern Ireland as part of the Republic.

The Council of Ireland was a major stumbling block for Ulster unionism. While the Ulster Unionist Party (UUP) refused to make a clear statement on it, more hardline unionists declared themselves violently opposed to it, seeing it as one step on the road to Dublin rule. The Vanguard Unionist Party was set up as a paramilitary body willing to fight against the setting up of this power-sharing executive, and declared itself ready to 'liquidate the enemy' should any attempts be made to pass the legislation. It began to achieve results when, after elections to the assembly, only twenty-four pro-White Paper unionists were elected, as opposed to twenty-six anti-White Paper unionists. Brian Faulkner's UUP pro-White Paper minority joined with the SDLP and the Alliance Party to form an executive. The power-sharing executive was set up on 22 November 1973, with Brian Faulkner as leader, and Gerry Fitt of the SDLP as deputy leader.

With the Assembly and Executive established, the Irish and British governments began to debate the ancillary issues, such as the Council of Ireland and the reform of the RUC. The result of these talks was the Sunningdale Agreement, the main points of which were:

1  A Council of Ireland to be established. This council would be concerned with economic and social co-operation, and would comprise members from both the Irish parliament (Dáil) and the Northern Ireland Assembly;

2  Reform of the mainly Protestant RUC;

3  A review of security measures (such as the internment of suspected terrorists without trial, a policy that had seen many innocent Catholics imprisoned without recourse to normal police and judicial procedure).

The Ulster Unionist Council rejected the Sunningdale Agreement, and Brian Faulkner was forced to resign from the party, to be replaced by the hardline, anti-Sunningdale Harry West. Faulkner continued in his capacity as leader of the Assembly, with a new party, the Unionist Party of Northern Ireland, but his position was becoming precarious. A British general election all but sealed his fate.

Faulkner's new party was ill-equipped to fight a general election, a weakness exacerbated by the conspiracy among anti-Sunningdale unionists not to run against each other in Westminster constituencies where they would normally be in opposition, thereby strengthening anti-Sunningdale unionist numbers in the Assembly. The Sunningdale Agreement was looking less and less safe. Only one pro-Sunningdale unionist won a seat, with the other eleven going to the United Ulster Unionist Council (UUUC). The British Labour Party won the election, with Harold Wilson as Prime Minister; Merlyn Rees was appointed Secretary of State for Northern Ireland.

The UUUC, after a conference in Antrim in 1974, stated its opposition to the Sunningdale Agreement and called for it to be scrapped. In order to ensure the death of the agreement, they used the Ulster Workers' Council, which had been established the previous year. On 15 May 1974, two days before the planting by loyalists of three car-bombs in Dublin and one in Monaghan, the UWC began its general strike. It used its considerable support from loyalist paramilitary groups, such as the Ulster Defence Association (UDA) and Ulster Volunteer Force (UVF), to intimidate anyone who didn't support the strike, and, for three days, Northern Ireland was crippled. It was believed that MI5 was also supporting the strike.

⌘　⌘　⌘

In 1972, the Fianna Fáil government, under Taoiseach Jack Lynch, was proposing a Bill called the Offences Against the State (Amendment) Act. The Bill proposed tougher new legislation to deal with both republican and loyalist paramilitaries in Ireland. Until then, suspected paramilitaries had been tried in ordinary courts where intimidation was rife. The government of the day felt that too many terrorists were avoiding justice. Something had to be done. The then Minister for Justice, Des O'Malley, proposed the new Bill, which stated that 'where an officer of the Garda Síochána, not below the rank of Chief Superintendent, in giving evidence on proceedings relating to an offence … states that he believes that the accused was at a material time a member of an unlawful organisation, the statement shall be evidence that he was then such a member.' It seemed to many to be uncomfortably close to internment, and met with huge opposition not least from civil liberties groups who denounced it for being draconian and for contravening civil rights at a time when they were being fought for so desperately by Catholics in Northern Ireland.

The opposition at the time was Fine Gael. Led by Liam Cosgrave, Fine Gael was a traditionally anti-republican party. And in Liam Cosgrave it had a traditionally anti-republican leader. He urged his colleagues either to support the Bill or, should they find they couldn't, at least to abstain from voting. The more liberal members of the party felt that they couldn't endorse the Bill on moral grounds. The more opportunistic in the party saw it as a chance to topple the government and bring in a Fine Gael/Labour coalition.

However, it was Fianna Fáil who held all the cards. Knowing that, were the Bill to be defeated, Fianna Fáil was in a better position to fight a general election than were Fine Gael or Labour, the government was in a win–win situation.

Cosgrave was in a bind. In supporting the Bill, he was saving the life of the government — something his colleagues would surely never stand for. Whether or not the Bill was passed, Fine Gael seemed to be headed for a new leader. The party was in turmoil and Cosgrave faced political death. It would take something huge to give him back his political career.

On 1 December 1972, just before the vote on the Bill, two bombs exploded in Dublin. The window panes in Leinster House rattled, and the TDs inside were shaken. As they sat stunned in their seats, word went around the chamber about what had happened. It was alleged that the IRA had exploded two bombs in Dublin city centre. The tide of the debate turned instantly. What had been a controversial and divisive Bill suddenly became a political necessity. Immediately Cosgrave had gone from being yesterday's man in Fine Gael and in politics to being the opinion leader in the party.

After an adjournment of an hour, the Dáil reconvened, and the Bill was endorsed by 69 votes to 22. Cosgrave managed not only to keep his seat but also to consolidate his power-base within the party. By the time the next general election came around, in February 1973, Fine Gael was in a much better position to fight it, and the party entered government with Labour, in a coalition which was to last until 1977.

The bombs had saved Cosgrave's political life, but they had taken the lives of two CIÉ employees. George Bradshaw, a bus driver, and Thomas Duffy, a conductor, were in the CIÉ Club on Earl Place. The first of the two bombs to explode that day went off outside the Liffey pub on Eden Quay, while the second went off in nearby Sackville Place. When the first bomb exploded, a young garda ran into the club and told everyone to evacuate the building. When Bradshaw and Duffy ran out, they ran straight into the explosion of the second bomb, which killed them both.

The news of the bombings which had filtered through Dáil chambers was followed by the allegation that the bombings had been the work of one of the wings of the IRA. However, this information was incorrect. As Don Mullan points out in his book, *The Dublin and Monaghan Bombings*, it would not have been politically expedient for the IRA to explode bombs in Dublin city while the Dáil was debating a Bill which would have detrimental effects on the IRA's own ability to work freely in the Republic. Both the Officials and the Provisionals soon denied responsibility. The IRA had not carried out the bombings.

That left only one other option. The Liffey bar was a known Sinn Féin haunt, and the party had just held its Árd Fheis in nearby Liberty Hall. It appeared far more likely that loyalist paramilitaries were responsible.

Seven weeks later, another bomb exploded in Sackville Place. This time, one man was killed — a Scottish conductor working for CIÉ. Loyalist paramilitaries were again blamed. But suspicions were raised. Previously, no one had believed that loyalist paramilitaries had the wherewithal to carry out such an audacious bombing raid. Conspiracy theorists in the country concluded that British security forces, in particular MI6, had taken a hand in the operation.

This was not unheard of. In 1973, two brothers, Kenneth and Keith Littlejohn, were caught in Britain and extradited back to Ireland for a litany of offences committed during their time in the country. Their list of crimes was extensive: bank robbery, fire-bombing and attacks on garda stations. In his book, *The Dirty War*, Martin Dillon makes the point that people recruited as undercover operatives are nothing like James Bond. Generally they are recruited because they are petty criminals capable of fitting into the seedy underbelly of any society. The Littlejohns seemed to be those kinds of characters. Kenneth had been a member of the British parachute regiment, but had been court-martialled and discharged for robbery. He spent his time out of the army in and out of prison for various offences. Kenneth had spent time in Ireland before returning to London and hooking up with his brother, where they claim they were recruited by British intelligence to carry out subversive activities in the Republic, for which the blame would be laid on the IRA, thereby causing a PR backlash against that organisation.

The brothers were sent to Co. Louth, a border area known for its republican activity. They made their presence and their support for republican ideals known there. Their known criminal pasts were the perfect cover for their roles. No one would suspect that someone who had been in prison and had robbed a bank at gunpoint would be a spy for British intelligence. Kenneth Littlejohn, though, wanted to live the life of the James Bond-type spy, and when he later relayed his stories back to journalists, he would beef them up to make his role seem more important than it actually was. While most of what he said could be taken with a pinch of salt, what is unquestionable is that the Littlejohn brothers were, in the words of Martin Dillon, 'with official sanction associating with terrorists and, as impeccable sources have confirmed, undertaking basic terrorist roles in the border areas of Newry and Dundalk.'

After a bank raid on Grafton Street, Dublin, in which the bank manager's family was held hostage and £67,000 stolen, the Littlejohns, with their accomplices, fled the country. They were caught in Britain and held in Brixton Prison while extradition proceedings were held. Their lawyer in Britain claimed that they could not be extradited because their crimes were of a political nature. They claimed to have been working for MI6 and the Secret Intelligence Services (SIS), and said that their handler had been a man called John Wyman a.k.a. Douglas Smyth.

Wyman had been operating in Dublin under a number of aliases, Douglas Smyth being one of them. He had stayed in the Burlington Hotel from where he ran a number of British intelligence agents who operated in the Republic. His contact was a sergeant from Garda Special Branch called Patrick Crinnion. At the end of 1972, as the Littlejohns were being extradited, Wyman got worried and tried to phone his man in Special Branch. Crinnion wasn't in at the time and the garda who took the call was suspicious of Wyman. Crinnion was put under surveillance, and both he and Wyman were soon caught. Both men were given sentences of only three months in prison, and both were released on good behaviour. According to Don Mullan, 'it was the quid pro quo for the extradition of the Littlejohn brothers.'

The Littlejohns were tried, and Kenneth received twenty years, while Keith received fifteen. Their part in the story was only a sidebar. The important discovery was that British intelligence had been found to have been operating within the Republic of Ireland.

*The Days Leading up to the Dublin and Monaghan Bombings*

In the days leading up to the planting of three car-bombs in Dublin and one in Monaghan, the tension on both sides of the border was high. On Wednesday 8 May, the IRA announced that British politicians were now official targets in their war. The announcement was provoked by a statement the previous day by the British army, in which it claimed that British soldiers had the right to shoot bombers dead even if those bombers were children. William Craig, leader of the Vanguard Unionist Party, said that sectarian killings were 'understandable and excusable if they were done to maintain the rule of law'.

This statement was made on the same day that an organisation to which Craig was closely connected, and an organisation which itself was closely connected to rather shady paramilitary bodies — the Ulster Workers' Council (UWC) — made a statement announcing that it would 'paralyse industry' if it had to, in order to kill any attempts at power-sharing between nationalists and unionists in Northern Ireland.

In a press conference on 14 May, the British government revealed that it had seized IRA plans to occupy much of Belfast forcibly, and to foment sectarian strife, thereby making it easier to take over and control the whole city. The plans were met with much scepticism, and many claimed that the whole thing was a fraud engineered by British security. Even Sammy Smyth, spokesman for the UDA, claimed that he didn't believe the British, and suggested that the plans had, in fact, been part of an elaborate SAS operation.

The IRA claimed that the plans were not, in fact, intended to start a civil war in Belfast but were, instead, defensive in nature, and designed to protect nationalist areas. Journalist Robert Fisk, who then wrote for *The Times*, had written almost two years previously:

> The Provisional and Official IRA have been holding informal talks on a local level in Belfast to plan a joint defence of Roman Catholic areas in the event of attack.

In Westminster, a ban on Sinn Féin and the UVF was lifted. According to Merlyn Rees, Secretary of State for Northern Ireland, the purpose of the order to lift the ban was 'to allow these organisations to take part in political action ... lifting the ban in no way condones violence.' Whatever the purpose of the lifting of the ban, it meant that as the UVF bombers drove across the border and on to Dublin on 17 May, they were secure in the knowledge that they were doing so as a fully legal and legitimate organisation.

As this was happening, Merlyn Rees flew into Dublin to meet with Irish Minister for Foreign Affairs Garret FitzGerald. The meeting, which took place under high security, was to discuss what was to be done about the situation in Northern Ireland where the first experiment in power sharing was slowly being strangled by intransigent unionists who had by now called their much-threatened general strike and were crippling industry and commerce.

*In the Republic*

On 17 May 1974, the Coras Iompar Éireann (CIÉ) bus drivers in Dublin were on strike over a management decision to change the number of days in the working week. The bus strike had been raging for weeks. The bus drivers were split between people who supported the decision to delay the planned switch to a five-day week, and those who did not. There was considerable bitterness between the factions and several different drivers' unions were involved. Newspapers of the day carried reports on the strike, which was having a considerable impact on normal life in the city. One even had a feature article on hitching lifts from strangers, a mode of transport that was, out of necessity, being used by many people living in the outlying suburban areas of Dublin.

As a result of the strike, there were no buses running in Dublin city on 17 May, and there were no long queues at any of the numerous bus stops in the city centre. At 5 p.m., quitting time in most offices in the city, people either left work and walked home or tried to make it in time for the overcrowded trains. By the time the bombs exploded, most people had already left for home, and were either packed onto a train or walking. It is cold comfort for the hundreds of families affected by the disaster, but that bus strike saved countless lives.

*Explosions*

On the morning of 17 May 1974, in the midst of one of the most significant periods of political activity in Northern Ireland's history, a group of loyalist paramilitaries from the UVF set off on a deadly mission to bomb the Republic. They stole four cars, three of which would be used to bomb the city of Dublin, and one of which would be used to bomb the town of Monaghan, thereby causing a diversion that would allow them to slip over the border unnoticed after their murderous deeds had been carried out.

Led by Billy Hanna, a member of the Ulster Defence Regiment (UDR) and a Korean War veteran from Co. Armagh, the group included some of Northern Ireland's most infamous killers. Robin Jackson, known for years as 'The Jackal' because his real name could not be printed for legal reasons, was a psychopathic mass-murderer who found a niche for himself in the Northern Troubles. Wesley Sommerville and Harris Boyle were members of the gang that, the following year, would slaughter the pop group, 'The Miami Showband', as the musicians returned from a gig in Belfast.

The UVF men made their way across the border and down to Dublin and, just before 5 p.m., parked their cars and left them. According to contemporary newspaper reports, the first bomb exploded at 5.27 p.m. on Parnell Street, just beside Conor Cruise O'Brien TD's Department of Posts and Telegraphs. Two of his own employees, Patrick Fay and Anne Marren, were killed instantly in the blast. As the dust was settling on Parnell Street, a bomb exploded outside Guiney's department store on nearby Talbot Street. Then the third bomb exploded, across the river on South Leinster Street, right beside Trinity College and within a few hundred yards of the seat of Irish government, Leinster House. It was not yet 5.30 p.m.

An *Irish Times* reporter described the scene in vivid detail.

Parnell Street, with small shops and working class folk had pathetic heart breaking reminders; the bodies and the maimed had been rushed off in ambulances by 5.45pm but the terrible smell of death could not be so easily erased.

There littering the roadway with the debris of smashed cars and the broken glass were the personal paraphernalia of the dead and injured, shoes, scarves, coats, shopping bags, even a bag of chips.

Women were crying because they heard that one of their children or a relative had been taken away to hospital. Some were demented with grief and I heard one woman say in a sobbing voice 'He'll never be back.' In the confused and chaotic situation it was not easy to be a comforter.

Little pools of blood splattered the roadway and the upholstery of one wrecked car was badly stained.

In the *Belfast Telegraph*, Alan Watson noticed the difference between the aftermath of the bombings in Dublin and the aftermath of any bombing he had seen in Belfast. Dublin, suffering the worst atrocity of the bombings, was stunned and seemingly paralysed, while in Belfast the atmosphere was always one of resilience and determination.

Like so many events in Ireland the terrible story of last night's murderous bombings will be handed down from father to son, from mother to daughter for many years to come.

But in Dublin this morning few people had the courage or the will to talk of 'our Bloody Friday'.

I walked the devastated Talbot Street the morning after the bombing where seven people died and dozens were mutilated in a split second of searing terror. The people, like the buildings, had all expressions wiped from their faces. The gutters, which last night ran with the blood of Irish people, were damp and ugly.

## IN CONTRAST

I had strolled down part of this very same street last Saturday night during a weekend in the city. Young couples laughed and the sound of horse-play echoed between the walls.

Seven days had passed and what a difference they had made. I thought last Saturday of how lucky the people down here were with their crowded streets and occasional drunk — such a contrast to the stark nightly tension of downtown Belfast.

But now that had changed. How long would it be, if ever, before the people of Dublin could forget the sight of limbless bodies strewn amid the rubble of Guiney's?

A young girl in O'Connell St. became ashen faced when she saw the title of the Carlton Cinema's feature film 'Horror Hospital'.

## HORRIBLE SCENES

Nobody I spoke to really wanted to put the blame for the slaughter on anyone. An ex-army man said he had to agree with what the Taoiseach said last night — anyone who practised or preached or condoned violence must bear a share of responsibility for the outrages.

'I was here last night,' he said. 'I will never forget the horrible scenes; women and children — and men — were wailing.'

'I was just around the corner at the Labour Exchange and I got here in seconds. I thought it was the end of the world — and I don't think much different this morning.'

## IN A DAZE

He and others who hung silent over the barriers stared at the street where rush hour became death hour. Dozens of evening newspapers which had been used to cover the torn and bleeding bodies lay sodden on the pavement.

Shop workers knocked out their shattered windows — but they did it in a daze, so unlike the 'we'll work on' spirit of Belfast in 1974. This was Ireland's worst single atrocity and the mood of the people reflected it.

I had never known it here like I had known Belfast, Derry or Armagh — fear lurked in every door.

Unfortunately, Watson vastly overestimates the public's capacity to remember their own tragedies.

*Aftermath*

After the bombings, the government reaction was, to say the least, confusing.

In early statements, it blamed the IRA for having what Liam Cosgrave and Attorney General Declan Costello described as 'moral responsibility' for the bombings. That phrase and the idea it described would continue to crop up in newspaper reports for days afterwards. No form of blame, however, was ever attached to loyalist paramilitaries, although they too had a significant part in the internecine war raging in Northern Ireland at the time, and in spite of the overwhelming evidence that some loyalist group had indeed carried out the bombings. The Garda Síochána knew within weeks that the UVF had carried out the bombings, and early newspaper reports stated clearly that loyalist paramilitaries had been responsible. The press soon dropped this line as the campaign to assign moral responsibility to the IRA gained momentum, and the garda information was never released or acted upon.

After the bombings, the immediate reaction of the government was not to rush to help the victims but to condemn the IRA. They used the opportunity to arrange mass arrests of any known republicans south of the border, and to intern them without trial in the military prison in the Curragh Camp. Plans began to be considered for a separate wing in Portlaoise Prison to deal with republican prisoners (a measure that was indeed carried out soon after), while soldiers were ordered home from abroad to patrol the border — firmly bolting the stable door.

It is more than a little odd that the most effective measures taken by the Irish government in the wake of the bombings were not to find the perpetrators of the largest loss of life on Irish soil since the death of forty-six people in an accidental German raid on Dublin's North Strand during the Second World War, but to use the opportunity to arrest men involved in the republican movement — men who were entirely innocent of the bombings.

Cosgrave formed a Cabinet Security Committee consisting of Conor Cruise O'Brien (who, along with losing two members of his department in the bombings, had almost lost his daughter who had been seconds away from walking out onto South Leinster Street from a gate at the rear of Trinity College); Paddy Cooney, the Minister for Justice; Paddy Donegan, the Minster for Defence; and Jim Tully, the Minister for Local Government. The purpose of this committee seems to have been not the organisation of the investigation or the pursuit of the truth in an incident which right from the start looked murky and problematic, but rather the initiation of a campaign of covering up the real blame for the bombings. The building of a wing in Portlaoise Prison to deal with republican prisoners seems to have been the only political legacy of the events of 17 May 1974, as neither that government nor any subsequent government has ever adequately dealt with the matter of the bombings. However, in the weeks after the atrocity, so much confusion arose from statements made by members of the cabinet that the truth has never fully emerged.

Prior to the bombings, there had been other incidents in Dublin in which British intelligence involvement was suspected. In 1972, a bomb had exploded on Kildare Street while the Dáil was debating a new special powers bill to deal with republican paramilitaries. The responsibility for the bomb was laid on the IRA, and the bill was enacted. It later turned out that the bomb was planted not by the IRA, but in fact by elements of the British security forces (including MI5 and the SAS) who were in Dublin at the time.

There was no day of mourning for the victims of the bombings. The government refused to have one, saying that there had already been 1,000 victims of the Troubles. This decision suggested that the greatest single atrocity of the Troubles, and the largest mass murder on Irish soil, did not warrant a day of mourning, because it might have offended those who had already lost loved ones or been injured by previous bombings. It would be echoed many years later when the Taoiseach, at that time Fianna Fáil's Albert Reynolds, refused to erect any sort of commemorative monument for the victims of the bombings, saying that it would be 'invidious' to single out any one atrocity for special attention.

In the Dáil, the bombings were a political issue for the months of May and June. Politicians soon began to lose interest in the whole issue, however, and, after June 1974, the number of related questions being asked in the Dáil had declined substantially. The investigation had not been officially closed — it had been mothballed. Forensic material had vanished, with some going to the Dublin county dump and some going to the RUC forensics lab from which it would never return.

The RUC was doing less than its level best to uncover the truth, as discussed by Don Mullan in his book, *The Dublin and Monaghan Bombings*. Mullan deals with just one example of this — the interviewing of William Henry whose taxi had been hijacked and used in the bombings. The RUC officers who interviewed Mr Henry left glaring omissions in their questioning, failing to ask him even for a proper description of the men who had abducted him. In his own research into the Garda/RUC investigation, Mullan was thwarted at every opportunity, and bureaucratic red tape was used to prevent him from getting at the truth.

Within weeks, the Garda Síochána had names, addresses and photographs of the bombers and were intimately aware of how the bomb-cars had been driven from Northern Ireland and parked in the four places in Dublin and Monaghan. They knew also that the men were members of the UVF. However, they could not interview the bombers, and had to pass the information on to the RUC, who did nothing with it. Many gardaí at the time believed that this was because of sectarianism in the RUC. It is undeniable that the RUC's inaction at this time prevented the investigation from making any headway and prevented the Garda Síochána from securing convictions. RUC investigators had themselves actually come to the same conclusions regarding the identity of the bombers, yet they failed to take any action on it. A *Sunday Independent* report from 26 May 1974, regarding the investigation on both sides of the border, quotes an unnamed but high-ranking garda involved in the bombings as saying:

> The trouble is that the ordinary rank and file of the RUC dare not make inquiries into the particular affair. They have their own sources of information inside the ranks of the UDA and UVF and UFF but any attempt to get information as to the men and/or women who came to Dublin to plant the bombs could well lead to the death of the policeman. Every turn these RUC men make they are afraid of being shot.

This contrasts starkly with the later evidence that the RUC had already made a full list of those who had been involved in the bombings. The RUC clearly had made the inquiries already. Why was this senior garda source involved in the investigation under the impression that the RUC had been afraid even to ask their sources in loyalist paramilitary circles? Was he told by the RUC that the information couldn't be obtained? Was he told to make people think that the information was harder to come by than it actually was? The Garda Síochána had not needed to risk the lives of its members to get the information. They had simply carried out basic police work, and within weeks had come up with a list of suspects.

The Northern UWC strike continued until 28 May, effectively killing the Sunningdale Agreement. While the UWC, under the control of elected MPs and paramilitaries, choked the life from democratic politics in Northern Ireland, their political masters in Westminster either couldn't or wouldn't do anything to stop them. Sunningdale lay dead. So did thirty-three people in Dublin and Monaghan. The former was remembered as the first experiment in power-sharing in Northern Ireland and the predecessor of the Good Friday Agreement that would come twenty-four years later. The latter were all but forgotten by official Ireland.

# DAY OF THE BOMBINGS

In the minutes before 5 p.m. on Friday 17 May 1974, in every factory, office and bank in Dublin city, employees were watching the time. The weather was warm and the weekend was on its way. The majority were probably thinking of how they would best spend those two short days off. Anyone who didn't have a car or hadn't already arranged some form of transport was more than likely considering how best to get home in the middle of the bus strike. All were watching the clock ticking towards quitting time. As Dublin's workers counted the minutes, three cars were being parked by a team of UVF volunteers, which had made its way across the border unnoticed; each car contained a massive bomb. No one in Dublin city but they and their accomplices knew anything about it. Certainly none of the employees knew any of this as they watched the hour hand chase the minute hand around the face of the clock.

At the same time, Billy and Edward O'Neill, seven and four years of age respectively, were on the balcony of their Dominick Street flat, fixing bikes. Like the workers of Dublin, neither Edward nor Billy had any idea of the terrible carnage and destruction that was about to be wreaked upon their city, or the devastation that would be unleashed in their lives.

Edward and Billy's father was out working with their uncle, his brother-in-law, for the day. Edward Senior, known as Eddie, had finished early and was on his way home to bring Billy to have his hair cut for his First Holy Communion. Martha, the boys' mother, was with their seven-year-old sister Angela, who was having her hair cut for her First Holy

Communion as well. Denise, their nine-year-old eldest sister, was looking after one-year-old Niall in their home.

May is First Holy Communion season in Ireland. In the 1970s, it was a time of great excitement for any family with a child being prepared to make theirs. This excitement was doubled for the O'Neill family because both Billy and Angela were First Communicants. Billy was to make his in the local church and would be taken there by his father, while Angela would make hers in the convent and would be accompanied by her mother.

Angela had been chosen to do a reading at her First Communion. The reading was to be from St Paul's epistles to the Corinthians, but Angela was having a little difficulty getting it just right. Every time her father put her up on the table in the middle of the room to practise her reading, she would instead say, 'A reading from St Paul's pistols' — much to his delight. He was particularly looking forward to hearing what she would come out with on the day itself.

There was to be a party in the house to celebrate the double First Communion. The party would also be a celebration for someone else in the family. It was Denise's birthday that day, and her birthday party and the Communion party were to be merged. The children, needless to say, were excited.

Eddie arrived home early, and he collected Billy to bring him to have his hair cut. Martha had left with Angela that morning and was still not back — hair salons on the day before a First Communion are always very busy. They had been there all morning. Martha had assumed that she would be home before Eddie and Billy left. She wasn't aware that he and Brian, his brother-in-law, had finished work early.

Back in Dominick Street, Eddie was having a bit of trouble getting Billy out the door for his haircut. The problem was not Billy, but Ed. At four years of age, Ed was, by his own admission, a daddy's boy. He idolised his father and was reluctant to let the man, a painter by trade, go anywhere without him. This occasion was no different and there was pandemonium in the flat that afternoon as Eddie tried to leave with Billy, while Ed tried desperately to force his father to bring him too.

Edward Senior was used to indulging his son. They had a game where Eddie would hide his son under his large Crombie overcoat and knock on the door of their flat. 'He used to put me under his overcoat and I'd put my legs around his waist and he'd knock on the door and he'd say "Oh, Edward's been taken by Jack Frost." He'd make this big thing of knocking on the door and make all these big exaggerated gestures.'

This time, Edward Senior wanted to get out to the barber's with his eldest son, but young Ed stood between him and the door, crying to be brought as well. Eddie tried to convince his son that he would be back soon, and tried as gently as he could to push him back into the flat and bring Billy to the van. The O'Neills' next-door neighbour, Mrs D'Arcy, was supposed to be babysitting Ed, Denise and Niall, but it looked less and less likely that Ed was going to consent to being left behind by his father. Being a persistent child, he managed to escape, sprinting down to where his father's van was parked, and he stood in front of it. In a rush to get Billy's hair cut, Eddie relented and allowed his second son to sit in the back, on the wheel-arch of the van, as they went to the barber's shop.

As they travelled, Eddie sternly warned his son not to mess around with the tools in the back of the van, probably mindful of the time that Ed had got himself covered from head to toe in blue paint, forcing his parents to spend hours scrubbing the boy to remove the paint from his hair and clothes.

When they arrived, Eddie parked the car and went around to the back of the van to open the doors, and his son sprang out of the back into his arms. Grunting under his son's weight, Eddie laughed and told him, 'You're getting too big for this.'

Eddie was a practitioner of martial arts and had made a number of friends during his time in his local karate club. One of them was a young man named Liam O'Sullivan who owned a barber's shop on Parnell Street. Eddie had never been in his friend's shop before but he decided to bring Billy and Ed there to have their hair cut. The decision would change the O'Neills' lives irrevocably.

Liam greeted Eddie warmly when he entered the shop, and they chatted for a while about karate and previous sessions in the club. Since Ed had kicked up such a fuss to go, it had been decided that he would get his hair cut as well. Eddie left the two boys in Liam's hands, and he and Brian went next door to the Welcome Inn pub for 'a lemonade or two' to refresh themselves after a hard day's work. Either Eddie or Brian would check in on the boys at regular intervals.

As the boys had their hair cut, they chatted. The two were close, and Ed remembers asking Billy if he would buy him any toys with his Communion money, and Billy telling him that he would. Next door, Eddie had finished his pint, and told Brian to order the next round while he went in to check on the boys. Finding them both finished, he paid and, it being his first time in the shop, he gave his friend a tip. Liam knew that Billy would be making his First Communion, so he took some money from the cash register and gave both boys a few pennies. Ed remembers Liam taking the money from the cash register and flicking it to him with his thumb and forefinger. Although he was only four, Ed has a vivid recollection of the money turning over and over in the air, catching the rays of the sun on its shiny surface, before he caught it in his hand and pocketed it.

Between the barber's shop and the Welcome Inn was parked a 1970 Hillman Avenger. Metallic golden olive in colour, it had been stolen from a security man by the name of William Scott, from Belfast. His home had been entered that morning by loyalist paramilitaries, who had tied him up. The car was then stolen and driven away while he was held captive, his captors playing cards upstairs until they released him at 4 p.m. By then, it was too late for him or the police to do anything about his car, which was in Dublin — loaded with explosives, primed, and ready to explode.

Because of the warmth of the evening, Liam had the door of the shop open to allow a breeze to blow in, and the two men chatted for a while, admiring a poster of Bruce Lee that was hanging on the wall behind the cash register. Eddie then left the shop with the two boys and walked back in the direction of the Welcome Inn, past the Hillman Avenger. Billy was on the right and Ed on the left, both hanging onto the pockets of their father's overcoat. Billy, being a boisterous child, was swinging from the lapels of his father's jacket, and managed to pull off a button, which fell to the ground and began to roll along the pavement. He scampered after it. Ed remembers:

> It was like it was slow motion and Billy was running after the button trying to catch it. The button seemed to be going in slow motion but Billy was running at normal speed. As he caught up with it, he bent

down and a big ball of flame just shot over him and it roared. The flame was roaring. My Da looked at me and it took me a long time to reconcile this with myself but he knew he was going to die. He looked at me and tried to push me behind him. People tell me there's no way I can remember that ... He knew he was going to die and I think it was the last act of a parent trying to shield me from it. There was a look of sheer terror. But I don't think his own safety or well-being came into it. As he was pushing me behind him, he was trying to reach forward and grab Billy, but there was no way he was going to reach him.

In the seconds after the explosion, there was silence. The only sound young Edward could hear was someone whimpering in the distance — not crying but whimpering. There was an acrid smell, almost like burnt pork, hanging in the air.

Then there came an eruption of sound — screaming, shouting, sirens.

Brian had run into the barber's shop in the aftermath of the explosion to see if Eddie and the boys had been caught up in the blast. Liam O'Sullivan, who had been cut on the head, and was bleeding down the side of his face, told him that Eddie had just gone out the door. The boys' uncle ran back out onto the street and found Ed lying on the ground with his clothes blown off him and shrapnel stuck in his face. Brian flagged down a man who was picking up children in his car to take them to hospital, and persuaded him to take another passenger. The car into which Ed was placed belonged to a man called Martin Coen. Ed remembers the sound of someone crying in the car, but cannot remember how many other children were there with him.

While Ed remembers little of his fellow passengers, he does remember the sight of his own wounds. Looking at his right leg, he could actually see the femur sticking out, and he could see right into the wound just above the knee of his left leg. He put his finger inside the wound and found that it was like sticking his hand into warm jam.

Ed had been blown from one side of the road to the other and had received horrific wounds to his face and legs. A piece of shrapnel was embedded in his face and had dragged the skin across until the bridge of his nose was almost visible. His father had been killed instantly, and his brother Billy had been seriously injured. Ed's memories of the moments after the explosion are scattered and selective. He does not, for example, remember being blown across the road. The feel of dust and grit at the back of his throat are vivid in his mind, and he could smell something he would later find out was the smell of cordite, but he can remember no pain at all.

Martin Coen had only just driven up to Dublin from Galway that day. He put Ed in the car with the other two children and raced to the hospital. He drove so quickly that he clipped another car along the way, but he arrived at the hospital safely. Ed O'Neill believes that he owes his life to the speed of Martin Coen.

The explosions had been heard all over Dublin. In the hairdresser's, Angela and Martha O'Neill had heard the sound, and Martha knew what it was. Although Dublin was far from the centre of the Troubles, it had seen its share of bombings in the previous two years, with the explosions in 1972 and 1973. It was an unmistakable sound. Martha remembers that one woman in the hairdresser's became quite upset.

> We heard the explosion. There had been two previous bombings and I lived on Dominick Street so I had known when those bombs went off. I knew what it was. In the hairdresser's that day there was a woman who thought [this bomb] had gone off near Green Street Courts [the court in which IRA prisoners stood trial] where there was a handball alley and she thought her children were in danger.

It was Martha, however, who had cause for concern. There was a strange atmosphere in the hairdresser's. Along with the almost-hysterical woman, there were several bad omens. 'There was a lot going on in '74. News of the bombings came on the radio, but it didn't mention Parnell Street.' However, it mentioned the other streets which had been bombed, and her brother was working nearby at the time and she was slightly concerned about him.

No one came to tell them that Eddie had been killed and the two boys had been injured. But Martha knew that something was wrong as they walked home.

I had a feeling over me, because when I was in the hairdresser's, the statue of St Martin fell. There wasn't a breeze out that day. It was a warm day and the hairdresser's door was closed, and it just fell and rolled to my feet. I always said a novena to St Martin. All the boys are called Martin and the girls are named after St Jude — the patrons of hopeless cases, because we tried so long to have a baby.

Angela, meanwhile, was completely oblivious to what was going on. 'We'd heard the explosion while we were sitting in the hairdresser's but I hadn't a clue what it had been.'

Denise O'Neill, at home with Niall, was waiting patiently for everyone to return. It was her ninth birthday and she had already received a large card and a charm bracelet from her daddy. She still has the card and the charm bracelet to this day.

There was fierce excitement in the house. More because of the Communions, because Communion was a big thing in the seventies and it was extra special because we had two of them, a boy and a girl, and Angela was doing a reading at hers.

Perpendicular to Dominick Street, where the O'Neills lived, was Parnell Street, and behind the flat in which they lived was a large timber factory.

There would always have been a lot of banging and we would have been used to loud noises. But this day, the place shook, the flat shook, the sitting room shook. And I can remember that vividly. Even though I was only nine, I got the feeling something was wrong. And when we looked out, we could see the smoke and people were panic stricken.

I don't know if I remember hearing the three explosions but I definitely heard Talbot Street and I definitely heard Parnell Street. Definitely. I ran out onto the balcony and I had Niall with me. You could see something had happened. I ran out on to the back balcony which overlooked Parnell Street. There were sirens and people running and there was a lot going on.

Denise didn't know it, but at this point, her father was already dead, and two of her brothers were seriously injured. However, she suspected something when her uncle Brian came up the stairs onto the balcony without her father, with whom he had been working and had gone to the pub.

> When I saw him, I asked him where my daddy was, and he said, 'He's helping to bring people to hospital in the van.' At the time, I didn't know what a bomb was. I knew that something had happened, but I didn't know what.

As Ed and Billy were being taken to hospital, their mother was making her way home from the hairdresser's with Angela. Martha recalls:

> As we walked home, I had a feeling. The place was deserted. It never dawned on me [why the place might be deserted]. I saw everyone on their balconies. No one on the street — everyone looking down on the street from their balcony. Mavis O'Toole, a neighbour of mine, came down the stairs to me and said, 'Eddie has been injured in the bomb.' Someone brought me down a chair. I asked if he was all right and I was told that someone had been talking to him.' So we went to Jervis Street Hospital and I'll never forget the sight. I never saw anything like it in my life. Coffins lined up against the wall and Jervis Street was packed.

When she went into the hospital, the sight was even worse. It was mayhem, and the staff were trying their best to separate the injured from the families, in order to bring about some semblance of order. In the relatives' waiting room there was complete hysteria. It was all too much for Martha. 'This Italian woman, Mrs Magliocco, was screaming. I just couldn't stay there.'

They were calling out the names of the injured, and someone shouted out the name of Edward O'Neill. Martha was shocked and had no idea whether it was her husband or her son. Soon after, she heard someone call out again, this time the name of Edward Junior. She was told that Edward had only forty-eight hours to live unless they could safely remove the piece of shrapnel without him bleeding to death. Then, as confusion continued to reign, someone called out that Edward Senior was dead.

I didn't know that he had gone and I didn't know that he had taken Ed with him. I can't explain to you how I felt. You'd have to feel it yourself. And I was six-and-a-half months pregnant.

When Martha found out that Eddie was dead and that the two boys had been injured, she was in deep shock. The doctors in Jervis Street decided to keep her in and sedate her. 'Whatever they gave me in Jervis Street, I was conked out. I signed myself out at two o'clock in the morning.'

Meanwhile, there was a lot of commotion in the flat in Dominick Street, and plenty of visitors. None of the children at this point knew that their father had been killed. Both Denise and Angela were at home waiting for their mother to return. No one told them anything, so Denise and Angela, probably believing all the excitement to be for them, went around telling people about Denise's birthday and Angela's First Communion. Both remember vividly the moment their mother told them that their father was dead. Martha had just come home. It was early in the morning, possibly two or three o'clock, and the girls were still awake and enjoying the attention being lavished on them and the money being given to them. They both spotted her coming up the stairs and ran down to meet her. Denise asked where their father was, and Martha told them that he was gone up to heaven with the angels.

Angela didn't realise that she would never see her father again. 'I was just interested in the fact that I had my Communion the next day and all the money I'd get.' The full implications hadn't dawned on Denise either.

There were hundreds of people in and out of the house that night and I was busy telling everyone it was my birthday and they were all giving me money. That was the big thing for me and I thought this was wonderful. I didn't know that because Daddy was gone to heaven, he wouldn't be coming back again. I think way back then we were a lot more innocent. Children were children and we didn't have the influence of television.

Martha's recollections of that night and of the days that followed are hazy:

[The] Rotunda Hospital called out to me and gave me valium. I didn't know what valium was. Then somebody was putting tablets into my mouth. Someone else was giving me tea with brandy. I'd never had brandy in my life. I didn't know whether I was coming or going.

It's hazy in my memory. People thought they were doing me good but they weren't. I mean, Denise should have been at that funeral and if I'd been in my right mind she would have been.

I had First Communions the next day. I thought my sister dressed Angela for her First Communion, but I did. I don't remember it. Between what Jervis Street gave me, what the Rotunda gave me, the tea with the brandy and the shock of the whole thing, I was out of it.

I vaguely remember the funeral. That's another thing I regret. Never seeing him in the coffin. So to me, he never died. I couldn't believe how my life had turned upside-down in a couple of hours. We were so happy that morning, looking forward to the First Holy Communions and Denise's birthday. Eddie was looking forward to it in particular because he wanted to hear about Angela's reading.

The day after the bombings, it was decided that, although Billy was seriously injured in hospital and would not be able to make his First Communion, Angela would.

I made my Communion the next day. I got up and got dressed and went off to the church. At that time, the boys and the girls made theirs separately and I was making mine in the convent and Billy was to make his in the church. The arrangement had been that my father would take Billy to the church and my mother would take me to the convent and we would all meet up after.

Instead, Martha brought Angela while Billy lay in hospital. He would make his on his return home months later, and the rest of the community in Dominick Street would turn out for it.

Angela even did the reading she was supposed to do at the mass. The story made the papers the next day. The *Evening Herald* of 20 May reported:

## FIRST HOLY COMMUNION DAY FOR
## VICTIM'S DAUGHTER

Mrs. Martha O'Neill of 59 Lower Dominick Street, Dublin, decided this morning that her daughter, Angela, should go ahead and receive her First Holy Communion.

She and other members of the family went to Dominick Street Church for mass at 10 o'c this morning.

But there was one empty place at the ceremony, her 39-year-old husband, Edmond [sic], was killed in last night's explosion at Parnell Street.

Mr. Peter Caffrey, Mrs O'Neill's brother, said that his sister decided to go ahead with the ceremony because this was what Edmond would have wanted.

Also missing in the church were Angela's brothers, Billy (7) and Edward (4). They were with their daddy at the time of the explosion and are now at Jervis Street Hospital.

The other O'Neill children — one boy and one girl — were being cared for by relatives in their top-storey flat at Dominick Street this morning, unaware that their father had been killed.

Mr O'Neill brought Billy and Edward to have their hair cut yesterday afternoon in preparation for Angela's First Holy Communion. They were on their way home when the bombs went off.

The *Evening Press* of 22 May featured a story about Denise's last birthday card from her father. The story also mentioned Angela's First Communion:

… Angela received Communion at King's Inn Street Convent watched by her mother, who was under heavy sedation.

'Angela read the first lesson at Mass and she nearly cried but she didn't,' Denise said.

Billy will receive Communion in hospital this evening …

Although the emotion of the day may have affected Angela when she stood up to read, the significance of the events still had not hit home.

I can remember being outside and being the centre of attention, which I was delighted with of course. I hadn't grasped at all that my father was dead. I just didn't know what that meant.

Angela also did the first reading at her father's funeral. She was the only one of the children who attended. Billy and Ed were still too sick in hospital and, because Martha was still in deep shock and unable to make the decision by herself, it was decided by other family members that Denise and Niall would stay with neighbours.

The *Evening Press* of 22 May reported:

### CHILD READS AT FATHER'S FUNERAL MASS

Seven-year-old Angela O'Neill, who made her first holy Communion last Saturday, read the First Reading at her father's funeral mass in St. Saviour's Church, Lwr. Dominick St. Dublin, today.

Her young brothers, Edward and Billy, were unable to attend the mass; they are being treated in Jervis Street Hospital for injuries received in the Parnell Street blast which killed their father.

Mr. Edward O'Neill (39) of 59 Lower Dominick Street leaves a wife, two daughters and three sons whose ages range from 18 months to nine years.

Relatives, neighbours and friends crowded into the Dominican church for the mass which was concelebrated by twelve priests.

A day or two after the funeral, some journalists from the *Evening Press* turned up on Dominick Street looking for a story. Seeing some children playing on the street, they approached them and asked where the O'Neills lived. Denise was one of the children playing on the street and told them that she was an O'Neill.

They sent me up to the house to get my birthday card and brought me off to Tara Street [where the paper had its offices] to have my picture taken. Without permission from anyone. They brought me over to Tara Street and then just let us walk home on our own. I don't think people realised that I was gone because so much was going on and they didn't until my picture appeared in the newspaper the next day.

Not only had these particular journalists, without anyone's permission, brought a nine-year-old girl away from her family, all of whom were distracted by their grief, and used her for a story and then let her walk alone across the city by herself, but they had allowed her to walk straight past the spot where her father had been killed only days earlier.

What hurt Martha even more was that she couldn't see her two boys. Ed was so badly injured that it was believed that he wouldn't make it. Both he and Billy were under very close observation, and it was three or four days before Martha could go to Jervis Street to see them. When she did eventually go, her brother and sister had to accompany her for moral support.

Martha O'Neill, six months pregnant and heavily sedated, could not cope with caring for her family in the days following the bombings. It was decided to send the children to stay with relatives while she recovered. Denise remembers:

> I was taken out of the house and sent to stay with my uncle. The two boys were in hospital but I didn't realise how sick they were. I still didn't realise what a bomb could do or what it was really. I knew that my father was in heaven but I didn't know that meant he wasn't coming back.
>
> I was taken out of the house on the Sunday and I wasn't at my father's funeral. An uncle decided that it wasn't the right thing for me to go to the funeral. The only person that was at my father's funeral was Angela — she was with my mother. We were taken from Dublin, myself and Angela, and sent to England for a short while.
>
> Because of what had happened, there was a lot of attention put on us. It wasn't something that we thought of or that we had experienced before. I was in my uncle's for quite a few weeks. Decisions were being made for my mother because she was shell-shocked. She had to come to terms with the fact that my father was dead, but she also had to deal with the fact that the two boys were injured, Edward quite badly.

Indeed, both boys were still in serious condition in hospital. Because he was only four, Ed has large gaps in his memories of that time, and some of his recollections are vague and seem to make no sense. He vividly recalls watching coffins being wheeled from the funeral parlour into the hospital on the evening of the bombings, something he can't have seen since he would have been in the middle of serious surgery at the time.

> The old A&E entrance to Jervis Street Hospital, there were barriers on both sides and big heavy plastic swinging doors and I remember sitting outside watching all the ambulances coming in. It's so vivid. Many people have tried to tell me it was just a dream, but it was so vivid. It was like people didn't see me, the place was mad. Right across from the A&E there was a chapel and lined up outside the door were the coffins and the lids were lined beside them. And as each person died, the porter would come out and the porter would put a coffin on the trolley and roll it into the A&E and I didn't know what it meant.

Martha tried to keep the children's spirits up throughout the whole ordeal by telling them that very soon they would have a new baby brother or sister. But tragedy was about to hit the O'Neills once more.

Three months after the bombings, as she approached her due date, Martha went to hospital for a check-up, and was told that she had dangerously low blood pressure. However, the doctors decided not to keep her in overnight. Denise remembers an ambulance arriving at the flats the next day.

> An ambulance came right up to the house. If anything like that goes anywhere, an ambulance or the Fire Brigade, hundreds of children will come out and swarm around it. I didn't realise it was for my mother until I saw her on the stretcher.

Martha had suffered a miscarriage. Before the miscarriage, she had been terribly upset by the thought that her husband would never see the baby she was carrying. However, because of medical protocol at the time, she never even got to see it herself. Hospitals now give the grieving mother time with the stillborn baby, but baby Martha O'Neill was taken away and buried without her mother ever seeing her. Having carried this baby for nine months, three of which were the most traumatic months of her life, she would never see what her child looked like.

> They just took her away. I've no memory of her. I've nothing. They took her and buried her before I even knew. She was a little girl. I can't even say who she looked like. I never saw my own child. What gave people the right to do that? Surely to God they knew you had to see this baby after carrying it for nine months. I never saw any of my children [who died] and that leaves you more brokenhearted.

It was much later in the summer that it dawned on Denise what her father's death actually meant. As often happens, it was brought about by the simplicity of a childish comment.

> We were playing out near the pram sheds and some child said something like 'You don't have a daddy.' It was then that I realised that he really wasn't coming back.

Edward and Billy were slowly recovering in hospital. Ed recalls that 'time just seemed to go.' For a child of four years of age who was being shuttled in and out of surgery and probably spent a good deal of his time under heavy sedation, this is not unusual. He spent six weeks in hospital initially and was in the same ward as his brother, Billy, who, although his injuries were not as severe as Ed's, stayed to keep him company.

> Because Billy wasn't as seriously injured as me, he healed quicker and [one day] my mother came into the ward and the doctor told her, 'I'll let Billy go home tomorrow.' When I heard this, I went absolutely hysterical and I got so upset that the doctors got worried in case I would hurt myself and kept Billy in far longer than he should have been kept in. But it was necessary to keep me in hospital.'

Although Ed's condition was quite serious and many of his wounds required extensive surgery, he has some good memories, mostly of the mischief he and Billy got up to: 'I remember one time in the corridors of the hospital we were racing around and the nurse caught us and took our slippers off us to keep us in bed.'

He also remembers a visit from his uncle Patrick, known as 'Whacker'. Ed was having the dressings on his wound changed and was crying in pain. Whacker stuck his head around the door saying, 'How are you today, big fella?' The nurse changing Ed's wounds asked him to leave, but then, seeing the calming effect it had on Ed to have Whacker around, allowed him to stay.

Ed had suffered horrific injuries. His left eardrum was perforated severely, giving him less than 20 per cent hearing in that ear. He received hundreds of stitches to a wound on the left side of his face which was caused by a piece of metal that lodged there when the bomb exploded. The scar ran down the side of his face, onto his neck. His legs were badly damaged, with the left thigh, knee and lower leg all wounded, while the right leg was broken. And these were only the more obvious injuries. There were many other cuts inflicted by flying debris, and these had to be stitched and sutured and to have foreign bodies removed from them.

# MEDIA REACTION

The word 'forget' comes up all too regularly in relation to the Dublin and Monaghan bombings. In 1996, when the families decided to give their campaign a name, they settled on 'Justice for the Forgotten'. When, in 1993, the journalists of Yorkshire Television were researching their documentary, they decided that a suitable title for it would be 'The Forgotten Massacre'. Clearly, the thirty-five people who died as a result of the bombings on 17 May 1974 had been forgotten about.

And those left behind, the injured and bereaved, were angry about it. Mostly, they were angry at being forgotten by the government. They were angry at the failure of the authorities to do anything about their loss and their hurt. No one has ever been convicted of the Dublin and Monaghan bombings, and no adequate investigation was ever undertaken into the unsettling rumours of British army collusion with loyalist paramilitaries, or of British and Irish government cover-ups of the bombings.

When the government appears to be hiding something so big, as it did in this case, one would expect the pressure to come from another angle — the media. We expect the media to act as the public's watchdog. We expect journalists to keep a close eye on those in positions of power, and to inform us if these people are abusing their power. The most famous example of such journalism is the case of Woodward and Bernstein, the two American reporters who uncovered burglary and phone tapping in the Watergate building, approved by the then US President, Richard Nixon. The two reporters discovered that Nixon had been engaged in unconstitutional behaviour, and the revelation and his administration's attempt to cover it up eventually forced him out of office.

Media theorists have long speculated about the influence that the media have on the public. They have examined the effects of various forms of media and attempted to assess to what degree people exposed to a particular medium might be influenced. They began to speculate that the news media, in particular, provided a type of forum in which the public could be informed of the actions of their elected representatives. This was a channel through which the public, who didn't see each decision being made as it was being made, could be made aware of what was being done on their behalf and, if they didn't agree, could take actions to prevent their government from making those decisions.

This, of course, was the theory. It was dependent on the media working independently and not being influenced or swayed by outside decisions. It relied on the media doing what we believe to be their job. A new theory arose, through Noam Chomsky and Edward Herman, which was called 'agenda setting'. According to this theory, the media are indeed a watchdog — in fact, they are the only watchdog the public has. And it is through the media that the public agenda is set. If something gets heavy coverage in the media, the public will know about it and the public can act upon it if they so choose. If the media do not cover an issue, the public will not know about it and they will be unable to act upon it, whether they would have chosen to or not. It is a simple theory, but it is one that has great resonance in the manner in which the Dublin and Monaghan bombings were treated by the media for thirty years.

⌘    ⌘    ⌘

In 1974, television was nowhere near as influential as it is now. Radio, on the other hand, was beginning to wane in its popularity. The main source of news and information was the printed press, so the press will be the main focus of this chapter.

As time went on, television became more powerful. As more people bought televisions, the programmes broadcast reached more people more easily, and this medium began to exert more of an influence. It was through television that the issue of the Dublin and Monaghan bombings was raised again. However, this did not even begin to happen until 1993, almost two decades later. By then, the damage had already been done, and the people of Ireland had forgotten — had, in fact, been allowed to forget — what horrors had been carried out in their capital city, and what injustices had been visited upon those who lost loved ones or suffered horrific injuries.

The responsibility to inform the public in 1974 lay with the print media, and they failed miserably.

⌘ ⌘ ⌘

All three bombs exploded after 5 p.m. on 17 May 1974, so no newspaper reports were available until the following day. The three main national dailies in 1974 were the *Irish Press*, *The Irish Times* and the *Irish Independent*. Unlike today, the Irish newspaper market was a much more divided grouping, and the *Press*, *Times* and *Independent* were all read by specific groups in society. The three taken together give a broad idea of what the general level of knowledge of the bombings would have been.

All three national daily newspapers were based in Dublin city, right at the centre of the bombings. The journalists of all three papers would have heard the bombs explode, whether they were in a pub next door or in the newsroom of the paper. All would have known exactly what it was — there had been bombings in Dublin in previous years, though none of this magnitude. And, after the story vanished from the papers, every journalist who walked, drove or took a bus to work would probably have had to pass one of the bomb sites on the way to work (the *Irish Press* was based on Burgh Quay, a point roughly equidistant from all three bomb sites; the *Irish Independent* is based on Middle Abbey Street, no more than a few hundred yards from Parnell Street, and almost within sight of Talbot Street; *The Irish Times* is based on D'Olier Street, which is five minutes from South Leinster Street, and within sight of the carnage of Parnell Street). Not one of the newspapers undertook an investigation of the events, or even followed up on the fact that there had been no convictions.

The coverage amounted to just a simple reporting of the events and then, when those stories had dried up, nothing. While the first week's editions of the three daily broadsheets dedicated a considerable amount of space to the bombings, it was generally of a poor quality, and very little of it left the reader with any real impression of the atrocity. No information on arrests is given; no suggestion is made of who might have planted the bombs; nothing is said other than the rather self-evident fact that a bomb exploded and killed thirty-five people, wounded hundreds more, and caused a lot of damage. It is right and proper that the victims should be given due coverage in the pages of national newspapers, but the print media at the time concerned themselves only with the human-interest angle. When, after a week or so, the human-interest angle had been over-exposed, they dropped it, leaving a vacuum in the coverage. No proper journalistic investigation of the story was undertaken, and there were only sporadic attempts to follow up the official Garda/RUC investigation. Within weeks, the Dublin and Monaghan bombings vanished from the pages of Ireland's newspapers and from the minds of the people of Ireland.

*The Coverage of the Day of the Bombings*
The shock of the bombings was reflected quite effectively on the front pages of *The Irish Times*, the *Irish Independent* and the *Irish Press*. In all three newspapers, the front page was dedicated to the story; only *The Irish Times* put any other news item on the front page with it (and even then only at the bottom of the page, taking one or two paragraphs).

The headlines reflected the mood. In the *Irish Independent*:
OUR BLOODY FRIDAY
DUBLIN'S RUSH HOUR OF DEATH
TALBOT STREET WAS LIKE DAYLIGHT HELL
WOMAN LAY DECAPITATED ON THE PAVEMENT
PEOPLE FELL LIKE NINEPINS

In the *Irish Press*:
HORROR HITS DUBLIN
CARNAGE IN PARNELL STREET
THE AGONY OF TALBOT STREET
IRELAND'S BLOODY FRIDAY

In *The Irish Times:*

## A PICTURE OF DEATH ON DUBLIN'S STREETS
## PATHETIC LITTER ON PARNELL STREET
## BODIES STREWN ON THE GROUND; POOLS OF BLOOD
## DUBLIN CAR BOMB HAVOC

All the stories from Saturday 18 May are concerned with the death, destruction and damage caused by the bombs. This is understandable. There hadn't been such a horrific catastrophe since a stray German bomb hit Dublin's North Strand during the Second World War. Journalists were shocked and horrified by what they saw. For many, while probably not the first time they had seen someone dying, it was undoubtedly the first time that most had seen carnage on such an extensive level. It is quite likely that most journalists were deeply shocked as they sat down at their typewriters to write the stories for the following day's edition.

It is quite evident in the type and tone of the news stories that were printed on the first day of coverage that this indeed was the case. Only one newspaper, the *Irish Press*, made any attempt to shed some light on the possible reasons for or causes of the bombings, or the identities and political backgrounds of the bombers. Two stories were written in the *Irish Press*, both of which appeared on the front page, which suggested that the bombers might have been loyalist paramilitaries. The Garda Síochána had, by 5 p.m., been informed by the RUC of the registration numbers of cars that had been stolen in Belfast on the morning of 17 May. Therefore, as they filtered through the debris and found the plates of those cars, the gardaí would have informed any journalist who asked that the cars had been stolen in mainly Protestant areas of Belfast. It doesn't necessarily follow that those cars were driven by loyalist paramilitaries, but it should have been the first clue in the investigation. As it turned out, the journalists in question simply stated their belief that the bomb-cars had been delivered by loyalists, and left it at that. The newspaper made no attempt to follow the story with any other stories of a similar nature. They simply left the issue in the capable hands of the government whose statements they faithfully reproduced in their pages.

The first of the reports mentioned above said that blame lay with 'some loyalist organisation in the North' and the second hinted at this by saying, 'one of the cars, a Hillman Avenger, had been hijacked in the Old Park area, which is a mainly Protestant district.' Nowhere else on the front pages of Irish national daily newspapers did this information appear. The rest of the paper dealt with the carnage that had been visited upon the victims and the city.

In the aftermath of the tragedy of 11 September 2001, Robert Fisk gave a series of lectures entitled 'September 11: Ask who did it, but for Heaven's sake don't ask why'. Fisk believed that it had become taboo to mention that aggressive US foreign policy had provoked an aggressive response. In Ireland, in 1974, the taboo question was not Why? but Who? To a great extent, it still is. For years, people had believed that the IRA was either responsible for provoking the bombings (according to the government line, the IRA's provocation of the bombings was more reprehensible than the bombings themselves) or that the IRA had actually carried them out. For more than twenty years, the question of who was to blame was not broached.

However, one cannot criticise any of the three newspapers for their first day's coverage. They had all just witnessed people lying dead and dying on the street, people with dreadful injuries crying for help, blood running in the streets. *The Irish Times*, the *Irish Press* and the *Irish Independent* all put the Dublin and Monaghan bombings first in the edition of Saturday 18. Each edition had pages and pages dedicated to the bombings. The coverage from the first day cannot be faulted. It is in the following weeks, months and years that Irish print journalism did itself a disservice.

After the shock of the first day, it would be expected that reason and journalistic training would take over for the second day's coverage (in all but *The Irish Times*, which doesn't and didn't have a Sunday edition). However, this simply didn't happen. As the days passed, the quantity of coverage decreased. This is not unusual. Stories have shelf-lives — some very short. However, the Dublin and Monaghan bombings stories were being pushed further back into the depths of the newspaper. The position of a story within a newspaper is indicative of how important the editor believes it to be. By this reasoning, the Dublin and Monaghan bombings were of little importance to the editors of the three newspapers.

The matter of blame is a rather contentious one. In the days following the bombings, there was considerable confusion and very little solid evidence. A number of reports in the *Sunday Independent* on 19 May, two days after the bombings, highlighted the confusion. A story, headlined, 'Loyalists condemn killings', was the first in any of the *Independent* stable of newspapers to deal with the issue of blame. It said:

> Although police on both sides of the border are keeping an open mind as to who was responsible for the bombings all evidence would seem to suggest that the massacre was the work of a group of Protestant extremists.
>
> All the cars used in the Dublin explosions were stolen earlier in the day in predominantly Protestant areas of Belfast while the vehicle used in the Monaghan blast was stolen from a car park in Portadown.
>
> The two main loyalist paramilitary organisations, the UDA and the UVF, have both strenuously denied responsibility as have both wings of the IRA, but nothing has been heard yet from the militant UFF, the breakaway group from the UVF who over the past year have claimed responsibility for most of the sectarian killings in the six counties.

All of this seems like quite good, if overly careful, journalism. It reports the garda position while adding certain salient points. Police were keeping an open mind about who was responsible, but the journalist who wrote the piece felt it was his duty to inform the reader that the most likely culprits were loyalist paramilitaries of some sort. It also points out that the UFF, who had claimed responsibility for most of the sectarian killings in Northern Ireland during that year, had not yet made a statement about the bombings. Although it was, in fact, the UVF, and not the UFF, who would years later admit to having carried out the bombings, this does not undermine the quality of the article. The journalist made certain assumptions based on the evidence available to him, and wrote his story. He was not afraid to suggest that blame lay with militant loyalists, and he put forward the UFF as being the possible culprit based on the organisation's track record. While these may seem like small points, stories that did anything of this nature were very rare in the bare two weeks of coverage given to the bombings. Stories like these should have been major feature articles, especially in Sunday newspapers. While there was nothing particularly ground-breaking about the information being presented, it was still analysis of the events and the evidence, and would have informed the public as to what was happening. Instead such coverage was all but buried and, in this instance, placed beside one of many stories blaming the IRA, thereby cancelling out any effectiveness the story had on its own. Under the headline 'Government keeping an open mind', was a story containing the following paragraph:

> The government yesterday was reluctant to read too much into the significance of the cars concerned being hijacked in largely Protestant areas. They do not have enough evidence to lay blame on any particular paramilitary body.

Initially this seems like prudence on the government's part. There wasn't enough evidence to blame anyone (the previous article had only suggested who could have been responsible; it did not blame anyone) and to do so would be rash and unjust. However, the last line of the article, 'they do not have enough evidence to lay blame on any particular paramilitary body' is in stark contrast with the statements which had already been made, blaming the IRA for having inspired the bombings. While attributing moral blame does not suggest actual blame, it does confuse the issue, especially when the same people make statements suggesting that no blame should be attributed to loyalist paramilitaries because of a lack of evidence, but encouraging the public to think that moral responsibility lies with the IRA. It's little wonder that so many people believed that the IRA had, in fact, carried out the bombings. This gross misconception began with these articles which all too faithfully parroted the government's statements.

Seven days later, and in the *Sunday Independent* again, there was another strange turn in the nature of the coverage when, in an article on page 8, there was a suggestion that the Garda Síochána 'didn't have a clue' who the bombers were.

> After the most intensive investigation in the history of the State, the Gardaí and RUC are still without a clue as to the identity of the mass murderers who planted the bombs in Dublin.

Officially the Gardaí say they are keeping an open mind as to the motives behind the crime but they have no hesitation in admitting the conviction that the people who committed them came from Belfast.

A high ranking Garda officer who is closely connected to the investigation told me he now believes the bombers were across the border two hours after the blast …

The trouble is that the ordinary rank and file of the RUC dare not make inquiries into the particular affair. They have their own sources of information inside the ranks of the UDA and UVF and the UFF but any attempt to get information as to the men and/or women who came to Dublin to plant the bombs could well lead to the death of the policeman making it.

'Every turn these RUC men make they are afraid of being shot,' said the Garda source.

The gardaí had, in fact, many clues and were following a definite line of inquiry.

All of the rest of the articles relating to the official Garda/RUC investigation had been based on press releases. It is a poor reflection on the journalists who were working on that paper that there was no questioning whatsoever of the official line for over a week during the investigation.

On 19 May, the *Sunday Press* provided another example of what could be done if journalists simply did their job. Under the headline, 'Monaghan: A time factor theory', the journalist explained how the bombers had made it back across the border by setting off the Monaghan bomb, and thereby dragging security forces across the border, thus giving them a chance to slip over at an under-manned border crossing. It was the first piece of analysis in any newspaper in the country.

The nature of the stories too seemed to betray a disinterest among the three newspapers in following up what was, and still is, the largest loss of life during the course of the Troubles, and the biggest mass murder in the history of the Irish State. There were, as has been mentioned, no journalistic investigations into the bombings. No journalists ever made their own inquiries, and there was precious little analysis of what information was available. Only the *Irish Press* attempted to put the pieces of the puzzle together, but in altogether too tame and timid a manner.

The reports on the official Garda/RUC investigation were simply regurgitated press releases, and if anything was known of the lack of RUC co-operation, the missing forensics, or any of the multitude of problems that dogged the investigation, no mention of it was made by Irish journalists.

This information would have been very easy to obtain at the time. However, as time passed, the information became harder to access, buried deeper in government files and unreliable memories. It has taken thirty years of pressure and two government inquiries into the bombings to uncover the tip of this iceberg. It could have all been prevented had the journalists of the day simply done some research.

Instead, in many cases, journalists merely acted as the mouthpiece for the official line. It is on the issue of who was to blame for the bombings that we see just how close the newspapers of the day were to the government. The Fine Gael-led coalition of the day was historically opposed to the republican tradition in Ireland. No one would criticise members of that government for condemning such a disgusting crime as the Dublin and Monaghan bombings. Nobody would criticise them for condemning the IRA's actions in Northern Ireland. However, the UVF committed this bloody act and seemed to get away without even being mentioned, while Fine Gael and Labour spent their time criticising the IRA for having inspired the violence, and the Irish public for having traditionally republican-leaning sentiments.

Their statements were misleading, incorrect and dangerous. Many Irish citizens, including those bereaved or injured by the bombs, believed for many years that the IRA had carried out the bombings. This can be directly attributed to the line which was instantly taken by Liam Cosgrave's cabinet in the aftermath of the bombings. And all three daily broadsheets at the time seemed to agree with the government that the IRA had 'moral responsibility' for the bombings, and that this somehow excused the loyalist paramilitaries who carried them out.

The IRA has been responsible for some of the most heinous crimes committed in the history of the Troubles. It is true that the organisation was involved in a tit-for-tat war with both the British army and loyalist paramilitaries of various hues. However, it is twisted logic to suggest that the IRA held responsibility for the bombing of Dublin and Monaghan, and it was simply wrong of the government to lay the blame at that door. No blame was attributed to the UVF. There seemed to be a sickening double-speak when it came to the bombings. Government members were only too happy to excoriate the IRA, but when they were asked who had carried out the bombings, they claimed that there was insufficient evidence to make any sort of statement. It was a line parroted in the Irish print media, where the only mentions of loyalist blame were fleeting.

Some of the articles try quite explicitly to blame the IRA. John Healy, writing in *The Irish Times* under the pen name 'Backbencher', wrote, exactly one week later:

> I am as always thankful for the smallest of mercies. And thanks be to God we didn't try burning down Kevin Street Sinn Féin like we burned down the British Embassy after Bloody Sunday. We're coming on.
>
> So is the Backbencher corpse count. And if the Provo collectors keep a low profile for a week or two, not to worry lads it'll all blow over, it always does. Our memories are blessedly short and it is only myself who sees the stick of gelignite and the fuse sticking out of the bottom of the same collection boxes.
>
> The Irish betimes are a most tolerant people. In a few weeks' time 'the lads' will be back at the GPO within sight of Talbot Street and the decent plain people of Ireland will plant dynamite pennies in the collection boxes and will have gone on their way before the next round of bombs go off to kill and maim.

The final sentiment seems initially to be a sound one. Supporting Sinn Féin financially would, no doubt, help the IRA to murder their next victims, and to collect any money in the line of sight of the Talbot Street bomb site would be incredibly disrespectful to those innocent victims of that bomb (and there is no doubt that republican activists did it anyway, eventually).

However, this is not Healy's main argument. His main argument is not as simple as 'Don't be a link in the chain of violence' or anything so high-minded. Healy begins the whole article by suggesting that the IRA was to blame for the bombings — by reminding the reader of the time when Irish citizens burned down the British embassy following the killing by the British army of unarmed civil rights marchers on Bloody Sunday, and by suggesting that the same citizens might have burned down Sinn Féin's Kevin Street offices had they not had a little more restraint, he clearly implies that the IRA actually planted the bombs. After a week of parroting the government's line of argument on 'moral responsibility', Healy decides to confuse his readers even further.

This is made all the more bizarre when you realise that only a few days earlier, Healy had made the following statement in his Dáil report:

> There are times when I wish that some of the men who sit as deputies in Dáil Éireann had to face the problems of the men and women in the Northern Assembly where they have real political problems to face and solve, and one of those times was yesterday ...
>
> Already the memory of the horror of Dublin's Bloody Friday is fading fast.

His attack on the government for its lack of action over the bombings rings hollow when you are aware that, only days later, he would write an article with the seeming intention of obfuscating the issue of blame for the atrocities.

Only one article in any of the three papers criticises this tendency. In the *Irish Press* of 27 May, an article appeared under the headline, 'Bombings — Laying the blame'. The journalist who wrote it attacked the government's position of holding the IRA responsible for the bombings in Dublin and Monaghan through stating that the bombings had been directly incited by IRA violence in Northern Ireland. He described a chain of violence, stretching back through Irish history, which made it possible to 'excuse A's guilt by citing B's crime'. To illustrate this, he suggested that Declan Costello, who the previous day had made a statement saying that the IRA bore 'a very heavy burden of responsibility for what has happened', was himself part of the chain and therefore responsible for the violence by having given a speech at the grave of Michael Collins. It is the only article which challenged the prevalent argument.

Before two weeks had elapsed — that is, before all of the victims had been buried — all stories about the bombings, however small or seemingly insignificant, had vanished.

The *Irish Independent* had kept the story on the front page, in some form, for eight days, and had dropped it from the paper entirely after thirteen days. The *Irish Press* kept it on the front page for slightly longer, with the story vanishing and then reappearing on alternate days. However, it too dropped the story completely before two weeks had elapsed. *The Irish Times* followed a similar pattern, keeping it on the first page for the first week, relegating it to the inside pages for the second week, and dropping it altogether after that.

## Press Coverage of the Yorkshire Television Documentary

By 1993, the bombings were completely out of the minds of most Irish journalists. It had been nineteen years since the atrocity had taken place, and the personnel in the newspapers had changed considerably. Successive governments had consistently ignored the whole issue, and the public had forgotten almost totally. Meanwhile, the campaign that had been started by Denise and Angela O'Neill was only in its infancy.

However, Yorkshire Television was finishing a documentary on the bombings, which had taken two-and-a-half years to make. The team had uncovered facts and evidence about the bombings, and about the subsequent handling of the bombings, that had never previously been released into the public sphere. Such a documentary should have received enormous coverage in the print media. It did not.

In the days leading up to the broadcast of the programme, there was much speculation about what exactly it might say. The documentary was the first to suggest that there might be 'a more sinister reason' for the nineteen-year silence on the bombings. It asked why there had been no conviction, no arrests and no admission of responsibility from any group (it was only after the documentary, when compelling proof had been produced that the UVF had committed the bombings, that that organisation admitted responsibility).

Some of the allegations were shocking. There were admissions by garda officers who had worked on the case that they could have caught the perpetrators — that, in fact, they had known exactly who was responsible, but that they had been held up and stymied in every way possible by the RUC.

The documentary was due to be screened on 6 July. On Sunday 4 July, there was some rather muted coverage. On page 45 of the *Sunday Press*, a television preview advised readers to watch the documentary. In the *Sunday Independent*, a front-page story by Joe Tiernan gave more details about the bombings. Tiernan, as will be discussed later in the book, was not a *Sunday Independent* journalist, but one of the Yorkshire Television team who had broken ranks and sold the story to the paper.

The next day, the *Irish Independent* contained one story, on page 6, running under the headline 'Government may review Dublin bombings inquiry'. The *Irish Press* had a story on page 1 about then Lord Mayor of Dublin, Gay Mitchell, who had, on his last day as Lord Mayor, called for a new inquiry into the bombings. Mitchell, a member of Fine Gael, would later suggest that enough had been done by the media and that the matter should be left alone. When the Barron Inquiry published its report, he was one of the first people to criticise Mr Justice Barron for having the temerity to suggest that the Fine Gael government had not done enough at the time of the bombings.

On Tuesday 6 July, the day the programme was broadcast, there were no stories whatsoever about the documentary.

The next day, on page 7 of the *Irish Independent*, there were two pictures which had the headline 'Dublin 1974 … and Newtownards 1993'. The pictures showed the carnage wreaked by one of the Dublin bombs and a bomb that had gone off in Newtownards that week. The caption read, 'Devastation: The Streets of Dublin after the 1974 bombings … and Newtownards yesterday — a police investigator walking past some of the wreckage caused by the IRA bomb late on Monday. The Dublin bombings were the subject of an investigative programme last night on ITV's *First Tuesday*.' No mention was made of who was responsible for the Dublin bombings, only that the IRA had been responsible for the bombing in Newtownards. The sentence structure leads the reader to believe that the IRA was responsible for both. No article accompanies the text to clear up the confusion.

*The Irish Times* had a front-page article headlined 'Loyalist bombers of 1974 named'. There was also an article on page 3, under the headline 'Portadown UVF unit suspected of 1974 bombings'. Both articles are simply reports of what had been said in the programme the previous night.

In the *Irish Press*, there was a picture of the O'Neill family and the Doyle family watching the documentary. Both families had helped in the making of the programme. The *Irish Press* gave most coverage to the programme, with page 6 dedicated to the story. The *Press* had, however, moved to tabloid format by this stage, and so the stories were brief.

The next day, an article appeared, which quoted senior garda sources who dismissed the findings of the programme, claiming that it had produced very little fresh evidence which could secure a conviction. In *The Irish Times*, there was a similar article in which a senior garda source claimed that the programme had not contained 'a shred of evidence'. Although it is probably true that all the information had been known to the Garda Síochána already and that none of the evidence was admissible in a court of law, the purpose of the documentary was not to secure convictions, but to highlight the manner in which the investigation had been handled. Therefore, the backlash from the anonymous 'senior Garda source' must count as an attempt to discredit the programme. Once again, the Irish print media were only too happy to reproduce what their sources in authority had told them, to the detriment of the programme and the campaign.

There were no articles at all on the programme in the rest of the week's newspapers. It had, once again, fallen off the radar screen.

*Family Reaction to Media and Lack of Public Interest*
The families bereaved by the Dublin and Monaghan bombings were done a great disservice by the print media and, later, the broadcast media in Ireland. While television and radio — but mainly television —made more of an effort to cover the bombings, they did so only when inspired to do so by outside events. When the Barron Report was published in December 2003, there were cameras from RTÉ and TV3 to cover the event. In 1993, RTÉ made a programme called *Friendly Forces*, but it was only in response to new information which had been raised by the Yorkshire Television crew who had spent two-and-a-half years researching the issue.

Television would have made it easier to make more people aware of the bombings, because it reached a wider audience, but it didn't seem to be bothered investigating it. It is true that the Yorkshire Television documentary took two-and-a-half years to make and cost a huge amount of money in the process, but this was only because the whole affair had been left to lie for so long. Had the investigation been started when it should have been — directly after the bombings — there would have been no need for such time and expense.

Tim Pat Coogan, who was editor of the *Irish Press* at the time, has said that his newspaper simply didn't have the resources to fund such an investigation. But this does not excuse the newspapers of the day from shying away from even questioning the official line on the bombings. There was little or no analysis of the facts at hand, and no attempt to bring new facts to light. To be fair to the *Irish Press* and its journalists, it was the only newspaper that did attempt to analyse the facts to hand (twice), and the only newspaper to question the tendency to confuse the issue of blame (once). However, this simply wasn't enough. Whether the funds were there or not, the most important element of a serious investigation appears to have been missing — the will to carry out the investigation.

Martha O'Neill wanted just to get on with her life after the bombings. The only time the print media ever visited her or her family was around the anniversaries of the bombings. And even then, they somehow managed to get it wrong. One year in particular, she was visited by a newspaper journalist and his cameraman. They sat with her, asked her ridiculous questions such as 'Do you miss your husband?' and she spoke to them. She told them that she missed him most around Christmas, when they used to put up new wallpaper and decorate the house. She missed preparing for Christmas with him. The following day, a picture appeared in the paper of her looking pale, drawn and haggard, and it was accompanied by an article which suggested that she lived in a cold, dank hovel with no man around to decorate it for her. Nothing could have been further from the truth, and she was furious at the time.

The victims of the bombings, it seemed, were nothing more than space-fillers for Irish newspapers — they could be trotted out on the days around the anniversary, and then put back in the drawer until next year.

Denise recalls the aftermath of the 'Hidden Hand' documentary made by Yorkshire Television. 'That was the most important piece of journalism about the bombings but it had absolutely no impact on the public whatsoever.' It had no impact on the public because the media gave it no coverage whatsoever. It sank without a trace, and along with it the momentum for the campaign.

> After the documentary it [the campaign] died a death again. The only time the media wanted to know was around the fifteenth, sixteenth, and seventeenth. That was the only time you ever heard from them.

# DOMINICK STREET TO PORTLAND COURT

In the early 1970s, Dominick Street, like most of the large housing projects in inner-city Dublin, was a close community. The O'Neills had many friends among the families in their building, and, when news of Eddie's death broke, they all rallied around the stricken family. On the day itself, they came to offer sympathy and support and do what they could, even if it was nothing more than simply making tea for those who were grieving. The O'Neills' neighbours did not leave them alone in the aftermath of the bombing, even if their government was determined to do just that.

Even months later, the rest of the families in the flats were only too happy to lend some support to the O'Neills as they tried to deal with the devastation that day had caused. Denise recalls the support they received from their neighbours at the time, epitomised by the turnout for Billy's Communion celebration as soon as he was released from hospital.

It was sometime late August. There was a garden in Dominick Street flats with a statue of Our Lady. So all the boys and girls who had made their Communion on the day all dressed up for Billy's Communion. Our neighbours were always quite close to us and my mother's family would come over and help us. At the time, people were generally supportive.

However, as the years rolled on, Dominick Street became a less pleasant

66

place. Drugs, particularly that drug of the working class — heroin — began to alter the face of the once-tight community. Soon, people were moving out in their droves, and some parts of Parnell Street and Dominick Street became virtually no-go areas.

Martha had been forced to go out and work menial jobs in order to replace the regular income of which Eddie's death had robbed them. What little money they had received in compensation was quickly spent on her husband's funeral and the medical costs for Ed and Billy. She worked with many other women in similarly dire situations, but she never shied away from hard work. It was a work ethic she had always possessed. She and Eddie had met in Birmingham, and both had worked and saved there so that they could afford to go home to Dublin. Now she was forced out to work again, but in the worst possible circumstances — in the absence of her loving husband.

In the 1970s, the Irish economy was in serious trouble. Many foreign manufacturers were threatening to move their factories to other countries, inflation was climbing (within a year of the bombings it would be at 20 per cent), and dole queues were lengthening daily. It was not a time to be plunged into financial difficulty.

The government was signally unwilling to help. By 1990, the Department of Justice reported that £600,000 had been paid out in compensation in 142 awards. While that might seem like a lot of money, it should be remembered that businesses were awarded millions for damages caused to their premises. The damage done to the lives of citizens of three nations was deemed to be worth only a fraction of that.

Denise, as the eldest of the O'Neill children, became acutely aware of the impact of her father's death on the family.

I knew very early on that it was a huge loss in our lives. From the day he died, our lives changed. Even from the simple things like taking us out every Sunday on trips in his van. I missed him an awful lot, but I only realised what it meant that he was dead when I was a teenager. When I got older, I missed him more when he wasn't there for milestones in my life like my debs and finishing school. Your father is very central to these events in your life. It was then that it started to impact on me what a loss he was.

Life changed dramatically for us. He was the breadwinner and my mother had always been at home. It had a huge effect.

Martha had been used to making her money stretch since the very beginning of her relationship with Eddie in Birmingham. This was a skill she put to great use in her husband's absence. She worked a series of jobs to support the family, while also striving to be there for them at the important moments in all of their lives, and her will was the only force keeping the family going. It would have been easy for the family to go under, disintegrate and fall apart completely. It is a testament to Martha O'Neill that her five children never had to endure such hardships, while families that hadn't lost a father and breadwinner in such tragic circumstances were doing just that.

While Martha was extracting every iota of value from each pound she earned, the children too had to pull together to make sure things were as easy as they could be for everyone. However, there was no thought of Martha ever being unable to support her family. When Edward and Billy came up with an idea to help out, she put a very abrupt end to it.

I remember when I was eight or nine we got a paper round and my mam was out working and we used to buy the *Sunday World* and go around selling them in the pubs in the area and my mam went mad [when she found out].

Nonetheless, Denise realised that life was difficult for them.

My mother had to go to work almost immediately. She had always worked from that time on. Backbreaking work, anything that put food on the table. Like the majority [of people in Ireland in the 1970s], we weren't rich. People just worked and looked after their children and their home. We never went without, in material terms were never short. My mother was a fantastic provider and she was meticulous about her home.

Within a few months, the stress of the loss of her husband claimed the thirty-fifth victim of the bombing when Martha's unborn child died before she went full term. Baby Martha O'Neill was officially recognised as a victim of the bombings only thirty years later when Judge Barron named her in his report. It was a pain Martha O'Neill carried around with her from the day she entered the hospital.

Two deaths is a huge burden for any family to bear, but the worst of it wasn't over. Edward and Billy were still seriously ill in hospital. Their siblings were rarely allowed to see them, and Billy was kept in for longer so that Ed wouldn't have to stay in hospital on his own. Denise remembers going to see the boys for the first time.

> I was terribly shocked at the sight of Edward. This would have been quite a few weeks after. He was like a rag-doll. Edward was always a quiet little boy but he was even more quiet. Billy asked me where my daddy was. We weren't really allowed go up to see them most of the time. People thought it would be too distressing to see them.

The loss of her father was devastating for Denise on a personal level.

> As the eldest child, I was very close to my father. His loss had a huge impact on my life. I missed him terribly. I missed him as a person. Our lives would have been completely different. My mother would not have had to go out and work. We wouldn't have had to help out around the house so much. I, as the eldest, took on a bit of responsibility as the boss, the mother. The others did what they were told. I still boss them around now, but they don't do what I tell them any more! The loss of him was impossible to measure. He was a lovely man, a gentleman; he lived for his family; he worked very hard. Sunday was a family day. It was for the children — mass on a Sunday. If there was good weather, we would be off.

Denise would be haunted by the death of her father in many different ways for years after.

> I was fourteen or fifteen before I walked up Parnell Street. I always had cause to walk up Parnell Street [she lived right beside it], but I would have walked around it. I don't remember the first time. But I

walk up it now and I can see an image of him in my mind. It's still tough to walk — I get an awful feeling. Particularly now because I've got to know other people who were injured and you think, 'That's where so-and-so died and that's where daddy died and there's where his van was parked.' It's eerie to walk past and think about it.

Initially it was his absence that most affected her — the very fact that he wasn't there. As time went on, she would begin to think more about the exact nature of his death and, as her late teens approached, it began to upset her greatly.

I used to think a lot about how he died, thinking, 'I hope he was not lying there.' I would have thought about it a lot to myself. As I got older, thirteen or fourteen, I tended not to talk about him to my mother because you didn't want to be upsetting her. So you tended not to talk about him. Or in front of Niall as he got older. You'd suppress your feelings and try to blank it. I wasn't constantly thinking about it, but I was constantly being affected by it. You'd try and blank it and when you get older you realise that decisions you make about simple little things are affected by the amount of energy you spend blocking out other thoughts. And it's because he wasn't there. My father wasn't there. It wasn't until I was much older, my late teens, that I realised the senselessness of the killing.

The purpose of the campaign that Denise and Angela started was not to get compensation for their father's death but finally to bring the events of that day to light. They wanted justice, not money. However, the pittance they received from the government at the time (a criminal injuries tribunal was established in the wake of the bombings) served as a more than adequate inspiration for them in later life. Angela remembers when she received the money the government had put into a post office account for those bereaved by the bombings.

Government aid was almost non-existent. He [Eddie] was killed in the bombings and that was it — you got up and got on with it. Compensation was awarded at the time — Denise and I would have received three hundred pounds each as compensation for his death in post office bonds which we got when we were 18 but that we knew nothing about before. At 18, I thought I was loaded, with £300, but when you look back on it, you think, 'What an insult.' When you're being compensated for such a great loss throughout your whole life — not that money was an issue — but that was pittance.

Three hundred pounds each for the loss of the most important man in their lives. The symbolism was not lost on Angela. Three hundred pounds — thirty ten pound notes — seemed disturbingly close to Judas' thirty pieces of silver.

Apart from dealing with their grief and coming to terms with his loss financially, they also had to deal with the reality of the injuries to Edward and Billy. Denise recalls,

When Edward got older and children were nasty to him, they called him 'scarface' and he got a terrible time. And then I'd have to go down and play mammy with the children and say, 'Don't you call my brother "scarface".' He developed an awful stutter. And his injuries were so visible. He suffered throughout his teens over that, going to clubs and that. I'd have to step in and defend him a lot. I'd defend him and say something really childish like, "It's not his fault he was in a bomb."'

Although he'd been badly scarred by the bombings and had spent months out of school in hospital at a vital stage in his development, Ed never received counselling for his trauma and was not given any sort of help to make up for the missed months of schooling. He was seen by a psychiatrist, and this was a legal obligation that had to be fulfilled in relation to an insurance claim lodged by Martha's solicitor. The psychiatrist's report, the result of six sessions between him and the now five-year-old Ed, deals in less than a page with the enormous trauma suffered by the child in witnessing the murder of his father and coping with his own massive injuries. In four paragraphs, the psychiatrist manages succinctly, but inadequately, to describe the effects of a trauma that would haunt Ed O'Neill for the rest of his life. Had it not been needed for insurance purposes, Ed would never have undergone psychiatric evaluation, however little time may have been spent on it.

Under the heading, 'Information from Mrs. O'Neill (Mother of the Patient)', the psychiatrist writes:

> Mrs. O'Neill told me that Edward was injured and his father was killed in a bombing incident in May, 1974. Edward was in hospital for five weeks. He was a normal six-year-old at the time of the accident. Since the accident Mrs. O'Neill said that he gradually became aggressive, irritable and difficult to control. She herself has been depressed and irritable.

The report is incorrect from the beginning. Ed was five when the report was published, and four at the time of the bombings, yet the psychiatrist writes that he was six when the bombings took place. The bombings, the biggest mass murders in the history of the state, are referred to as 'a bombing incident in May, 1974', as if he had forgotten the whole thing and now had been vaguely reminded of it by his contact with one of its tragic victims. It was symptomatic of the way the bombings were regarded by most people in the country. This psychiatrist was not the only one who could remember them only as 'a bombing incident in May 1974'.

Under the heading, 'Examination', six sessions are distilled to their essence in five sentences.

> Edward presented as a co-operative overactive boy who related well with me and with the children and the Staff in Our Lady's Hospital. He is of low average intelligence. He said that he gets upset when he thinks of his father. He said that he fights a lot with other children. He said that he has a bad temper.

After six sessions, Ed O'Neill, clearly physically and mentally devastated by the worst atrocity in the history of the state, is summed up in five sentences. The psychiatrist's conclusions are as follows:

> This boy suffered serious emotional trauma as a result of the nature of his father's death, the loss of his father, his own hospitalisation and

his mother's depressive reaction. The combination of these factors would lead to long term emotional conflict in any child. Edward has had a reactive emotional disorder. It is probable that he will always suffer to some extent from emotional conflict as a result of the trauma that commenced in May, 1974.

Correctly, Dr Stack points out that Edward O'Neill, like every person who saw the carnage wreaked by the Dublin and Monaghan bombings on that day, would 'always suffer to some extent from emotional conflict as a result of the trauma'.

It was at this point that Ed O'Neill was beginning to grow up and realise some of the harsh realities of life in Dominick Street. He returned to school having missed months of crucial schoolwork, and he became very shy. He had developed a very bad stammer, and, as a result of this, the scars on his face, and his shyness, he became a target for bullies who tormented him constantly.

> I was in St Mary's Christian Brothers School and I used to get an awful time when I was a kid. I was regularly getting beaten up, and they'd all stand around shouting 'scarface, scarface'. I used to hide behind the big dumper bins during break-times and lunch-times because I didn't want to get beaten up. That smell of stinking rotting rubbish in the sun … I still can't walk past a rubbish bin on a warm day without gagging.

The Dominick Street flats in which he lived were also an unforgiving place. He remembers one incident in particular involving a local bully, who, according to Ed, was a 'bad young fella'.

> I think I would have been six at the time. I remember a group of him and his friends were into robbing cars. The school was pretty close to the flats and if Billy couldn't walk me home, I'd walk home myself. This time it was raining and I had an anorak over my head and my school bag on my back and he came up and punched me in the forehead. I started crying and said, 'Leave me alone, I'm gonna get my big brother after you.' Billy was forever getting me out of scrapes.

He [the bully] took my shoes off me. I don't know why but he made me walk home in the rain with no shoes on. I was crying and standing in a puddle and he got straight face to face with me and screamed at me, 'What are ya gonna do about it? Get yer oul' fella after me? Yer oul' fella's dead!' And I remember the spit flying out of his mouth and I could smell alcohol off his breath. He was fourteen or fifteen and I was six or seven. And I remember putting my hand up to wipe it off. He screamed at me and punched me in the side of the head.

Ed's mother wasn't home. At this stage, she'd got a job in a canteen of a local factory, and Ed let himself in.

While Ed was struggling with bullies at home and in school, he was also struggling with his mind. At nights, he would wake up screaming, dreaming that he was back on Parnell Street, with his skin and hair on fire. Whenever he woke up, he would be petrified, and drenched in sweat, believing that he could feel his skin burning and smell that burnt-pork smell again. It tormented him for years.

Ed believes that the effect the bombings had on him growing up made him something of an introvert. He recalls one New Year's Eve when he was seventeen years old. Everyone in the family except him was getting ready to go out, and Martha asked him if he was going out, too. She spent the night trying to convince him to go out and enjoy himself. Eventually he rose, saying, 'Actually, I *was* invited to a party', and he began to get ready. His mother was delighted, thinking that he was going out with friends. In fact, there was no party. He got ready and left the house for a local pub, where he sat on his own under the only telephone in the place while everyone else was enjoying themselves. He had three pints, then went home and told his mother that the party was great.

The children's lives were not easy. Growing up with a father-shaped hole in their lives could never be described as easy. But they all agree that their mother went out of her way to make sure that they had every possible compensation for the loss. According to Angela:

Growing up was a struggle without my father in an emotional sense. He was a great family man. But we never did without as a result of it. I certainly think our lives would have been different with him, but we didn't have sad Christmases or have no Easter eggs at Easter. We were compensated for the loss by our mother, but there was a price to pay for that because she had to go out and work hard to give us these things. I think she sometimes felt she had to give us extra because he wasn't around. I know that moving house was something they had wanted to do around the time he died. And my mother could not do that by herself. And we might have even gone on to third-level education.

The O'Neills left Dominick Street in 1985. Ed was fifteen years old and he was so happy he ran to the new house in Portland Court, behind the Big Tree pub, and got the dustpan and brush and swept the place out. The already close-knit family was even closer after eleven years of struggling and scraping to survive.

# EDDIE O'NEILL

*He was taken so young from his family. You'll never pass what's for you.*
*You won't go a day before you're supposed to.*

Martha O'Neill on Eddie's death

The film, *Schindler's List,* uses colour only once. It is the colour red — the most vivid and remarkable colour possible in the otherwise (intentionally) miserable grey and black world evoked by Spielberg. Red is the colour of the dress worn by the little girl Schindler sees from his balcony. The German industrialist watches her intently as she passes below, and the impression made upon him is remarkable. The next time we see that dress, it is lying across the top of a large pile of corpses. The girl is dead. The effect is stunning. It makes us, the viewers, together with Spielberg's Oscar Schindler, realise that every corpse in that pile was an individual. Every one of those people was as unique as that girl in the red dress. Every single one of them had a life and hopes and dreams that were cut short. By focusing on the death of one individual, we realise the scale of the devastation.

For more than thirty years, we have watched news reports, bulletins and newsflashes on television, listened to broadcasts on the radio, and read stories and features in newspapers and magazines about people whose lives have been permanently shattered by death or injury related to the Troubles. In such a long time, these stories began to develop a pattern and vocabulary of their own, and it became easy to forget that behind the stock phrases and the labels placed on the victims, there is a human being whose life has been ended by a bullet or a piece of shrapnel, or in some other equally horrible way. It is easy to forget that, as the newsreader relates the story and then moves on to the weather or that day's sports results, there is a mother or father somewhere in Ireland grieving for a lost son or daughter. Usually, in the past, there was more than one.

The purpose of this chapter is not to single Eddie O'Neill out as the most important victim of the Troubles, or the most interesting, or to suggest that his family was any more affected by his death than any other family in Ireland in this terrible period of our history. Nor is it the purpose of this chapter to catalogue the thousands of victims of the Troubles. This chapter sets out simply to highlight one life, in the hope that it may serve as a reminder that every single life lost in the Troubles was the life of an individual, like Eddie O'Neill. By showing the impact the death of one man had on the lives of so many people, perhaps we might come to realise how huge the scale of carnage has been over more than three decades of the Troubles.

*Martha O'Neill*
Martha O'Neill was pregnant with a baby girl when she lost her husband. The loss of Eddie was so traumatic that she also lost the baby. Eddie was 39 when he was killed, but Martha was several years younger. Insurance assessors informed her that she wouldn't get as much money as another woman in her position because she was young enough to remarry.

> Eddie was a wonderful man. We'd a great relationship, a great partnership and a great life. I didn't have dishwashers or washing machines. We didn't have luxury items. We didn't need them. We had a great family life. We worked very well together. We had our rows, like every couple, but we loved each other.

When Martha was still a teenager, her father decided to move to Birmingham. The reasons for the move were never made clear to her. As a child, she had spent much time playing on the beach or in St Anne's Park near North Bull Island, a large nature reserve on an island in Dublin Bay. To the teenaged Martha, it seemed ludicrous to move from somewhere as pleasant and comfortable as her home, to the dull red-brick and smog of industrial Birmingham. She always longed to return to Dublin.

Martha was a Caffrey, and her uncle was the owner of Caffrey's Sweets. Her father was a talented man who could turn his hand to almost anything, and had a wide variety of jobs in his time, including painter, decorator, plasterer, sweet-maker with his brother, and musician. When he was working with his brother in the factory, he would regularly turn his own kitchen into a small sweet factory where he would make chocolates, cakes, Easter eggs and all sorts of confectionery, much to the delight of his young family.

However, his real talent lay in music, and he performed in show bands all over the country, and could play the mandolin, the guitar, the piano and just about any other musical instrument he was left long enough with. Given his ability to turn to any job so readily, Martha doesn't know why he decided to move the family to England. All she knows is that one day she was living in the fresh seaside area on Dublin's North Strand, and the next she was living in smog and smoke amid ugly factories in England's grim north. It was not a complete disaster, however.

Eddie O'Neill was living in Birmingham when the Caffreys moved over there. He was a painter and decorator who worked for Baxter's where Martha's brother was employed. Eddie and Martha were introduced to each other at a social club in 1958. At the time, there had been a spate of murders in Birmingham, so no young ladies were allowed out in the town on their own without a chaperone. So it was that Martha came to attend the social club with her brother. Although she was very young — only sixteen — and Eddie was twenty-four, the pair just clicked.

In a very short time, they were a couple. Eddie was a boxing enthusiast. In Dublin, he had been an amateur boxer and had achieved some success when he was younger. He trained regularly and followed boxing religiously. Martha herself became interested in boxing through Eddie and recalls the piles and piles of copies of *The Boxing News* she kept for him in a wardrobe in their house in Birmingham. Through Eddie, she came to have an extensive knowledge of the sport. He used to come around to listen to fights on the radio which, because they were being fought in America, were on at two in the morning. Her father would set the alarm and everyone would get up to listen to the radio.

Eddie and Martha became man and wife in Birmingham on 31 December 1960. Martha had just turned eighteen at the beginning of that October. Eddie was the grand old age of twenty-five. 'I have no idea why we chose New Year's Eve,' Martha says. 'He just asked me to marry him and I said yes. I was only going out with him for a year at that stage.'

They planned to have a large family, and they started straight away. However, luck was not with them. Martha became pregnant, but the baby, a boy, was premature, and he died at birth. The next child, a little girl, arrived the following June, but she died when the umbilical cord got tied around her neck.

Martha couldn't stay in Birmingham. She had still never quite got over the shock of moving from the seaside town of Donnycarney to the smoky, smog-filled ugly industrial town of Birmingham. The couple had been saving since their marriage for the move back to Dublin. Martha was great with money, a talent that she would turn to good effect after Eddie's death. Eddie and Martha came home in May 1962.

Back in Dublin, they moved into a flat in the blocks on Dominick Street, just off Parnell Street, and before too long began the family they had wanted so much.

While Martha and Eddie had wanted a large family, they were beset by difficulties. According to Martha, in the thirteen years they were married, she was pregnant thirteen times. The children they had were precious to them. And Eddie doted on them. When he wasn't out working, he was bringing them places and giving them the most enjoyable life he could. Sunday was his day to bring the children off on trips in the van. They would polish their shoes the night before and leave them lying in a row at the door, ready for mass the next morning. After mass, they would all troop into the van and go off with their father.

Martha found it almost impossible to live without Eddie after his death.

It took me an awful long time and for three years I just couldn't cope. I'd go up to Glasnevin and I just wanted to bring him home with me. I couldn't bear leaving him there.

Death is an awful thing. To lose anyone is the worst feeling in the world. And I had to get over the fact that I was still pregnant and he would never see the baby. That used to kill me.

In the end, Martha herself didn't even see the baby, who was taken away immediately. On top of this, she had been keeping the spirits of the children at home bolstered with the hope that soon they would have a new baby brother or sister.

> Billy and Edward developed two very bad stammers after the bombings and couldn't talk. Edward would ask, 'Will the baby be ready today?' with a really bad stammer. The thoughts of coming out of hospital with nothing and telling those little children that [the baby was] dead ... and the Rotunda Hospital said that the bombing wasn't the cause of my baby dying. It *was* the cause of my baby's death.

### Denise O'Neill

Denise O'Neill was the eldest child in the family, and her father called her the apple of his eye. It was her birthday on 17 May, the day her father was killed. She still has the charm bracelet and the card that she got from him on the morning of her ninth birthday.

As with the rest of the O'Neill children, she remembers mostly the fun she had with her father. He seemed to spend whatever free time he had either in the karate club or at home playing with his children. When he wasn't playing with his children at home, he was bringing them out in his van for trips to various places around Dublin and beyond. They would go to the beach sometimes where they would practise martial arts together, or they would go to the Phoenix Park where he had hung a swing on a tree for them.

Denise is happy to talk about her father, but she keeps some memories of him to herself. Some memories would be made less special if they were shared with the world.

She used to go to work with her father on Saturday mornings. When he would go to a site to pick up his gear or clean up after a job, she would pretend to hide in the back of the van and he would pretend not to see her. Then, once they had arrived, she would jump out and try to surprise him while he would do his best to pretend that he was surprised by her.

He loved playing practical jokes. He'd eat his dinner and pretend to look away and you'd steal a bit of his meat and he'd look back and say, 'Oh, where's it gone?'

She also remembers his kindness, and not just to his children. He was highly regarded by the people of Dominick Street, especially the older people who lived there. He would go out of his way to make sure they had things and, if the weather was inclement, he would bring coal or logs for their fires and food for their presses. This kindness was never forgotten.

To his daughter, Eddie O'Neill was a giant. 'From a child's perspective, he was a very big man. He had big hands,' Denise remembers. In fact, he wasn't a huge man, but left a huge hole in his family's lives when he was killed.

Things were very different when he was gone. You'd hear him [when he was alive] whistling coming up the balcony. You'd miss his van not being parked outside the flats. Simple things. His number 6 cigarettes. He was missed. My mother's life was made so much harder when he wasn't around.

Denise missed the affection he would lavish on all of them daily.

He'd always have one of us on his shoulder. He was a jolly person. He enjoyed his life, he enjoyed his family and he enjoyed his children.

As Denise grew up, the big moments in her life, although always joyful and happy occasions, were saddened by the knowledge that there was one guest missing who probably would have enjoyed the whole event more than anyone else.

He wasn't there when you got married or made your confirmation or you turned sixteen or you passed your school exams. And you'd think about him at these times.

As a child, Denise didn't realise that the fact of her father's being dead meant that she would never see him again. She laughs when she says this, suggesting that she might just have been a particularly stupid child, but it is easy to see how a child could fail to grasp the finality. For months after the bombings, the children were surrounded by people. As Denise puts it, 'We were never given the chance to realise he wasn't there. My mother's family were very good, looking after us in the months after his death.'

As time went on, they just came to live with the situation and cope with it. The realisation struck her only some years later when playing with another child:

> I was out the back playing with some child and there was an argument over a ball or a skipping rope and, kids being kids, she said to me, 'You don't even have a daddy.' I remember how it struck me. That's what death meant. They're never coming back.

For the first time, Denise began to see death as being the end of life, as opposed to her father's simply being 'with the angels', as her mother had explained it to her.

Martha O'Neill did her best to ensure that her children never suffered more than they had to. It was difficult. The man who had brought so much fun and love to their home would never again walk through the door. And Martha had to work doubly hard to be mother and father to her children. Denise recalls:

> My mother always went out of her way to make up for the fact that he wasn't there — emotionally and materially. At Christmas we always got more than we asked for and more than we should have expected from her.

As the 1970s turned into the 1980s, Martha had another problem to be concerned about. Cheap heroin was beginning to flood into Europe from Afghanistan, and Ireland was no exception. Inner-city Dublin was soon filled with the drug, and it began to turn what had been close communities into ghettos. Dominick Street was one of the hardest-hit communities. It changed from being a place where almost every neighbour had come out to help Billy O'Neill to celebrate his belated First Communion, to a place where junkies and addicts roamed the balconies, and thievery and muggings were an everyday occurrence. 'You only had to look out on the balcony to see a handbag being snatched or something,' Denise recalls. 'It was awful.'

While Denise believes that it was only a small number of people in Dominick Street who earned the area its criminal reputation, the fact is that people soon began to flee the community. The O'Neills would soon follow, but nonetheless they lived in the area during one of the worst scourges to hit Dublin's inner city. Denise has great admiration for her mother for bringing them all up safely during that time, and is eternally grateful to her for it. 'I don't know how she managed it,' she says.

*Angela O'Neill*

Angela was only seven when her father was killed. Most adults will remember very little of what happened to them up to and probably for some time after the age of seven, but Angela's memories of her father are very clear. As people grow older, their memories grow more selective. Things that seemed important to them as children, and as teenagers, seem less so as adults. The mind files those memories away in deep storage, only to be recalled when something drags them forward. As most people grow older, memories of their childhood will fade, and memories of what they did with their father when they were six will begin to seem less vivid, until eventually they think they've forgotten completely. They haven't, of course — the memories are just in deep storage. However, for Angela O'Neill, her memories of her father are few, and each one is precious.

She remembers how fit and strong he was. He'd enjoyed some success in his youth as an amateur boxer and always kept himself in good shape. Once — Angela doesn't know what age she was at the time — he was working out in the flat, wearing his karate outfit, and he turned around and announced, 'I'm going to live until I'm 100.'

Not all Angela's memories are as heart-rending as that. Most, in fact, are simple memories of a man who adored his family and took life with more than one pinch of salt.

> I remember the fun … he used to get in on our practical jokes. We once bought a false rasher and a plastic egg and handed it to him on a plate with a knife and fork and him breaking his heart laughing at it and we believed that he thought they were real in the first place. We

would say the rosary every evening like most Irish families and we would all kneel along the sofa with our heads down. And he used to stand in the corner with a belt in his hand making sure no one would mess, but of course he'd never lay a hand on us. But there was one time that Billy and I put a small piece of newspaper on her [Martha's] head and every time she'd bow her head the piece of paper would fall off so we'd put it back up there. We thought it was hilarious and he was standing in the corner with the belt in kinks laughing, supposed to be stopping this sort of thing from happening.

Eddie O'Neill was passionate about martial arts and passionate about his children, and it was inevitable that the two would mix.

Denise, Billy and I did judo and he'd be upstairs doing karate. And every Saturday morning during the summer, he'd have us down on the beach practising and running with our suits on on Portmarnock Strand. At home, he'd throw the mattress down on the ground and have us practising our throws onto it. But, of course, we all gave that up when he died.

He was generous too, Angela recalls:

I remember we used to get presents at Easter time. And I remember one Easter, Denise got a record player and I got a big yellow duck — it was bigger than me at the time.

These memories are tinged with sadness by Angela's knowledge that she never got to know her father as an adult. Although she has heard stories from his friends and relatives about what he was like, and gathers that he was the same fun-loving, easy-going character she remembers, Angela regrets that she never got to see him in an adult context.

My uncle, my mother's brother, adored him and would often tell me about times they had and the laughs they had. Our relationship would definitely have changed and I'd love for him to have lived so that we could go for a pint — to see the man as opposed to seeing the father.

The O'Neill family was strong before Eddie's death and remained strong after it. There is no doubt that, although he was with his children for only a short period, he left an indelible mark on their lives. While his and Martha's plans were put on hold, the drive she instilled in them was balanced by the sense of fun that had always been in the house thanks to Eddie. His influence was all-pervasive, even in death.

While things would have been different for the O'Neills had their father been around, Angela doesn't believe that they would have been much better off materially. While money probably would have been slightly more available to them, Martha's efforts were Trojan, and they never went without. As she points out, they were probably the only children in Ireland at the time to get presents at Easter.

But no quantity of presents can compensate for the loss of their father. No quantity of gifts can relieve Angela O'Neill's need to hold onto the few precious memories she has of her father. Neither Angela nor the rest of the O'Neills want material compensation for the loss of their father. They want something for him instead — justice.

*Liam O'Sullivan*
Liam O'Sullivan was the last person to speak to Eddie O'Neill before he died.

> The first time I met Eddie was in the [martial arts] club in Church Street. Shotakan was the particular style of martial arts. I knew him only a couple of years but I felt as if I knew him all my life, I got on that well with him. I was eighteen or nineteen when I met him and we were training down there and I got to know him. He was a very nice guy.
>
> I knew him to see prior to that, but we got very close down in the club. I knew very little about him before I met him. We used to train and spar together in the club and he was always there. I was training every night I could and he was always there.

Liam had been training in various forms of martial art since the age of fifteen. Although young when he met Eddie, he was already at a fairly high level. He had tried shotakan, kenpo, and tae kwan do, and has continued practising martial arts all his life. Eddie, by contrast, had been training for only a year or two, but because of his background in boxing, his physical fitness and his dedication to the sport, he was already quite good.

> Eddie was almost forty at the time and I was only eighteen. He was only starting. But he did a lot of boxing before that and he was quite handy at the boxing. He was very popular with all the lads and very well respected. There were quite a few guys around his age and maybe a little bit older at the club.
>
> He was a very modest sort of a fella. I knew he was handy, because he didn't go around bragging and I suppose that's the reason we hit it off. He was very fit for his age. Any time I was there he was there so he obviously enjoyed it that much. He was very interested in it.

In spite of the age gap, the two men were drawn to each other through their love of karate and their dedication to the sport. Over the two years or so that they knew each other, they never spent much time talking about anything other than training in the club. Liam never knew much about Eddie's family life, and Eddie never asked Liam about his. However, Liam believes that they would have become closer friends had fate not intervened.

On the day of the bombings, Eddie had brought the two boys to Liam's barber's shop to have their hair cut. Within seconds of stepping out the door, he was dead. It was his first time to go to the shop. Liam says:

> I always felt a tremendous amount of guilt for that. And from what I believe it was just a spur of the moment thing — he needed to get the boys' hair cut and he said, 'I'll bring them down to Liam.'

Liam was nineteen in 1974. He had just taken over his father's barber's shop on Parnell Street and was making a great success of it. The difference between Liam and other barbers in Dublin at the time — his father included — was that Liam could style hair. In the 1970s, long hair was in vogue, and the old-style barbers simply couldn't handle the new demands that were being made. So, when Eddie O'Neill walked into the shop that

Friday, it was humming with business. So many heads of hair had been washed that day that Liam had been forced to turn on the electric heater in the shop in order to dry some towels. The day itself was already a very warm one, so the front door of the shop was open to allow a breeze blow through.

Eddie came into the shop with the two boys around 3.30. And we were having great craic talking about a few sessions we had up in the club. Brian was with him — a brother-in-law of his. I had this poster of Bruce Lee up on the wall and of course he was mad into it. Brian decided to go out for a pint. I was up to my eyes in work — the place was packed. The lads got their hair cut and, as they were going out, I gave one of them a few pence because he was making his Communion. I flicked them a few bob. And then he gave me a couple of bob as a tip.

Just as he was walking out the door, I bent over to plug [the heater] out and just as I bent down, the bomb went off. I thought for a second it might have been the heater exploding. I had Perspex in the window rather than glass and two pieces came in and a piece of the car came in and cut through the top of my head and stuck in the wall — we tried to get it out with a pliers later but it wouldn't come out. There were a good few people in the shop injured and then Brian came in and said, 'Where's Eddie?' and I said, 'Eddie's okay — he's just gone out.'

Although for a few moments Liam thought that it was the heater that had exploded, when he turned and looked out the window, he realised what had happened. The shop around him was in ruins, and many of his customers were injured. Had Liam not bent down to plug out the heater, the piece of the bomb-car that cut his head and lodged in the wall above him would have lodged itself firmly in his body.

Realising what had happened, he went outside:

I went out and there were bodies all over the place and Eddie was just in the side of the garage and his clothes were all torn off him. There was a piece of glass after piercing him and going through his heart. There was a young fella on the petrol pump, Derek Byrne. He'd have been fourteen, and he remembers that I got towels and put them around him and I vaguely remember something stuck in him. Apparently when the explosion went off, the hose whipped up and stuck in his shoulder. I don't remember taking it out of his shoulder, but he swears that I took it out. And then he asked me for a cigarette and I took one out and lit it for him, with petrol lying everywhere. My father came out of the shop and there was a fella decapitated outside the chipper that was only three or four doors up. We got out of there. I still wasn't sure if Eddie was dead or alive. I was brought to hospital myself. Derek Byrne was left in such a bad way that he woke up in a morgue.

Following Eddie's death, his friends from the club were devastated. He had been very well respected, and no one knew how best to commemorate his death. Liam thought that the best idea would be to run a tournament in Eddie's honour, but the club decided instead to present a black belt to Martha. It now hangs on the wall in her sitting room.

It was only when Eddie died that Liam realised how little he actually knew about his friend's life outside the karate club.

Anything we knew about each other was the training and we were so into it, that was all we'd talk about. We were still very good friends even if it was just on that level. Maybe under different circumstances if that hadn't happened and the bomb had never happened we would have gotten to know each other even better than we did. I felt as if I'd known him all my life — even if it was only through the training. We never even got the chance to go out socially, but I'm sure we would have.

Just like the O'Neills, Liam was left to fend for himself after the bombings.

Our shop was destroyed and we only got £270. I had been saving to buy a house but I had to put all the money into the shop and I still went off and got married in the end. We had to move into a rented house that we shared with someone else. That was not what we'd planned.

The whole incident changed Liam's life. Apart from the fact that he had lost his friend and had his own life turned upside-down, he felt tremendous guilt about having brought Eddie down to the shop. Eddie never would have been on Parnell Street had he not known Liam, and he wouldn't have been in the path of the bomb had Liam not had that poster of Bruce Lee that he had stopped to chat about.

> I used to go out quite a bit, I was a young man with a lot of money but there was a lot of anger in me. I used to feel like I was nearly hoping for trouble to come my way. And I later found out that a good friend of mine was feeling the exact same way. We were aggressive and we didn't understand why. And no one gave us counselling at the time.

The guilt about Eddie's death and the memory of the carnage had a huge impact on Liam as a young man. In the absence of proper counselling, he found solace in martial arts.

> It's not just physical training; there's a lot of mental training as well. Martial arts teaches you not to be aggressive. I was of a high standard. I was probably more advanced than most. I put so much time into it and I just had the talent.

However, the mental discipline of martial arts worked only up to a point. What he really needed was counselling. When the Justice for the Forgotten Campaign started, there was somewhere to go for the first time to discuss his feelings about the bombings. Liam went and spoke to a counsellor called Áine Grealy, who was with the campaign for a brief period. 'I got on well with her and I was comfortable with her,' he recalls. After Áine Grealy had left Justice for the Forgotten, Liam decided to go and organise his own counselling.

> I attended another counselling session in Beaumount hospital. I have recurring dreams about it [the bombings]. It's seldom a week would go by without me having a dream about it. In the dream, I remember running down Parnell Street, running over all the bodies and trying to get away from it. Then I'm at the back of a church and looking at

all these coffins. Some nights it just goes and goes and I'd wake up exhausted.

Through bad training techniques, Liam developed arthritis and couldn't work as much as previously. As his own father had done in 1974, Liam passed the shop over to his son.

Liam remembers the first time he met Ed O'Neill Junior as an adult. Liam was sweeping up outside his shop and a young man pulled up on a motorbike. He took off his helmet and asked Liam, 'Do you know who I am?' He introduced himself and they have stayed in contact ever since.

> I gelled with young Eddie, but I never really tried at all, it just happened. Eddie is very like his father; he reminds me an awful lot of him. He looks like him. Very like him in the face. He's bigger than his da, but he looks like him. He has the same personality as his father. Very friendly, but he's nobody's fool either. That's the reason I get on with him, I suppose. We just chat about things in general. It's usually just about the bombings, but that's because it's the biggest thing in both of our lives.

*Edward O'Neill*

On Father's Day 2003, Ed O'Neill Junior visited the grave of his father, Edward Senior. It is his habit to visit the grave regularly — every Father's Day, Christmas Day, his father's birthday and the anniversary of the bombings. He visits to pray for his father's soul. On Father's Day 2003, he promised his father that this year he would see justice — that no one deserved to die as Ed Senior and thirty-four others died; that no one deserved to be treated as those families were treated after the bombings. And for the first time in twenty-nine years, Ed O'Neill cried for his father.

⌘　⌘　⌘

Fairly soon after his Leaving Cert, at a time when jobs were still difficult to find in Ireland, Ed got a job with J.T. Collins and Company, an insurance broker on Baggot Street. Most people might have made a life for themselves, realising how lucky they were to have a job in such difficult economic times. Ed O'Neill simply could not.

> The normal life that I tried to lead was a mask, and as things started to go haywire, the mask started to slip. Underneath it all, I was just hurt and angry. At that period, I was not a very nice person.

Ed used to get very depressed around the anniversary of the bombings, which was also his sister's birthday, but he tried hard to keep the mask from slipping. He kept telling himself that he had to get things together, and, for a while, it worked. Although he was getting on well at work and he had even earned a promotion, underneath the mask his life was in turmoil.

The problem, he soon came to realise, was Dublin. Every day he had to live and work in a city that held nothing for him but bad memories and pain. The very city was a reminder of how his father had been murdered and how he had been injured. He went to Sydney with his brother, Billy. He worked first in Qantas Airways and then with the New Zealand Insurance Company. In Australia, he had a couple of sessions with a psychiatrist who had done a lot of work with veterans of the Vietnam War, and who told Ed that he showed a lot of the same symptoms as those veterans. It was the first time that Ed heard the term 'post-traumatic stress disorder'.

While Ed was away from Ireland, he picked up work where he could, and used the money he earned to pay his way. He travelled to Melbourne where he stayed for a few weeks in a small hostel, and placed a notice in a window, looking for travel companions. Together with an English couple, he went to Canberra, Adelaide, across the Nullarbor Plain, and into Perth. He later travelled all around South East Asia before going to the United States and South America. In Panama in 1991, sitting with a bottle of beer in one hand and an apple in the other, watching an American warship coming up the Panama Canal, Ed decided that it was time to go home. He had spent more than a year travelling.

Ed never told anyone that he was coming back home. He returned to Ireland dressed in flip-flops and Bermuda shorts, with a rucksack and a poncho, and it was raining heavily in Dublin. His mother had been having difficulty sleeping for the days preceding Ed's unannounced arrival, so on the night of his return, unaware of her son's plans, Martha took a Valium and went to sleep. When Ed arrived, he went up to her room, tapped her on her shoulder and said, 'Ma, it's me.' His mother glanced at him, said, 'Oh, howya Edward?' and promptly fell back asleep.

Ed's anger had not subsided during his travels. However, he was now able to direct it towards different ends. The time away from Ireland, away from the city in which his father had been killed and he had been injured, had given him perspective and mental stability. He was still angry but he could now put his energy into projects such as helping his sisters with their burgeoning campaign for justice.

Ed went to college as a mature student. He earned a degree in Business Studies at Dublin City University. However, he was beginning to get very ill. The physical effects of the shrapnel in his body and the considerable injuries he had sustained were taking their toll. He suffered from serious dizzy spells and severe nausea. He had always suffered from these to a mild degree, but now his condition was getting progressively worse. He had to undergo many operations to remove shrapnel and to get rid of fatty tissue that had grown around scars.

He was also still being haunted by the memory of the bombings. It had taken him twelve years to walk down that part of Parnell Street again.

I used to unconsciously avoid it — I'd walk up to the Garden of Remembrance and down Denmark Street or walk around from the other side. This particular day, I didn't think and I just walked down it and this car backfired and I had to be prized down from a lamp-post by Billy. I'll never be comfortable on Parnell Street, but I've learned to direct my feelings in other ways.

Ed feels that it could all have been different. 'I feel that if I had been given adequate counselling to deal with this then my childhood and my adolescence would have been a lot happier.'

*Edward O'Neill Junior on his Father*

People would walk up to me on the street and say, 'You are Eddie O'Neill's son, aren't you?' I would always react with a certain degree of suspicion before answering, trying to figure out who they were and what their motives for the question were in the first place.

Most of the time, I would answer positively and say, 'Yes', although still somewhat suspicious. But generally people would then elaborate and tell me they knew my father from a long time ago when I wasn't even around on this planet. There were many occasions when I would actually end up going for a pint with some of those people as they would go further into their memories for me. I used to sit sometimes in awe at the stories that would come of these perfect strangers.

It was like I held the memory of my father in a mythical Thor-like esteem and would happily sit there for hours, or indeed as long as these strangers would give me, while the story would be played out. There was a common thread running through all of these stories. My father, although a physically imposing man, was widely recognised as being a gentleman of the highest quality. It's funny, but many people seemed to assume that I had already heard the stories of what kind of man he actually was. There was one, though, that I would like to tell.

We had an old woman living in the flats where we came from, who was called Powderface. I am sure my father knew her real name but the kids in the flats all knew her as the former [Miss Powderface]. This old lady suffered from a breathing difficulty which required oxygen and regular hospital trips.

Some years after his death, this old lady called me to her, saying she wanted to tell me something. Somewhat gingerly, I approached her. She told me that before my father's death he used to regularly bring her to hospital, sometimes carrying her all the way through the Mater Hospital as her doctor was regularly shifted around the grounds due to the lack of space at the time.

She said she always tried to let on that someone else was picking her up but he always insisted that it was no trouble. He would leave her sitting waiting for the doctor then he would go and seek out her new supply of oxygen and have it brought back to his van before going back for her. He would then go back for her and wait while the doctor examined her and let her go.

Old Powderface told me that he used to make a point of dropping in and he would always bring a bag of coal and a bag of logs for her as a coal fire was the only form of heating she had at the time.

She went on to tell me that she was not the only person he helped out. He would try to call on lots of the old folk in the flats, sometimes on the silliest of pretences, but always to give these people a little bit of company and maybe have a few cups of tea in the process.

She told me that many times she told him to spend the money on his children and his wife, to which he always replied with a joke of some kind that he was only spending what he could afford.

There was another time when I was around eighteen or nineteen years old and I was going through a very difficult period. I was drinking heavily and many times ended up picking fights with people that I knew would give me the beating of my life. It's hard to describe the emotions that were circulating around my head at the time. I had no fear of anyone or anything. I wanted to hurt myself but was too much of a coward to do it by my own hand. It's difficult to describe to anyone who has not gone through this series of emotions or experienced the sense of loss and grief that had completely encircled me, but anyone who has will know exactly what I am talking about.

I was sitting in the Parnell Mooney Pub on Parnell Street when a man approached me and said, 'Sorry, but are you Eddie O'Neill's son?' Somewhat aggressively, I replied, 'Who wants to know?' He sat down beside and said, 'My name is Mick Travers and I knew your dad very well from the karate club. Can I sit with you for a few minutes?'

'It's a free country,' I replied.

He began by telling me that many people in Dublin [in the 1970s and 1980s] thought of him as a hard man. He worked the doors of a few pubs around Dublin. He told me that 'me and your aul' fella sparred in the club a few times and I knew he could hit me very hard.' He went on to say, 'I was standing there and his big fists were coming at me from all directions and I hardly got a bloody punch in.' He finished up by saying, 'It was a pleasure to have known your aul' fella — he was one of life's true gentlemen.'

Even now, thirty years later, the fact that he is not around upsets me greatly. I do feel that I have been deprived the guidance of a true gentleman. As Mick remarked to me as he was walking away, 'Gentle when stroked, but fierce when provoked — that was Eddie O'Neill.'

He should have been there to see his grandchildren born. I should have had the chance to go to him seeking advice about girls and my first car. I know people die all the time and it's tragic, but the circumstances of his death make it all the more painful to endure.

I don't think that any of us — men, I mean — ever grow up ... we will always be daddy's boys. I miss him. Even now, nearly thirty years on, there are some times when I just want him to put those big arms around me and give me a hug and tell me everything is going to be okay. I still desperately miss him. Is that silly?

# GETTING STARTED

*'A phone book and some newspaper clippings. That's how it started.'*
Denise O'Neill

*'We were all aware of the Dublin and Monaghan bombings and we all assumed that the terrorists had been caught and that someone was in prison somewhere. We never asked the question of anyone though.'*
Denise O'Neill

*'I always had a great interest in the Troubles in Northern Ireland. I was well aware of the divide at a very young age. Denise and myself would always speak about it together. It was in my early twenties that we decided to ask questions and get an explanation for ourselves.'*
Angela O'Neill

Moving to Portland Court, the O'Neills finally started a phase of their lives that had been delayed by the tragedy of the bombings. It had always been Eddie and Martha's intention to move out of Dominick Street to a house of their own. However, without Eddie around, that plan had to be delayed. In other circumstances, the move might never have taken place. It was a triumph of Martha's will that eventually the family did manage to make the move.

In the meantime, while the O'Neills had been getting on with the everyday business of living, those men who had inflicted such pain and misery on them and on the rest of the families bereaved by the bombings had been free to continue their campaigns of death and destruction. Not one of them was ever arrested or charged with the bombings. Not one of them was even questioned. As far as the law was concerned, these were innocent men. Men like Robin Jackson were free to act on whatever murderous impulses drove him. Robin Jackson died not in a prison cell where he should have been, but in a hospital bed, of natural causes. Two governments, in Britain and Ireland, made sure — either by intent or by neglect — that the perpetrators of the atrocity would continue to live their lives as free any other man.

None of the O'Neills was aware of this or the irregularities with the garda investigation which had effectively allowed their father's killers to escape back across the border.

The Garda Síochána had behaved rather bizarrely when it came to conducting the investigation. It is easy to suggest that they were simply unprepared for the sheer scale of the disaster, but that doesn't explain away all of the irregularities which seemed to hamper the investigation. To start with, not one member of the gang that had carried out the bombing was ever arrested or brought in for questioning. During the whole investigation, in fact, only one man was brought in for questioning, and he was released when he was found to have had nothing to do with the bombings. Moreover, there was an alarming lack of care taken with key forensic materials from the very moment the gardaí stepped onto the scenes of the crime.

Some journalists have speculated on the issues, and many experts have been called upon to give their opinions, yet no one has proved conclusively what happened. Plenty of theories abound, but no one has yet been able to say what happened. The report of the Commission of Inquiry into the Dublin and Monaghan Bombings, headed by Mr Justice Liam Hamilton and later by Mr Justice Henry Barron, failed to provide anything even close to a definitive answer, and, it could be argued, failed to draw the obvious conclusions from the evidence it had gathered.

Ed O'Neill claims that, in the course of his own inquiries into the matter, he was informed by a former member of an Garda Síochána that the investigations into the bombings were officially wound down. He was told that gardaí at the time were making headway in the case (they had at this stage, with the aid of the RUC, compiled a list of suspected bombers), and were frustrated with the order to let the case drop. This seems to be supported by evidence found by Glyn Middleton's 'Hidden Hand' team, who interviewed a number of gardaí who were on the case and who said, variously, that they could easily have caught the perpetrators.

However, in his report on the bombings, Mr Justice Barron states that the problem lay not with orders from the top preventing the investigations from going any further but with sheer ineptitude on the part of gardaí. It is quite possible that both have an equal part to play in the thirty years of inaction in the Dublin and Monaghan investigation.

In the hours, days and weeks following the bombings, eyewitnesses were rounded up, and they were shown pictures of the suspects and even brought to suspects' houses. What emerged from all this was the information that not only were known loyalist paramilitaries involved in the bombings, but that there were significant numbers of officers and NCOs from the British army operating in Dublin during the early 1970s.

In his report of the Commission of Inquiry into the Dublin and Monaghan Bombings, Mr Justice Henry Barron refuses to draw from these findings any conclusions regarding collusion. However, he does accept that on previous occasions there had been illegal actions carried out with the aid of British security force personnel in this State and that, although no evidence exists now to prove it, it is quite possible that this is what happened in Dublin and Monaghan also.

The closest example is of the Dublin bombings of 1972 and 1973. Both were inspired, if not in fact carried out, by members of the British security forces, and there is compelling evidence to suggest this. Furthermore, the Dublin and Monaghan bombings were carried out by loyalists who, it has been alleged, were being 'run' by a British army officer called Robert Nairac. Nairac successfully ran the three men both before and after the Dublin and Monaghan bombings. He was later killed by the IRA.

In his report, Mr Justice Barron refers to journalist Joe Tiernan's book, *The Dublin and Monaghan Bombings and the Murder Triangle*, in which the author alleges that the same officers who were running Billy Hanna had been involved in the planning of the bombings of Dublin in 1972 and 1973. Although Barron does not deal any further with these allegations in his report — perhaps because of Tiernan's refusal to discuss the allegations with the Inquiry — he does not suggest that these possibilities have been ruled out or that they are false. In fact, he later says:

> A finding that members of the security forces in Northern Ireland could have been involved in the bombings is neither fanciful nor absurd, given the number of instances in which similar illegal activity has been proven.

It is necessary to understand that in this context 'proven' means 'proven beyond all reasonable doubt', in a legal sense. Most of these allegations cannot be proven in that sense, and that, of course, is the main problem with the Barron Report. In any case, it is because of the important work done by journalists such as Joe Tiernan, Glyn Middleton and Don Mullan that these processes have begun at all.

The garda investigation produced many leads but none seemed to be followed up. Many people were identified as known UVF members. David Alexander Mulholland (who died in his home in England the day Mr Justice Barron's report was published) was clearly identified by more than one eyewitness. He was well known to the Garda Síochána and the RUC, and a clear dossier of his career was already in the possession of both forces. According to garda files, he is described by Chief Superintendent John Joy as follows:

> David Alexander Mulholland of 114, Ulsterville Park, Portadown. This man is a member of the UVF and has a history of involvement in car bomb explosions in Northern Ireland. He is 35 years of age, 6 feet in height, well built, blue eyes, light brown hair, turning grey, round large features, very pale complexion.

With all this information — his past history in car bombings in Northern Ireland, his known membership of the UVF, an organisation that was one of the prime suspects in the bombings, and having been positively identified by a number of eyewitnesses as having been in the Parnell Street bomb-car — this man wasn't even brought in for questioning. Incredibly, Mr Justice Barron suggests that the reason for this was that one of the eyewitnesses insisted that Mulholland spoke with an English accent, and this affected the veracity of her identification.

For a man who had been steeped in this investigation for so long not even to suggest in his official report to the government that readers should remain sceptical about the decision to dismiss what is otherwise an airtight identification simply beggars belief. As any criminal who wishes to keep his identity secret will attest, an accent is the easiest, and probably the first, thing to change. If David Alexander Mulholland came to Dublin driving the car containing the bomb that would later kill Eddie O'Neill and seriously injure his two young sons, would it not seem possible that he would use a different accent in order not to arouse suspicion? A car from Britain driving around the streets of Dublin might be less suspicious than a car from Northern Ireland. Wouldn't it make sense, then, that Mulholland might try to pass himself off as a Briton, rather than allowing himself to be clearly identified by his accent?

In any case, Mr Justice Barron doesn't fail to identify Mulholland as the driver of the Parnell Street bomb-car, but his assertion that the accent was the reason he wasn't at least brought in for questioning by the gardaí or the RUC does not in any way absolve the Garda Síochána of gross negligence (or worse) during the investigation.

Another eyewitness account described by the judge makes his assertion even more difficult to understand. A man entered a café on Cavendish Row, claiming to have been in Arnott's on Henry Street when the bombs exploded (this happened only minutes after the bombings, and all witnesses claim that the character seemed less than perturbed about the death and carnage that had been wreaked) but according to the waitress, he didn't have enough time to get from Henry Street to Cavendish Row, and he couldn't have known where all three bombs had exploded (in conversation with the people in the café, he mentioned the third bomb which had exploded on Nassau Street). The key element was that, of the people he spoke to in the café, none could quite pin down his accent. One said it was English, while another couldn't decide whether it was English or Northern Irish. It would seem to have been a case of an Englishman speaking in a Northern Ireland accent or, more probably, a man from Northern Ireland speaking in an English accent. In any case, the man identified in the café was almost certainly putting on an accent. Yet Mr Justice Barron does not seem to think that this is a possibility — nor does he seem to think that it was a possibility with David Alexander Mulholland.

On that day, there was also an identification of a number of British army officers and non-commissioned officers (NCOs). A former British army NCO who had absconded from the army had come to Dublin where he was hiding. He later told gardaí that, around the time of the bombings, he had been out on the streets of Dublin and had seen a corporal he knew from the British army driving around Dublin. The source had hidden, assuming that the corporal was looking for soldiers who were absent without leave, and had thought no more of it. However, after the bombings, his suspicions were aroused, and he went to the Garda Síochána, and gave a statement and a description of the corporal. He told the gardaí at the time that the corporal was an Australian who hated the Irish. His description of the corporal was shown to other eyewitnesses who verified it. The gardaí had contacted the British army about the corporal but had received no reply.

Another piece of information was recorded on the day of the bombings. Before the explosions, gardaí had received a number of calls about a white van with English registration plates, parked outside the Department of Posts and Telegraphs. The gardaí didn't follow up the calls until just after 5 p.m. They reached the place and were told by eyewitnesses that the van had gone in the direction of Sheriff Street. The bombs exploded less than half an hour later, and gardaí found the van in Dublin Port, containing a British army uniform. Irish army intelligence claimed that gardaí later arrested a British army officer on a ferry going to England, and found weapons in his bag. There is no reference to this in any Garda report.

*Forensics*
Forensic material is one of the key elements in any investigation. The investigation into the bombings raises serious questions relating to the handling of the forensic material, and there is disparity between certain reports, and therefore doubts about the claimed chain of custody of the material. The material was collected on the day of the bombings and brought to Garda HQ. There the technical team worked on the material, examining it and finding nothing.

Journalist Don Mullan, in his examination of the forensic investigation, found a number of worrying facts. The Garda Síochána, having investigated the materials in Garda HQ, sent only a small amount of it to Dr James Donovan in the Irish State Laboratory, choosing instead to send most of the material to Dr R. A. Hall in the Department of Industrial and Forensic Science in Belfast. Interestingly, the garda who was said to have delivered the material, Detective Sergeant Jones, 'emphatically denies' that he did so, according to Mr Justice Barron's report.

Dr Donovan told Mullan that there was absolutely no reason why the bulk of the material should have been sent to Belfast. The Irish State Laboratory was perfectly capable of carrying out an investigation into the materials collected after the bombings.

Dr Hall, meanwhile, is critical of the length of time it took the Garda Síochána to send the material to him in Belfast. Whether or not it should have been sent is a moot point, but in any case, the material was finally received by Dr Hall on 28 May 1974 (eleven days after the bombings), by which time most of the chemicals for which the forensic scientists would look would be gone from the material. Indeed, as Mullan points out, in his report to the Garda Síochána, Dr Hall gives a stern lecture on proper handling of materials of this nature. Needless to say, neither Dr Donovan nor Dr Hall found anything of significance on the material they received.

No reason was ever given as to why Dr Donovan was given only some of the material from one bomb site, Parnell Street, while Dr Hall was given the majority of the material, but much later. If speed was of the essence, as the gardaí surely knew, then it would have made more sense to give all the material to Dr Donovan. As it was, Dr Donovan was finished his investigation and had filed his reports before Dr Hall had even received the material in Belfast (Dr Donovan filed two reports, on 24 and 28 May, while Dr Hall only received the materials on 28 May).

Mullan conducted an extensive investigation into the official forensic examination of the bombings. Speaking to forensic chemists, police and army experts (from the United States) he formed a clear picture of an investigation that had not adequately dealt with the materials at hand. Mr Justice Barron, in his report, is critical of the level of amateurism with which the Garda Síochána dealt with the forensic materials. Mullan concludes a little more harshly. Following his interviews with Ed Komac, a retired US army major, Mullan writes that Komac is convinced that the operation was a military one, based on a number of issues. For example, the fact that no fragments of any timing devices were found around the bombs suggested that the Jock-Clock, an improvised timing mechanism invented by a Scottish member of the UVF (hence the name), was not used, and instead a more sophisticated timing device was employed.

Mr Justice Barron's report includes the results of the forensic examination by the Irish army Explosive Ordnance Disposal team, which points to the use of commercial or military explosives, rather than home-made explosives (home-made explosives would have been typical of loyalist bombs at the time, and the use of a different type of explosive would suggest outside help).

Because of the delay in getting the forensic material, Dr Hall could make no firm conclusion regarding the type of explosive used but he does list typical loyalist improvised explosives.

Through a combination of a lack of RUC co-operation and the inaction of the British and Irish governments, the investigation had been quite effectively railroaded in the months following the bombings. Although it remained open, it was inactive, and evidence (that hadn't already been destroyed) lay gathering dust, while suspects continued to murder and kill throughout the Troubles.

The O'Neills were unaware of any of this. They were busy coping, and assumed that justice had been done, although they hadn't seen it being done. As they entered their twenties, the two eldest children, Denise and Angela, began to organise the victims into a support group, bringing together all those bereaved and injured by the bombings.

They weren't on their own for long though. A number of other people had interests in the bombings that extended beyond the passive. In his spare time, John Morgan, a former Irish army officer, was looking into the issues surrounding the bombings, and finding out that things weren't as they seemed. And Kevin Walsh, a union official who had been present at the bombings on 17 May, was beginning to realise that the dead of that day had received no commemoration of any sort — not even an official day of mourning in the days after the bombings. Meanwhile, an RTÉ journalist, Joe Tiernan, was investigating the bombings and would soon join forces with some journalists from Yorkshire Television who, led by

Glyn Middleton, concluded that there was something decidedly strange about the Dublin and Monaghan bombings.

All of those who began their own investigations into the bombings realised that trying to get convictions was futile. Many of the bombers were dead, some killed in the Troubles, some killed by their fellow paramilitaries, others having died of natural causes. In any case, these men were simply pawns in something much bigger. The arrest and imprisonment of the men who drove the bomb-cars on 17 May 1974 was no longer the primary concern for the O'Neills. They were about to ask those in authority some very hard questions indeed.

⌘  ⌘  ⌘

It is one of Martha O'Neill's greatest achievements that the children she raised did not just survive, but prospered. All of them — Denise, Angela, Billy, Edward and Niall — grew up in a loving and comfortable environment. Almost every opportunity that could have been afforded them was. All of the children received a full education and went on to build families of their own. Undoubtedly this was Martha O'Neill's intention all along. However, what she had never planned for was her children's desire to follow up on their father's murder. All five of her children, at some stage, have been involved in the campaign for justice, and Denise, Angela and Edward have been with it from the start. If justice is ever done in this case, the fact that Martha O'Neill harboured no bitterness, and instead got on with her own life and the lives of her children, will have a lot to do with it.

The very first step in the O'Neills' own campaign was a small but highly significant one. The family had never discussed the bombings at home — Martha didn't discuss them in front of the children in case it upset them, and the children didn't discuss them in front of Martha in case it upset her. As children, all of the O'Neills had become aware that the bombing that had killed their father had not occurred in a vacuum. All were aware of Irish history and of the Troubles in Northern Ireland, and they knew that the Dublin and Monaghan bombings were a part of those Troubles.

Denise and Angela discussed it among themselves and soon came to the realisation that their father had not been killed by a bomb, but had been murdered by bombers. This distinction, so self-evident to us now, was one that would change their lives and those of many others. It took them all some time to come to this conclusion but all of them know that this realisation was the start. Murder is a crime, and therefore someone should have been held accountable for it.

It was a while before they took the next step. Many years later, in the mid-1980s, Denise was working in a solicitor's office on Abbey Street, and took her first step in the campaign for justice for the victims and survivors of the Dublin and Monaghan bombings.

> I remember sitting in work in Abbey Street one day and phoning the garda press office. I don't know what prompted me to do it, but I rang to find out what the story was with the bombings, to see who had been sent to prison. I remember being absolutely struck dumb when I was told that the files were still open and that no one had been prosecuted. Thirty-three people had been killed and no one had been sent to prison. And that horrified me. It had never been discussed at home; it was just assumed that someone had been sent to prison for it. And that was when I got angry.

That first phone call was quickly followed by more. The O'Neills had started and were intent on continuing.

> Myself and Angela would travel around and we went to the library and read microfiches of old newspapers and we got telephone books and tried to match up newspaper reports with the addresses. [At that time] we didn't know anyone else who had been injured in the bombings.

Although they were starting to bring together the families who would soon provide the base for a campaign, there was still no official recognition of their efforts Denise recalls:

> It took a huge amount of personal time and expense. But you don't worry about those things at the time. There was a group in the North

called Relatives for Justice — Fr Denis Faul was involved with them. We were invited to various different meetings up the North and we'd go and listen.

Trade union official Kevin Walsh, who had been on his way to pay his union dues on the day of the bombings, had been deeply affected by the carnage and the devastation caused by the three bombs on Dublin on that day. He had watched the newspapers regularly around the anniversaries of the bombings to see if there would be any sort of commemoration ceremony or mass at which he could pay his respects. When none was organised, he decided to do it himself.

In 1990, he managed to organise a commemorative mass in the Pro-Cathedral. He tried to bring together some of the families of the victims by placing ads in the newspapers. Denise was at work the morning of the mass and was reading through the paper when she saw the ad. She leapt up and ran straight to the Pro-Cathedral where she met Kevin Walsh.

Walsh had also been writing to various Lord Mayors of Dublin and to Dublin Corporation, in an effort to have some sort of monument erected in memory of the victims. The year after the commemorative mass, he enjoyed some level of success. The Lord Mayor of the day, Michael Donnelly, had decided to erect a stone outside the Garden of Remembrance on the seventeenth anniversary of the bombings.

Meanwhile, Denise had also been in contact with the Lord Mayor's office regarding that year's commemorative mass, and it was arranged to have the unveiling of the memorial stone, followed by the mass and then a reception afterwards at which the Lord Mayor would attend.

Thus, through the offices of the Lord Mayor and the efforts of Kevin Walsh, Denise O'Neill and Angela O'Neill, the relatives of the victims of the Dublin and Monaghan bombings began to come together. Denise had already brought some of the injured and bereaved together for the first time:

I had been in contact with Michelle Byrne, who had lost her mother, and I had contacted another girl called Marion Bradley whose sister Josie had been killed, and a couple of the injured.

The memorial stone, however, was quite small, and the relatives and Kevin Walsh would later complain that it had been erected in the wrong place and that it was an insufficient memorial for such a huge disaster. Moreover, in spite of the publicity that the bombings were now getting, there was still no attempt being made to re-open the investigation or to set in motion a new investigation.

Denise had already started sending letters to people to find out what had happened. 'Haughey was in power and I started to write to him,' she recalls.

An Taoiseach
Charles J. Haughey
Dáil Éireann
Leinster House
Kildare Street
Dublin 2

21 March 1991

Dear Mr Haughey,

I am writing to you in the hope that you can give me information in relation to the 1974 car bombings. My father Edward was killed in the bombings and my brothers Edward and Billy were seriously injured.

Over the last few years I have made unsuccessful attempts to ascertain why the investigation regarding the bombings was never brought to a satisfactory conclusion. The recent coverage of the Birmingham Six case has made me realise that the killing of the 33 people on the 17th of May 1974 in Dublin and Monaghan can no longer be left on the shelf and that justice must be given to the dead, injured and bereaved.

We are now approaching the 17th anniversary of the bombings and I feel that as the bombings resulted in the largest mass murder in the history of our State that something must be done before another 17 years go by.

I am sure you will appreciate how strongly I feel in relation to this matter and any information you can give me in relation to same would be greatly appreciated.

Yours Sincerely,

Denise O'Neill

Edward too had been trying in his own way to help the campaign along. He vividly remembers his own political awakening. He was in primary school and, during one rainy break period, his class was kept in and the teacher turned on the radio. A news story about a UDR man who had been shot dead by the IRA prompted him to ask the teacher what was going on. The teacher told him as best she could and it sparked off in Ed an interest in Irish history. As soon as he was old enough, he joined Capel Street Library and began to study it on his own.

In 1985, Ed started secondary school at St Vincent's in Glasnevin. Seeing the efforts his sisters were making, he decided to try his best to give a hand. His mother had bought him a Honda 50 motorbike and, on his lunch-break from school, he used to drive down to the Dáil on Kildare Street and stop TDs to try to solicit help. No one was interested. One particular TD, having listened to the story patiently and made vague promises to help, as he walked away, said to the fifteen-year-old Ed, 'Now, remember us at election time.' Most were totally unhelpful. Ed can count on the fingers of one hand the TDs who actually helped him.

This was the other side of the campaign. While Angela and Denise, together with Kevin Walsh, had success in getting masses said and memorials erected, politicians did not want to do anything more constructive. Very few politicians replied to Denise's letters, and there was no progress being made in the attempt to uncover the truth about what had happened.

However, the campaign had come to the attention of the Irish National Congress (INC). Nora Comiskey knew an old friend of the O'Neills, Mavis O'Toole. Mavis had asked Nora, a founder member of the INC, if she would go and help with the campaign in any way she could. Nora went to the first commemorative mass in the Pro-Cathedral and met with the families. She felt that Denise and Angela were somewhat wary of her, but she believed it was with good cause, as the INC had a reputation of being connected to the republican movement. In any case, the girls warmed to her in the end.

According to Nora, not all of the families were as politically savvy as the two O'Neill girls. She herself had always been a very political person, with a strong interest in human rights and civil rights issues, but she was surprised by how uninformed some of the people within the campaign really were. She remembers one person asking her if the IRA had been responsible for killing their relatives. She was stunned that someone could be so naïve as to think that it had been the IRA.

The people in the campaign weren't the only ones who seemed to know very little about the campaign at the time. The families would have to fight a campaign not only against the governments of Ireland and Britain, but also against the apathy of the Irish people. Nora went out on the streets with them when, in the early 1990s, they began to protest at the lack of official recognition of the bombings. She remembers trying to get signatures on a petition which would be sent to the government of the day, along the same lines as the book of condolences for the victims of the Enniskillen Remembrance Day bombing, which had occurred in 1987, killing eleven people. She was amazed at people's reactions. Many just walked by, telling the families who were taking their first steps in what would turn out to be a very long campaign for justice that they should just let the whole thing drop and that it was all water under the bridge.

Denise remembers, in 1987, the father of Marie Wilson, who died in the Enniskillen bomb, telling the media that he forgave his daughter's killers. She recalls:

My mother said that ten years before that. She told us to pray for the people who did it. She told us God would deal with them.

Yet the Irish public, who had been so outraged by the Enniskillen bombings and so touched by the forgiveness of Gordon Wilson, seemed not to want to hear anything about the Dublin and Monaghan bombings or from those bereaved by it. Years of having been fed propaganda or simply told nothing by the Irish media meant that the public simply didn't realise that justice had never been done. They were happy with the story they had been told.

In 1974, the government had gone out of its way to attribute to the IRA what it called 'moral blame' for the bombings. Any suggestion that the UVF had carried out the bombings was drowned out by the argument that the atrocity had been inspired by IRA violence. Neither Denise nor Angela was a supporter of the republican cause, and they certainly did not support their methods. However, they were astute enough to realise that there was simply no political expediency for the IRA in bombing Dublin. The Provisional IRA was very much a Belfast organisation and had very few ties to Dublin. However, it had a certain amount of support in the Republic of Ireland, and to commit such a heinous act as this would result in a lot of lost support.

Angela recalls that they spent years trying to persuade people of this fact:

> We believed for a long time, or rather we had been led to believe, that the IRA was responsible. We couldn't understand that — why would they come to the South and blow up their own? But the ordinary people in Ireland were happy to believe the IRA was responsible. In the early eighties, Denise and I and some other people stood outside the GPO and tried to gather signatures for a petition to hand in to the Taoiseach's department asking for a full public inquiry. We knew that this was the only way to get to the truth. We gathered thousands of signatures, but some of the responses were incredible. People who would have been around at the time and witnessed the carnage asking us, what were we doing, why were we doing it and saying, 'Let bygones be bygones', and 'Sure, the IRA were responsible for that and everyone knows that.' [And asking] why would we be going out looking for answers and [saying] it was a waste of time and a waste of money.

The government did not stop at simply confusing the issue of who was to blame, however. On 22 May, Conor Cruise O'Brien claimed that the Irish people had no right to condemn the atrocities carried out on 17 May when they had for so long condoned a campaign of terror in Northern Ireland carried out by the IRA. Cruise O'Brien, then Minister for Posts and Telegraphs, had lost two employees, Anne Marren and Pat Fay, in the Parnell Street explosion, and had almost lost his daughter in South Leinster Street. One wonders if he would have made the same statements had he lost his daughter rather than two employees.

Denise and Angela were both very young when they started the campaign, both still coming to terms with the death of their father, and having had to spend their formative years without his influence in their lives. Her twenties were a very angry period in Denise's life. This wasn't helped by the brick wall into which they continually ran in their efforts to start the campaign. Angela, too, found it frustrating trying — it seemed in vain — to arouse in other people any interest in the campaign for justice. But the belief that there was something more to this spurred her on:

> I was finding out things. You find out that the gardaí knew, and you wonder, 'Were our lives so meaningless to them? Were we just pawns in a political game? Does it mean nothing to nobody?' It was, and still is, very frustrating. It can make you very bitter if you allow it. You have to be very careful. I try to see good in people, I try not to find fault in people, but when you see things and learn what happened and realise, you're stuck for words. You meet so many politicians who tell you it's awful but do damn all about it.

None of this deterred the girls from continuing. Angela and Denise had moved from simply talking about the bombings among themselves at home to actually doing something about it. They realised that nothing would happen without a significant support base. They knew that they needed the other families around them. All of the bereaved families and the survivors would, they felt, make a formidable group and one that no government could ignore.

> Myself and Denise had been doing some small bits of research in the ILAC Centre Library. We had been trying to get names and addresses and trying to form a group. We knew that's what we had to do — bring a group together to get some power behind us. We'd been

writing to Charles Haughey, who was then Taoiseach, and Garda HQ at the Phoenix Park. We wanted to know if the files had been closed and if anyone had been caught. We were told that the files were never closed and that they had not been closed because no one had ever been caught. The more questions we asked, the more we came to realise that we were not going to get answers.

They were beginning to realise that something bigger lay behind all the official platitudes about the bombings of 1974. Denise remembers reading an article in a Sunday newspaper about an SAS officer who had defected and had sold his story to the media. In the article, he mentioned the Dublin and Monaghan bombings. It was the first time she had heard any suggestion of SAS involvement in the murder of her father.

Politicians, however, still seemed to be uninterested. None wanted to know about the allegations of conspiracy and very few were willing even to go to commemorative masses.

> Seán Haughey, who was Lord Mayor of Dublin at the time [in 1994, on the date of the twentieth anniversary mass for the victims of the bombings], and Tony Gregory, who was always very good, turned up.

It was a non-issue and this was reflected in the turn-out. One incident in particular sticks in Angela's mind:

> Mary Robinson was President at the time and didn't attend and later flew to Warrington to sign a commemorative book.

That the President had gone to Warrington was not a problem. That she had refused to go to a mass in the Pro-Cathedral to remember thirty-three people, thirty-one of whom were Irish citizens who had been murdered in 1974, seemed a massive, official snub. It was not the first and it would not be the last.

Nevertheless, despite the continuing lack of official recognition and the ignorance of the Irish public, the campaign was beginning to take shape. There was a core group committed totally to the uncovering of the truth behind the bombings, and the group had continued to grow since the first meeting outside the Garden of Remembrance on the seventeenth anniversary.

Each year as the anniversary came up, we would advertise and try to contact people, and there was some media coverage and more people started to come on board and it began to get stronger. The initial group that came together wanted justice desperately. The Masseys, the O'Briens, Tim Grace, Mrs Fay. Every year, the group grew.

For seventeen years, the bereaved and the injured had never even met each other. Although they lived in the same small city, sometimes in close proximity to each other, each family had suffered alone. For Angela, the coming together was important for everyone involved, even though initially it didn't bring about a re-opening of the investigation.

Finally there was a place where a group of people who'd suffered the same ordeal could come together. Even if it was only once a year on the seventeenth of May. As a group there was a huge solidarity. Even with those who weren't involved in the political lobbying.

For Martha, the early days of the campaign were the best. Before any of the splits, it was just the families together. While some worked hard to see justice done, the rest could be content with meeting and talking about their loss — something they had never done before. Martha rightly credits her two daughters with this:

Denise and Angela were wonderful. The girls got in contact with all the other families and when I met all the other families, I felt very much healed. I knew a lot of people had been killed but I didn't know how many. When I met Frank and Tim Grace and all the rest — for seventeen years you were alone because you never knew anyone else. But when you met all the families, you weren't alone. Frank was talking about his lovely daughter. Mrs O'Brien about her son and her daughter-in-law. That's when we started to heal.

The healing was necessary. It was important for the families to come together and meet each other and speak to one another. However, in order to be fully healed, the families needed to see justice done. They needed a public tribunal of inquiry. More recognition was needed and, unbeknown to the two girls, it was on its way.

# THE HIDDEN HAND

As magazine articles were being written and the campaign was beginning to take shape, the Dublin and Monaghan bombings came to the attention of journalist Glyn Middleton, who worked for Yorkshire Television's *First Tuesday* programme. *First Tuesday* was broadcast, as the name would suggest, on the first Tuesday of every month, on ITV. At the time, ITV's reputation for investigative journalism was peerless. Even the BBC, the world leader now in news and investigative journalism, was in the shadow of ITV. Moreover, there was considerable interest in Irish affairs. Journalists working for the programme had already made heavily funded programmes on the Guildford Four and the Birmingham Six cases. According to Middleton:

> Yorkshire television at the time had a fantastically independent reputation and were pretty fearless when all kinds of anti-government programmes were made. It was regarded as fairly untouchable.

He had previously worked on a documentary on the Stalker affair, which had been seen by an Irish man called John Condon. Condon had been very impressed by the programme, and had sent to Middleton a magazine article on the Dublin and Monaghan bombings, suggesting that it might be a good subject for an investigative programme.

Intrigued by the subject, Middleton pitched the idea to his direct superior. He recalls being warned the it might be a tough investigation to crack; both men assumed that the subject matter would have been investigated by other journalists and other organisations since 1974, and that all attempts to find new evidence or come up with a new angle on the story must have come to nought. With this in mind, they assumed that they would find it difficult to get any new leads and new information. No one realised at the time that there never had been any real and concerted attempts to conduct an investigation into the bombings. While it would take Yorkshire Television considerable time, effort and money to look properly into the Dublin and Monaghan bombings, the team was to find itself the first actually to investigate the story, and information would therefore be easier to come by than they initially expected.

Middleton was slightly daunted when he realised that he and his team would be the first to look into the bombings. Knowing that the investigation he was about to undertake might very well not uncover the final truth, and aware that he was relatively new to the job he was in, he was at great pains to point out to his superiors that this was far too large a case to be resolved in one hour of television, whether or not two-and-a-half years had been spent in researching it. He recalls discussing it with his boss who told him:

'You're not going to solve this. You're not going to end up with the names of the people and be able to go out and arrest them the next day. The best that you'll get is a better understanding and a better insight into a subject that seems to have gotten less and less attention.'

My boss at the time had done three programmes on the Guildford Four and he told me that they learned more about those bombings every time they did a programme. He didn't expect me to come back with the definitive version but if we came back with some interesting information and some new perspective on it that it would still be valuable.

Middleton was not an expert in Irish history and he needed to research the topic. The difficulties he encountered in simply gathering information on the Dublin and Monaghan bombings were an awakening for him. He bought books on Northern Ireland and was surprised to find so little about such a massive and recent event. He interviewed experts on

Northern Ireland and the Troubles and found that they knew as little about the bombings as the books could tell him. The distinct lack of information about the bombings would later inspire him to call the documentary 'Hidden Hand — The Forgotten Massacre'.

There were, however, some small titbits of information, and Middleton made use of them. *Now* magazine, in May 1990, had carried an article about the bombings, for which journalists Frank Doherty and John Byrne had interviewed two gardaí who had been involved in the investigation. One of the gardaí had told the journalists, 'I have no doubt that there is a much bigger can of worms here than anything connected with the Birmingham Six.' Prior to that, in April 1989, in an article in *Dublin Diary* magazine, journalist James Carruthers had raised the spectre of the Dublin and Monaghan bombings. The article centred around two brothers who had been deeply involved in the British spy-ring operating in Dublin in the early 1970s. The brothers are never named but it is quite clear, reading the article with the information to hand today, that the men in question are the infamous Littlejohns. The article suggested that the brothers had carried out the Dublin and Monaghan bombings, along with a loyalist paramilitary by the name of William 'Frenchie' Marchant. The assertion that the Littlejohns had been involved in the bombings was incorrect. However, Marchant was correctly identified as one of the key members of the bomb-team.

In the *Dublin Diary* article, Middleton came across the name of Joe Tiernan. Tiernan was a researcher with RTÉ's *Today Tonight* programme, and, in investigating the bombings, had spoken to the Littlejohn brothers. Middleton got in contact with Tiernan and asked him if he would like to be involved in a Yorkshire Television investigation into the bombings. Tiernan had already amassed a considerable amount of material on the bombings, which Mark Ackerman, another producer on the programme, analysed. According to Middleton, the material Tiernan had gathered was of great benefit to the investigation. He says of Tiernan: 'He worked very hard on both sides of the border in difficult circumstances.'

Former Irish army officer John Morgan also came to the attention of Middleton's team. Morgan had for some time been tugging away at loose strings surrounding the bombings, hoping that the whole thing would unravel. He gave what help he could to the Yorkshire Television journalists. Although lacking a journalistic background, he did not lack an inquisitive mind. According to Glyn Middleton, 'His great strength was getting other people interested. He didn't pretend that he had the story but he thought it was worthy of a closer look.'

The *First Tuesday* team started off by spending several months in Northern Ireland, trawling around the UVF and UDA heartlands, gathering raw intelligence. Realising that no one was simply going to spill the beans to them over a cup of tea, they decided to immerse themselves in the community, trying to compile an accurate dossier of information on what was known about the bombings. Then they went south to do the same and compare the information they had gathered.

The *First Tuesday* team was the first group of journalists of any kind to manage to co-opt the assistance of the Garda Síochána. Middleton is still not sure why.

I think that by going down with a large body of information, not going cold and asking them to dig into their files … Perhaps it was lucky timing, perhaps it was the amount of times we pestered them so much, perhaps it was because we were an English company taking an interest in it, perhaps someone from higher up put pressure on them, perhaps it was the reputation of *First Tuesday* for integrity in Irish affairs.

We had tremendous access to people. I went to have a meeting with Garret FitzGerald and no one stood in the way if I wanted to speak to anyone. Maybe it's because nobody knew we were doing it. I just made a list of police officers involved and turned up on their doorsteps. They welcomed me, took me in and talked to me; some pushed me away but we got a lot of help. The Department of Justice and Garda Síochána were the only two that could really have helped me in any way, and I think the decision was made jointly between them.

Through John Morgan, Middleton got in contact with the O'Neills. The former army officer had already given Denise and Angela whatever information he had gathered in relation to the bombings. He was one of the first people to give them any information about their father's death. According to Middleton:

[He] did his own investigation into the bombings, was one of the first people to do any research on the bombings. He knew all the facts already. He was an important character in the history of the campaign.

The team had amassed a huge body of information, and Middleton felt that they were on top of a very powerful story. The only thing they needed, he believed, was the human side of the story.

Once we thought that we had a reasonable amount of information about the bombings and that there was a programme there, we then realised that we had to personalise it. We wanted to find some key people.

Middleton decided that the O'Neills would be one of the human faces of the Dublin and Monaghan bombings in the programme.

As the producer, I decided we needed two or three people who could tell very personal stories. We always knew that the main thrust of the film would be down to the investigation but I was taken by Edward's story ... the boy caught up in the blast ... his father was killed, and to that day small pieces of the bomb-car were being taken out of his body.

I liked Martha; I thought she had immense courage; she told the story very well. Angela and Denise were articulate and I liked them.

According to Angela, when Yorkshire Television got in contact with them to tell them that they were planning to investigate the bombings for a documentary, there was an increased sense of hope and optimism within the group. Finally someone other than the families was interested; finally someone other than the families thought that something wrong had been done and that it warranted a proper investigation.

Denise believed that the information provided by Middleton during the making of the documentary was important to the continuing stability of the campaign. It strengthened and bolstered it. It seemed that finally they were getting somewhere.

Yorkshire contacted us and told us they wanted to make a documentary about it. We were involved in that for a year, maybe a year and a half. Glyn Middleton ... gave us all the information about the cars, the car park in Whitehall [where the bombers had parked and regrouped after crossing the border before driving on to Dublin city centre]. We knew all about that for years before it was aired. For three years prior to that, we had been going around to various constituency offices and writing to the gardaí and the Taoiseach and getting nothing — only one liners like, 'We received your letter and thank you for it.'

However, the internal troubles that within a very short space of time were going to tear the campaign apart were beginning to rear their heads. Middleton recalls:

Focusing down to a small group of people gave me headaches. Factions had arisen within the families, which was difficult and I could understand why. I think there'd been a history of rival groupings, and as an outsider you come into those and don't understand the sensitivities you're dealing with.

There was a very hostile screening of our film in the week before it came out. I came over to show the families and by that stage there had already been a schism. We thought it was important to show everyone at a private screening. I take a lot of responsibility for not smoothing that path. I think it was just down to personality clashes between people in the group.

At this point, Joe Tiernan had begun to get involved with the campaign itself. He had come in contact with the subject of the bombings on a number of occasions during his career and, through his work with RTÉ's *Today Tonight* programme, had spoken to a number of UVF men who had mentioned the bombings as part of interviews on other issues.

He was now beginning to work with the campaign, but his input was not appreciated by all of the families.

Denise recalls:

I remember him sitting in my mother's house, before 'The Hidden Hand' was to be aired, and he was talking about Hollywood and million-pound deals for this book he was going to write. That's not what we were interested in. We wanted to know why our government did nothing about the bombings.

The O'Neills were not interested in glamorous film premières; they wanted a full public inquiry.

Tiernan had requested that no one speak to the press about the documentary. On 26 May 1993, at a meeting in Wynn's Hotel on Abbey Street, he had told the families:

The programme is not ready yet but should be ready shortly, perhaps within a month to six weeks, and for that reason we are asking that this meeting be kept absolutely private and secret with no media involvement whatsoever.

Yorkshire Television, who have put a lot of resources and manpower into this project, have asked that no one speak to the press. If you are asked by a journalist anywhere, in Dublin or down the country about this meeting we would ask you to say 'no comment'.

We are not attempting to muzzle anyone. You have your own free will and you make your own choice but in the interest of this campaign, which we hope will last long after the programme has been transmitted, we would ask you to give us a chance to get this thing up and running …

Now some of you may wake up in the morning and expect to see this meeting all over the papers, and some of you may be disappointed when you don't. But I want to re-iterate that we are not ready for publicity yet. Even leaving aside the programme, my instinct is that we should wait till we build and consolidate. There is no point in cutting your record till you have your music properly rehearsed. Cheap, flash-in-the- pan publicity, like this issue has been getting each 17 May over the past few years, is no use. We must be prepared to organise a long, discreet, sustained campaign that will get us answers and justice at the end of the day.

Having given the families such strict instructions to maintain silence over the issue of the programme, Tiernan failed to follow them himself. One month later, 4 July 1993, he had a number of articles published in the *Sunday Independent*. Having told the families that it would be six weeks before the programme would be aired, his timing could not have been worse. The programme was within a few days of being aired and he had seriously jeopardised two-and-a-half years of work. Glyn Middleton was planning to show the programme to the families in the Royal Dublin Hotel the following day and the programme was due to be broadcast on Tuesday, 6 July. Now, however, everything was thrown into turmoil.

Denise remembers the panic she felt when she first heard about the articles he had published:

> I got a phone call on Sunday morning. Mark Ackerman [one of the producers on 'The Hidden Hand'] phoned me at 7 a.m. in the morning and said, 'Denise, can you get the Sunday newspapers?' I asked him what was wrong. He said, 'Joe Tiernan has just done a piece on the Dublin and Monaghan bombings and he's put the whole programme in jeopardy.' I ran upstairs like a lunatic screaming at Paul [her then boyfriend, now husband]. The shop beside me didn't open and the nearest place I knew where I could get the newspapers was from a newspaper vendor on Doyle's Corner in Phibsboro and I flew down to him and I was in tears because we needed this programme to come out and we needed people to see what had happened. I stood there on Doyle's Corner in a pair of slippers, pair of jeans and the top of my pyjamas and I was in tears when I opened the newspaper. I couldn't believe it. I got straight over to my office in Christ Church and I photocopied everything and I faxed it to them [the 'Hidden Hand' producers]. And I was thinking, 'That's it, we're done for, no one's ever going to know.'

Denise and Angela phoned the other family members and told them to buy the *Sunday Independent* to see the articles Tiernan had written. In spite of the potential damage to the programme, some of the families were delighted with the publicity. Angela recalls:

When we got down there, they were saying, 'Isn't it great?' I'm not saying that I'm any more intelligent than the girl sitting next to me, but you see that Yorkshire television have done this investigation. They've put so much work into it, something you've been trying to do for the last four years and have gotten nowhere. You see what they've done and you see the material they've got; you know that if it does nothing else, it's at least going to open eyes; there's going to be someone somewhere who sees that there is actually something here.

Angela couldn't understand why Tiernan had the articles published:

He knew this was a huge story; it was the first real research into the bombings and once he'd done the work for Yorkshire, he knew how big it was and how potentially big it could become.

In spite of this, he wrote articles for the following week's edition as well. Tiernan never gave a reason for selling the articles to the *Sunday Independent.* The other members of the group decided to stay with him while the O'Neills were effectively ostracised. Denise remembers:

At a public meeting in Wynn's Hotel, the campaign took another turn. There was a lot of talk about compensation and money, which is always something I felt soiled the campaign. I'm not saying people weren't entitled to money, but it wasn't the goal — truth and justice was what we were looking for. We wanted the truth; we wanted to know what happened. All of a sudden, you've got people on the prime-time news coming out of government offices talking about compensation. No talk of truth and no talk of justice. The impression then was that we were here for money. But the one thing I wanted out of all this was the truth behind our government's inactions. I, as an Irish citizen and Eddie O'Neill's daughter, have a right to know.

Glyn Middleton was extremely annoyed about the danger into which Tiernan had put the whole programme.

We all had spent a very long time on this documentary and had protected it — for us the big obligation was to make sure it went out — and Joe chose to go to the *Independent* with the story and let them run it, gave them information that didn't come from us. Joe didn't play any part in the editing of it — he was using the raw material he had worked on. Presumably he did it because he felt he didn't get enough prominence [in the documentary] or he thought that his efforts had not been appreciated.

Middleton, however, is reluctant to give any opinion on Tiernan's continued involvement with the campaign after he had finished with the programme.

I didn't know a lot about what Joe Tiernan was doing there. I knew he was involved in some way but he's an Irish citizen and he had a lot of material built up and he's entitled to do that as long as he operates in a fair way.

He makes it clear that it is not the way he would operate, however.

I try to make it a rule in television in whatever I do … that I make it clear to them that all I do is make a film and if that helps … great. I'll treat them fairly and honestly and with integrity but I won't be there forever running the campaign.

He considers himself to be a journalist, not an activist.

Maybe Joe has more of a right than me to stay with the campaign because he is an Irish citizen but I wouldn't.
I told the families that I didn't have all the answers. That programme was just a catalyst for their longer battle. I wasn't going to be here forever to tell the story but whatever I get, they were welcome to use it. I hope today those people will feel that we were fair to them.

Before the documentary had been aired, Joe Tiernan had put himself forward as the chairman of the new committee. Up until then, the campaign had been run on a very informal basis, without a chairperson, a secretary, a treasurer or a committee. People were understandably excited and there was a huge turnout at the meeting in Buswell's Hotel in Dublin at which the committee would be elected.

The campaign, now calling itself 'Relatives for Justice', had Tiernan as chairperson, and a committee comprising Frank Massey, Edward O'Neill, Jacqueline Wade, Michelle Byrne and Paddy Doyle. They issued press releases and wrote up a list of five demands. These demands were that the Irish government would set up an inquiry headed by a High Court judge or a Deputy Garda Commissioner; that the Irish government, through the Anglo-Irish Agreement, would prosecute the inquiry in Northern Ireland with the British authorities; that the Irish and British governments would set up a joint compensation fund to compensate bereaved families and injured victims; that the people responsible be arrested, extradited and brought before the courts; and that the British government would admit publicly that its armed forces had been involved.

Angela was not as happy as the other families to have Joe Tiernan as chairperson of 'Relatives for Justice':

> I stood up and was very vocal about how I felt and it ended up that there was a huge row. It was very sad to see family members fighting like that. It caused a huge split in the campaign.

The O'Neills weren't finished with Joe Tiernan yet, though. Angela came home from work one day to find that a message had been left by local gardaí instructing her to come down to Cabra Garda Station. Stories had been circulating in the *Evening Herald* and on television that relatives of the victims of the Dublin and Monaghan bombings had been receiving death threats in the middle of the night. Angela recalls:

> The gardaí had left a message for me to contact police at Cabra Garda station and they brought me in for questioning because he had alleged that I had been making the threats. [They thought that] I had been getting out of my bed at two in the morning — I had no phone in the house and mobiles weren't on the scene and I had a young child at the time — and going out to a call box and making death

threats against these people. Telling them they were going to die. This was what Joe Tiernan said. I absolutely broke down.

Angela was distraught and went straight to her solicitor.

> Enough was enough — it was getting dirty and serious. I'd never been in a police station in my life, and here I was being interrogated — it was quite traumatising.

Her solicitor wrote a letter, and Joe Tiernan sent a letter to Martha, apologising for any upset he had caused. In a temper, she tore the letter up. Angela couldn't believe that she had torn up the evidence.

> It was the biggest mistake she ever made. This was more vindication. The gardaí came to realise that it was all a hoax. [But] I would have liked for him … to have been charged with wasting police time.

Joe Tiernan stayed on with the campaign for some time afterwards. The O'Neills continued their own campaign for justice and truth, alone.

> We just went back to quietly working away in the background, going to anniversaries and that sort of thing. If we thought we could write to anyone and get a response, we would do it. But I felt the momentum for the whole public inquiry was lost. We were just called the 'victims and relatives of Dublin and Monaghan 1974'. They [Tiernan's group] were no longer looking for a public inquiry. We knew from the start that that was what was needed — especially then after the 'Hidden Hand' had produced such evidence. But he was going in a different direction altogether.

Glyn Middleton had found it a steep learning curve, coming to Irish affairs as a novice but working on such a difficult topic. He'd spent quite a bit of time on a drama documentary on the Stalker affair.

> I think it sparked an interest in Irish affairs. But I've not dedicated a life to Irish history and politics. We tried to keep a clear head about

what we could and couldn't do.

A lot of interesting but unprovable information came our way that simply couldn't be used in the film.

I think we thought at the time that it would have more impact in Ireland than in Britain. More Irish people would be interested in it and the audience was a fairly typical *First Tuesday* audience but, as we'd expected, it went pretty much unnoticed here. It was almost as if it was expected that there would be another controversy about a terrorist atrocity in Ireland. We assumed that the real interest would be in Ireland. We were slightly anxious about injunctions. We didn't release video previews to the press. We relied on their reaction when they saw it. I'm surprised that it has had such an impact in Ireland — I thought it would be the starting point of other investigations.

He was later asked by John Wilson – who at the time had been appointed Victims' Commissioner in the wake of the Belfast (Good Friday) Agreement – why the programme had had such an impact, and he said:

Whatever else you think it said, and whatever else you think it did, I thought it left a pretty clear message that the potential cover-up was almost a greater story than the bombings. I'd been in the files, I'd spoken to enough people, I knew there was eyewitness evidence against certain individuals although up to that point it had been denied. I knew that the gardaí had tried to take the investigation further but that it had not been — no one north of the border was interested in helping. And the officers that I spoke to told me that was passed up the line to their political masters. When you're a Garda Commissioner and the biggest investigation in the history of the Irish State is stopped somewhere along the line, you go and tell your political masters. But the politicians denied, to a man, that they knew about this.

For the politicians' assertions to have been true, Middleton says, you would have to believe that the police were lying. You would have to believe that the police investigation had been stopped and that they just didn't bother to notify their superiors.

In order to believe that, you have to believe they just said, 'Oh well, that's life' or that they did tell their political masters and that it was too embarrassing or too sensitive to raise with their counterparts.

Middleton also points to the rather odd behaviour of certain politicians around the time of the documentary.

Conor Cruise O'Brien made a rather personal attack on Olivia O'Leary, whose only role in the programme was to watch it and to write a two-minute introduction — that was an interesting reaction in itself. We never said that the politicians are lying and yet he took it that we were accusing him and his colleagues of either lying or covering up.

Any time the Dublin and Monaghan bombings are brought out in the media, Conor Cruise O'Brien is generally the first one to protest. When the Barron Report was published, he made a similarly vitriolic denouncement of the judge and his findings.

The O'Neills were delighted with the programme. It was the first time a lot of the information they already knew, and some they had never suspected, had been put before the Irish public and those in power. However, Denise was disappointed with the general reaction to the programme.

That was the most important piece of journalism about the bombings but it had absolutely no impact on the public whatsoever. I remember the week it aired we organised three weekends down by the GPO [with] the Masseys. I can remember people telling me, 'That was 25 years ago — why can't you let it go?' I wanted to punch somebody. This is where you get really annoyed and angry and frustrated. That something can happen like this on the streets of their own city and they just don't give a damn. It really did mean nothing to them. But then you'd get one person who'd say, 'I remember that day' and they'd tell you their story.

Once the furore about the documentary had subsided, the O'Neills went back to fighting for justice alone.

After the documentary, the general public forgot about the campaign again and the only time the media wanted to know was around the fifteenth, sixteenth and seventeenth. That was the only time you ever heard from them.

*Aftermath*

The government of the day — a Fianna Fáil government under Albert Reynolds — did its best to ignore the programme and its findings. The Minister for Justice, Máire Geoghegan-Quinn, claimed that there had not been enough new information in the documentary to secure any arrests and that the idea of a tribunal of inquiry into the affair was simply not an option. She suggested that the programme's finding had simply been strongly held suspicions. She seemed to forget that some of the gardaí on the case who were interviewed for 'The Forgotten Massacre' were adamant that the investigation would have produced results had it been allowed.

The opposition put plenty of questions to the government, but no answers were forthcoming. The official line was that the government would support the garda investigation, to which Máire Geoghegan-Quinn had referred as 'the proper and most appropriate form of inquiry in this instance'. In other words, the appropriate forum was an inquiry which did not have in its remit the ability to compel members of the government to give evidence.

The government, in essence, seemed happy to leave the investigation officially open, while not actually doing anything to further the process. It was an attempt to satisfy the families and had been tried successfully by every previous government since the Fine Gael/Labour coalition of 1974. Now, Yorkshire Television had made that impossible. Although the programme had had a limited impact on the public, it could not have been ignored by the government anymore. While it took some time, as all things related to the Dublin and Monaghan bombings seem to, the whole process had been given a massive push start, and, this time, it would not be stopped.

On 27 July, nearly three weeks after the documentary, the families managed to get a meeting with the Minister for Justice. The minister assured them that a garda investigation of the information would take place, but this of course was tainted by newspaper reports which had emerged days after the programme, in which senior garda sources were quoted as having said that there was no new information in the documentary. The families were not, as was promised would happen, kept up to date on the investigation, and there was considerable unease that the government was once again covering the whole thing up.

In 1994, Nora Comiskey put forward the idea of an unofficial public inquiry. Nora had been involved in the Cullyhanna Inquiry — a young man called Fergal Caraher had been shot by the British Royal Marines in Cullyhanna, Co. Armagh and no one had ever been convicted of the crime. The Irish National Congress had gone to Armagh to help the family, and the inquiry had turned out to be quite successful. High-profile civil-rights lawyers like Michael Mansfield, who chaired the inquiry, assisted in the process. Nora believed that a similar process would work for the Dublin and Monaghan bombings. Apart from the information that it had the potential to unearth, it would also be a hugely public event and raise the profile of the bombings. However, because of lack of funds, the idea of a similar inquiry into the Dublin and Monaghan bombings never got off the ground.

The twentieth anniversary came and went. At the anniversary mass, there was a record turn-out of politicians and dignitaries, yet no statement had been made about the garda investigation of the information presented by the documentary. The families' questions were still unanswered.

Nora Comiskey introduced a friend of hers, Margaret Urwin, to the families. Margaret had also been a member of the Irish National Congress and was enthusiastic about getting involved in the campaign. She began to work closely with the families.

Two years elapsed before there was any further progress on the issue. A new, Fine Gael-led, government was in power, and Nora Owen was the Minister for Justice, with John Bruton as Taoiseach. In 1995, the minister met with the families. Because the O'Neills were still outside the campaign and some bad feeling remained, she met with them in two groups. Nora Owen flatly told both groups that no new information had been discovered with which to further the investigation. A public inquiry would not be established as it might prejudice the case.

At the end of the meeting, the minister told the families that the case remained open, and said that if they came across any new information, they should bring it to her and she would have it thoroughly investigated. Effectively, the minister was placing the onus for the furtherance of the investigation on the families, rather than the Garda Síochána whose job it was to pursue such an investigation. It was a grave insult to families who had been fighting for more than ten years to try to get the authorities to take notice.

*Barron Report*

In Part Five of the report of the Independent Commission of Inquiry into the Dublin and Monaghan Bombings, Mr Justice Barron deals with the issues raised by the 'Hidden Hand' documentary. Having been dismissed by the Ministers for Justice during both a Fianna Fáil and a Fine Gael-led government, the programme was now about to receive a proper and accurate assessment.

Barron gives the background first.

'Hidden Hand — the Forgotten Massacre' was the title of a television documentary made by Yorkshire Television as part of its 'First Tuesday' series, and first broadcast on 6th July, 1993. The programme was directed by Glyn Middleton and co-produced by Glyn Middleton and Mark Ackerman. Its principal researcher was Joe Tiernan. Amongst those who appeared or contributed to the programme were:

1. Former secretary of State for Northern Ireland, the Rt. Hon. Merlyn Rees (now Lord Rees of Cilfynydd);
2. Former heard of British Army Bomb Disposal in Northern Ireland, Lieutenant Colonel George Styles;
3. Former British Army Captain and Military Intelligence Officer Fred Holroyd;
4. Former British Army Senior Information Officer Colin Wallace;
5. Former Irish Military Intelligence staff officer, Lieutenant Colonel John Morgan;
6. Former Irish Army bomb disposal expert, Commandant Patrick Trears;
7. Former Garda Commissioner Eamon Doherty;
8. Various unidentified Garda officers of senior and lesser rank, two

unidentified RUC Special Branch officers and one unidentified member of a British Army special duties unit.

He goes on then to summarise the programme and its contents:

The Hidden Hand film began with footage of a memorial service for victims of the bombings, overlaid with statements from eyewitnesses, survivors and relatives of the victims. From there the narration purported to describe how the bombings took place, beginning with the theft of the bomb cars in Northern Ireland. Some persons referred to in the Garda investigation reports were named as suspects, along with others not mentioned in the Garda reports but suspected by the programme makers as having been involved in the bombings. The four additional suspects were:

(1) Billy Hanna — a well known UVF figure from Lurgan, murdered outside his home on 27 July, 1975;

(2) Harris Boyle — a UVF member, killed on 31 July, 1975 when a bomb he was planting in a van belonging to the Miami Showband exploded prematurely.

(3) Robert McConnell — a part time UDR member and suspected member of the UVF, killed by the IRA on 5 April, 1976.

(4) A man known as 'The Jackal' — not named in the programme but known to be Robin (Robert John) Jackson, a well known member of the UVF. He was still alive at the time the programme was made, but died of natural causes in June 1998.

The focus then shifted to the progress of the Garda investigation, and in particular to what happened when the Northern Ireland authorities became involved. It was queried as to whether the RUC, the British authorities and the Irish Government had done everything in their power to expedite the Garda inquiry.

Having indicated that the evidence available to the Garda investigation team placed responsibility for the bombings with UVF members based in Portadown, the programme then considered whether that group had the capacity to carry out bombing operations of such size and apparent sophistication at that time ...

The remainder of the programme was given over to answering

the questions of where such assistance [assistance which was necessary in the wake of the programme's conclusion that the UVF did not, in fact, have the capacity to carry out such bombing operations] could have been found. Although no firm conclusions were reached, the programme clearly implied that the security forces in Northern Ireland were the most likely source for such assistance ...

Barron goes on to say that in the programme, allegations that British army officers were 'using loyalist paramilitaries as a "friendly guerilla force", advising them on potential targets and assisting them with weapons and planning ... centred on former British Army Captain Robert Nairac.' The makers of the programme, Barron says, suggested that there were links between 'Nairac and the Portadown loyalist terrorists. And also that in May 1974 he was meeting with these paramilitaries, supplying them with arms and helping them plan acts of terrorism against republican targets.'

Having suggested this connection, Barron says, the programme then attempted to explain why members of the security forces would want to help loyalist paramilitaries. The conclusion the programme came to, which Barron would later concur with, was that it was an attempt to bring down the Sunningdale Power-Sharing Agreement.

The programme broadcast snippets of an interview with Merlyn Rees in which he indicated that he knew about the actions of particular subversives within the British army in Northern Ireland. It had been under Rees that the Sunningdale Agreement had been negotiated, and he felt that the army had undermined his efforts in an attempt to prevent the Agreement from being implemented. The former Secretary of State for Northern Ireland is quoted as saying:

> It was a unit, a section, out of control. There's no doubt it reflected the views of a number of soldiers: 'Let's go in and fix this lot', and so on. But that it went on, and that it went on from Lisburn and it went on from the Army Information Service and those associated with it, I have no doubt at all.

Barron is also quite scathing in certain of his observations about the programme. As a judge, he requires a certain level of evidence before he can make an assertion of any sort. Therefore he is at odds with the journalistic practice of protecting sources, seeing it as undermining the veracity of the information provided. In his words,

> It is essential to realise that much of the information gathered by the programme makers came from unnamed sources. It is accordingly not possible to test the accuracy of the information directly.

He also points out that the programme-makers did not make it clear whether the bombs that exploded in Dublin were in any way connected to the bomb which exploded in Monaghan. He suggests that perhaps the Monaghan bombing was carried out by some opportunistic bombers who had decided to capitalise on the chaos caused by the Dublin bombings. It is a completely untenable theory and Barron later concludes that the bombings were, in fact, connected.

The programme-makers also, in Mr Justice Barron's opinion, gave a misleading impression of the level of Garda co-operation. Throughout the programme, they suggested that the Garda Síochána gave them files, when, in fact, a liaison officer had been appointed to trawl through the files on their behalf. It was up to the programme-makers to ask the right questions, therefore, in order to receive the right information. In other words, it was more hit-and-miss than the programme-makers would have wanted us to believe.

He also suggests that there were occasions in the programme when there was some confusion regarding the source of certain allegations and that, in the absence of actual statements of who had said what, the viewer was left to believe that the information had come from the Garda Síochána. In other cases, the information that was taken from the Garda files was incorrect or misinterpreted.

He also suggests that the strength of the identifications was overemphasised by both the programme makers and the gardaí involved. He refers to a garda quoted in the programme as having said that they 'could have taken them to court with such positive identifications', and says that this is not correct. Because of his distinguished career, Mr Justice Barron would be the best person to assess this. However, this garda was not the only one quoted who felt, quite strongly, that the investigation had been promising and that convictions could have been secured. In the end, no one was even questioned.

Mr Justice Barron, in suggesting that the identification of one of the bombers, David Alexander Mulholland, had 'inconsistencies which undermine the reliability of their evidence' is overstating the case somewhat. The inconsistency he mentions is, as has been previously stated, nothing more than a discrepancy of accent which could easily be explained — Mulholland may simply have affected a British accent in order to avoid identification as a Northern man acting suspiciously in Dublin on the day of the bombings. It is not the most airtight of disguises, but it seems to have worked as far as Mr Justice Barron is concerned.

Having made his comments on certain irregularities in the programme, Mr Justice Barron concludes:

> The principal achievement of the 'Hidden Hand' programme was to place the Dublin and Monaghan bombings once more at the forefront of the public mind. Although constrained by the limitations of the television documentary format and by lack of full access to Garda and RUC records, it succeeded in making the case that there were questions to be answered in relation to the conduct of the original investigation. The issues and allegations raised by it were the catalyst for a campaign by Justice for the Forgotten and others. It was as a result of that campaign that the Government set up this Commission of Inquiry. The Inquiry though focused initially on the claims made in the 'Hidden Hand' programme, has received a considerable amount of previously unseen information from a variety of sources. Accordingly, this report both encompasses and goes beyond the issues raised by the programme.

This is, of course, something of which Glyn Middleton was always hopeful. He realised at the time of making the documentary that he would never be able to deal with all of the issues in relation to the bombings (indeed, Mr Justice Barron's report, although it does exceed the 'Hidden Hand' investigation, leaves out a number of key elements in relation to the bombings). It was Middleton's hope that he and the team he assembled to make the documentary might inspire someone else to look into the matter further. Although it took more than a decade for it finally to happen, that is what the Independent Commission of Inquiry into the Dublin and Monaghan Bombings did. Middleton says of the programme:

> I'd like it to have gone further. I'd like to have been more definitive. I'd like to have fewer gaps of knowledge and I'd like it to have been able to do more for the victims who put a lot of trust in us to tell their story. But the reality was … that it was going to be that way. The problem with Irish stories is that you're always piecing it together and you're always missing pieces. We regarded it as being an important programme in terms of inching forward a very dark and intriguing event. We hoped that a lot people would build upon it.

The issues raised by the programme, according to Barron, fall into three main areas:

(1) The perpetrators:
The programme makers purported to give details of how and by whom the bombings were carried out which exceeded those contained in the Garda files. In some instances, their claims were based on inaccurate information as to what was in those files. But in the main, these claims are believed by the inquiry to have been based on information supplied by former RUC Sergeant John Weir, supported by information from unknown loyalist paramilitary sources.

(2) The investigation:
It was alleged that proper co-operation was not forthcoming from the RUC in relation to the pursuit of suspects in Northern Ireland. It was also alleged that the security forces in Northern Ireland had intelligence pointing to suspects for the bombings, but had failed to follow it up. These claims were based largely on information from former members of the security forces Fred Holroyd and Colin Wallace.

(3) Collusion:
As set out earlier, the programme made specific allegations of links between British Army officers and loyalists whom it suspected of having participated in the bombings. It also considered the issue of

collusion between elements of the security forces and loyalist paramilitaries in a wider context, and raised allegations of a conflict between those sections of the security forces who supported and opposed the Sunningdale process respectively. Again, Wallace and Holroyd were the principal sources for this part of the programme.

Barron also investigated in close detail the allegations made by Fred Holroyd, Colin Wallace and John Weir. These will be examined in a later chapter.

As acknowledged by Barron, the 'Hidden Hand' documentary brought much-needed momentum to the campaign. Although it was all but ignored by the public, it wasn't possible for those in power to ignore it. The families pushed the issue until, eventually, the government was forced to meet with them. However, it would be a long time before the pressure which began with the revelations in the 'Hidden Hand' documentary began to bear fruit.

# JUSTICE FOR THE FORGOTTEN

Yorkshire Television's documentary, 'Hidden Hand – The Forgotten Massacre', had raised the profile of the campaign considerably. The raised profile had, however, lead to bitterness, bad feeling and recriminations and, ultimately, almost sunk the campaign.

The 'Hidden Hand' programme was, at the time, the most important piece of journalism relating to the bombings in existence. But the later split had robbed the campaign of much of the momentum the programme had afforded it. Many of the families were understandably disheartened. The government, never too keen to act upon the information it had been given, seemed quite content to slip off the hook once again.

The original campaign that had come together under the O'Neills had now split into two groups. Both groups continued to lobby TDs, senators, presidents, taoisigh, the government and the opposition. They continued to phone people, write to people and try to make those in power aware of what had happened. There was considerably less vigour in their attempts, however.

On the other side of the campaign, after Joe Tiernan's departure two members decided to draft in outside help. In 1993, only a few months after the 'Hidden Hand' documentary and the acrimonious split, the Irish National Congress was contacted by Jackie Wade (Jackie's sister, Collette Doherty, had been killed on Talbot Street) and Alice O'Brien (Alice had lost four members of her family on Parnell Street — her sister, Anna,

Anna's husband and their two young daughters). The aims of the Irish National Congress were peace, unity and justice in Ireland. Through the INC, Robert Ballagh, Nora Comiskey, Thomas Cullen and Margaret Urwin became involved. Their introduction would bring much needed impetus back into the campaign.

The families, by now, had re-focussed their goals. While putting the men who had actually committed the crime in prison was still important to them and would provide much needed closure, more important now was a public tribunal of inquiry, which they hoped would highlight the actions of the British security forces in assisting in the carrying out of the bombings, and the inaction of the Irish government of the day and subsequent Irish governments in failing to bring anyone to justice — effectively covering up the bombings. And so the rump of the group that the O'Neills had initially brought together, with this new impetus, began to make headway and regain some of the momentum that had been lost after the split.

The group would soon begin to call itself 'Justice for the Forgotten', and it would be central to driving forward the cause of the victims and bereaved of the Dublin and Monaghan bombings, and finally forcing the government to take notice.

In 1996, the campaign, having received substantial funding from an anonymous businessman, decided to hire a legal team. Nora Comiskey had visited republican prisoners in Portlaoise Prison for many years as part of her work with the INC. Through her dealings with these men, she had come across a lawyer called Greg O'Neill. O'Neill had represented Peter Pringle who had been wrongfully convicted of shooting a garda, and whose conviction was later quashed. According to Comiskey, O'Neill was one of the few lawyers who worked on what she called 'national issues', and she felt that he would be a huge asset to the campaign. Through Greg O'Neill, Cormac Ó Dulacháin, a barrister, was introduced to the campaign. Justice for the Forgotten now had a legal team.

Both men were enthusiastic and eager to help the campaign. Their impact was instantaneous. The two lawyers advised the families that they should take the case to the European Commission because they believed there had been a breach of Article 2 of the European Convention of Human Rights.

However, before they could do this they went to the High Court in order to obtain the garda files from the investigation into the bombings in 1974. There was another reason for this – they were required to explore every avenue open to them in their own jurisdiction before they could bring the case to the European Commission. However, they were turned down in their request in the High Court and they took the case to the Supreme Court and were defeated there too. They had also met with then Minister for Justice John O'Donoghue, to ask him to release the files, and to ask for a public tribunal of inquiry. They received no help from the minister, who told them that only the Garda authorities could release the files, and said nothing about the tribunal. He pledged, however, to stay in touch with the campaign's lawyers on the matter. He did not.

By July 1999 the case had been thrown out by the European Commission on the grounds of the six-month time-bar on cases brought before it. There was no possibility of appealing this decision, and it spelled the end of any possibility of taking the case to the European Commission. The families had, once again, been frustrated by official red-tape and bureaucracy.

⌘ ⌘ ⌘

Don Mullan had been introduced to the campaign through the artist Robert Ballagh, with the intention of getting him to write a book about the bombings. Mullan, a journalist, had written a book on Bloody Sunday, which had been lauded for its investigative work on the theory that there had been a shooter on the walls of Derry on that fateful day. The work he did on that book is widely regarded as having heavily influenced the British government in their decision to re-open the investigation into the events of Bloody Sunday and overturn the verdict of the Widgery Tribunal. It later became the basis of an award-winning film about Bloody Sunday, starring Northern Irish actor James Nesbitt.

Apart from writing about Bloody Sunday, Don Mullan had also been involved in the campaign to re-open the inquiry into the events of that day. He had worked closely with the families, and he knew that they were central to any book he was going to write. So, through Urwin and Comiskey, he went to meet the Dublin and Monaghan families. Urwin would later help as a research assistant on the book.

When he met the families themselves, Mullan was struck by their dignity, but he also saw how difficult it was for them to sustain a campaign over such a wide geographical area. In his work with the Bloody Sunday families and his later work with the families of the victims of the Omagh bomb of 1998, he had come to realise that one of the keys to their success was the sense of community among the bereaved and wounded. In Bloody Sunday, almost all of the members of the campaign came from the same area in Derry, while in Omagh almost all the families came from the town itself or the surrounding countryside. However, with the Dublin and Monaghan bombings, the victims and the survivors were spread all over the country. Keeping the continuity in such a large and widespread campaign was difficult. And that was not the only difficulty that Mullan encountered. Through his interviews with family members, he came to realise that some of the bereaved families were missing from Justice for the Forgotten, in particular the family that had been instrumental in starting the whole campaign.

> The thing that surprised me at the time was that, through interviewing the families, I came to realise that it had been the O'Neills that had started the whole thing. People like Frank Massey would have talked about the importance of Angela and Denise in particular. [And] the dignity of Martha O'Neill was striking. An inner-city woman who was left a very young widow with two seriously injured young boys and one of her young girls due to make her First Holy Communion the next day . She herself was pregnant and from the trauma her baby was stillborn. Martha O'Neill's baby is one of the victims. But I was really taken by Martha O'Neill's dignity and strength and the fact that she had brought up really good kids. It was they who, when they were teenagers, asked the important questions of other families.

Mullan believed that the O'Neills' role in the beginning of the whole campaign was enormous and that their abilities would be of great benefit to the campaign at the time. He realised they should be involved in it once more.

[In the beginning] they sparked off amongst a number of the families the quest for truth and justice. It was extraordinary that the O'Neills were not involved at that stage.

Mullan had first met the O'Neills when he was working for TV3's *20/20* programme. He was making a documentary for the twenty-fifth anniversary of the Dublin and Monaghan bombings and he interviewed Angela O'Neill. He had been impressed by Angela's grasp of both the personal and political implications of the bombings for all the families. He felt that the absence of the O'Neills from the campaign that they had effectively begun was an immense loss to the work of Justice for the Forgotten. He worked to bring them back on board. and to heal any old wounds that remained from the aftermath of the 'Hidden Hand' documentary. He wasn't interested in how they had parted ways — he simply wanted to get all the families together in order to make the campaign as strong as possible. Having worked on the Bloody Sunday campaign, Mullan was aware of the need for solidarity. He also knew that, from time to time, the raw emotions that motivated people to spend their every spare moment fighting the government and the civil service would spill over and result in heated internal rows.

I wasn't that interested in getting involved in that side of it, I was more interested in getting them to develop their campaign along the lines of the Bloody Sunday model. And the Bloody Sunday campaign was so successful because it was based on the families. The families were in control and they made the decisions. The Bloody Sunday families had drawn up a simple statement with three demands which was the focus of every meeting they held. All party political matters were left at the door. One of the first contributions I made to JFF was to invite one of the Bloody Sunday families to Dublin to meet the families involved in JFF. Gerry Duddy was the brother of Jackie Duddy, the first fatality of Bloody Sunday, shared the experience of the Derry families. Following this he helped the Dublin and Monaghan families to draw up a campaign statement that was read at the beginning of each meeting, as well as calling out the names of the 33 people who were murdered. They were there for a very specific objective — to get a public tribunal of inquiry.

Eventually, the O'Neills were brought back into the fold.

*Victims' Commission*

The Belfast (Good Friday) Agreement had been signed in April 1998 and ratified on both sides of the border the following month. Seamus Mallon famously called it 'Sunningdale for slow learners'. It is one of history's ironies that the agreement which the Dublin and Monaghan bombings were supposed to kill was resurrected twenty-five years later, only to contain the seeds of a process which the families hoped would finally bring justice to those who were murdered.

The Belfast Agreement contained a section on Rights, Safeguards and Equality of Opportunity, paragraphs 11 and 12 of which referred specifically to the rights of victims. It was these paragraphs that Justice for the Forgotten seized upon. Having seen their attempt to bring their case to the European Commission fail when the Garda Síochána refused to hand over the files relating to the investigation, the campaign was intent on not letting this chance slip by.

The Minister for Justice, on the night before the referendum to ratify the Agreement, announced that the government was to establish a victims' commission under former Tánaiste John Wilson. The families met with Wilson on 25 September 1998. Don Mullan, who attended the Victims' Commission with the families, wrote that he

> was impressed by the sensitivity with which he listened and responded to various contributions, many of which were punctuated with expressions of deeply suppressed anger. This was the first time in almost a quarter of a century that a representative of official Ireland had sat and listened to their stories.

Before Wilson issued his report, there was yet another milestone for the families. For the first time ever, they met with an incumbent Taoiseach. The families were intent on pressing for a fully constituted public inquiry. According to Tim Grace, whose wife Breda was killed on Talbot Street, it was 'imperative that such a tribunal of inquiry be established'.

Those who attended the meeting felt that Bertie Ahern genuinely wanted to see justice done for those who had been killed, injured and bereaved. According to the minutes of the meeting taken by Justice for the Forgotten, the Taoiseach suggested a sub-committee which would work with JFF's legal team. He would not commit himself to public inquiry but, when pressed by Don Mullan on the issue, Ahern replied that he was not ruling out the possibility of a public inquiry. The families left the meeting with renewed hope. The hope was to be dashed by recommendations made by John Wilson in his report.

In the report, Wilson accepted that 'no one has ever been made amenable' for the bombings. He accepted that 'the Garda investigation had identified the probable culprits very quickly but that it then ran into difficulties.' He stated that it appeared that the gardaí 'did not receive all appropriate co-operation from the RUC' and 'that the Irish Government did not press the British Government on this point'. He even went so far as to accept that 'agents of a friendly Government may have had a hand in planning and executing the crime.' Wilson was made aware, by the families, of official attempts by the gardaí (cf. pp136-7) to prevent them from gaining access to the files in order to take a case to the European Commission. He was aware of how much pain and hurt the families felt after, at the time, a quarter of a century of having been ignored.

Yet, when he came to announce his decision and give his recommendations, he completely ignored the families' calls for a public inquiry. Instead, he proposed a private inquiry to be headed by a former Supreme Court judge. The families angrily rejected the proposal. Although they had waited a quarter of a century to see justice done, they were not willing to accept a private inquiry if it meant that they could not see justice being done.

In a press conference on 7 August 1999 they made their opinion on Wilson's announcment clear. In a press release issued at the conference they said:

> We are without reservation deeply disappointed that Mr Wilson has chosen to recommend a private inquiry as distinct from the public inquiry which was sought by Justice for the Forgotten in it's [sic] campaign going back several years ... we find it odd in the extreme that he did not see that the logical conclusion to be drawn from such findings was that any inquiry to be undertaken into the circumstances

of the bomb outrages and the adequacy of the security response thereto north and south of the border should be in public ... any tribunal of inquiry that is established must have the power to compet [sic – should read compel] the attendance of witnesses and not merely seek their assistance as volunteers to the process ... Justice to be done must also be seen to be done. For those who have been abandoned by the police and justice system in this state for twenty-five ... years ... any inquiry which compromises the principles of openness, transparency and accountability will not have any credibility. The victims and relatives require vindication – such vindication can only come from an open process in which they can fully participate.

Bizarrely, Wilson claimed that the families had never specifically asked for a public inquiry. This simply wasn't the case. Cormac Ó Dulacháin had made a submission to the Victims' Commissioner entitled 'The Case for a Tribunal of Inquiry' which had clearly stated, 'the victims and relatives of the Dublin and Monaghan bombings ... believe that a sworn public tribunal of inquiry is the only mechanism that can address their substantive needs ...' and 'the victims and relatives ... seek the endorsement and recommendation of the Victims' Commissioner for a Tribunal of Inquiry.' This was part of a larger explanation of the importance of the public inquiry in maintaining democracy. However, in spite of this documented evidence, Wilson continued to claim that the word had never been used. He maintained this view in an interview conducted by Don Mullan for TV3 on 11 November 1999.

On August 12 an interdepartmental group that had been suggested by the Taoiseach during his meeting with the families, met at Government Buildings. It was at this meeting that the families became aware that the government was intent on accepting John Wilson's recommendations. On 29 September this was confirmed when the Taoiseach announced that the government would be establishing a private inquiry. Justice for the Forgotten issued an angry press release:

The survivors and families have no faith in a private inquiry. The Government decision contrasts sharply with the public inquiry being conducted into the Bloody Sunday massacre in Derry.

There are clearly matters of public interest in the case of the Dublin and Monaghan bombings to warrant a public inquiry. The reluctance of the Government is bizarre and in the view of many may be explicable only in terms of maintenance of secrecy over that which should be revealed. It adds insult to the injury suffered by the bereaved and wounded ...

1. The relatives and victims cannot and will not engage in a private inquiry into mass murder and compromised police inquiry into these murders.

2. Justice for the Forgotten, as part of its ongoing campaign, will engage in what we see must be a preliminary examination with the chairman of the case for a public inquiry. We will demonstrate to the chairman of the inquiry the impossibility and inappropriateness of an inquiry into these matters being conducted other than in public.

3. It is clearly in the interest of public faith and confidence in our police and justice system that the facts are examined and brought out publicly in an open process which does justice to the concern of the bereaved and of the Irish people as a whole.

On 1 October Margaret Urwin was informed that the interdepartmental committee was to be disbanded and its work taken over by the Department of Justice. A week later, a meeting was held between the committee of Justice for the Forgotten and officials from the Departments of Justice and An Taoiseach at which Margaret Urwin took notes. According to Urwin, a senior civil servant told the members present that the Taoiseach was 'fully informed as to our opinions on a private inquiry'. Margaret herself raised the issue of the Irish government's inconsistency in calling for a public inquiry into solicitor Pat Finucane's murder and their insistence on a private inquiry into the Dublin and Monaghan bombings. Cormac Ó Dulacháin said that there would be serious difficulties with a private inquiry. He said that, while private inquiries can be effective in cases that require extreme sensitivity (he cited the Kilkenny incest case as an example), the case of the Dublin and Monaghan bombings would not be well served by a private inquiry. He pointed out that a public inquiry was as much about the process as the end result. In other words, it was vital to have the information released into the public domain.

The families, after another meeting the same month, decided that the only contact they should have with the private inquiry was to submit their case for a public inquiry.

The legal team requested that the government postpone the establishment of any inquiry until they had time to make a case for a public inquiry. The inquiry was duly postponed, and the legal team was instructed to make such a report.

In front of a Joint Oireachtas Committee on Justice, Equality, Defence and Women's Rights, on 25 November 1999 the families presented their written submission to the Committee. The submission was entitled 'A Trust Betrayed' and included five oral statements by family members, Don Mullan and Glyn Middleton. The Committee voiced their support for a public inquiry into the matter.

The government was beginning to realise that the families were simply not going to accept a private inquiry. On 16 December, Michael McDowell, then Attorney General, and officials from the Department of the Taoiseach all met with the families to try to hammer out a new deal. He told the families the government was devising a new strategy, similar in nature to the Public Accounts Committee Inquiry. Simply put, there would be a fact-finding stage in which a judge or other eminent legal person would examine the evidence at hand. The findings of that examination would then be given to a Joint Oireachtas Committee on Justice, Equality, Defence and Women's Rights and this committee would decide on the merits of a public inquiry.

Liam Hamilton, a retired Chief Justice, was appointed to 'undertake a thorough examination of the Dublin and Monaghan bombings and their sequel'. The families were told that it would take no more than a year and would be a part of an ongoing process which would bring about a full public inquiry.

The pressure Justice for the Forgotten had put on the government had worked. The idea of a private inquiry had been shelved.

In 2000, the inquiry was finally started and was officially titled 'The Independent Commission of Inquiry into the Dublin and Monaghan Bombings'. The legal team had already begun to work with the inquiry and had handed over a considerable volume of material to aid the judge in his investigation. The list included: a complaint sent to the European Court; documents relating to the High Court action; correspondence which had been previously undertaken between a member of the campaign and the Garda Commissioner; correspondence with then Chief Constable of the RUC Ronnie Flanagan; judgements of the High Court and Supreme Court; forensic reports from both Dr R. A. Hall in Belfast and Dr James Donovan in Dublin; and interviews by journalists (Don Mullan and Glyn Middleton) with eyewitnesses and gardaí.

The families were also told that the judge had been given all the files relating to the bombings, from the relevant departments. The inquiry was now under way and it was decided that the lawyers should be engaged on a full-time basis. The process was going to be a time-consuming one and they would need the legal team to devote its full attention to it. In June 2000, the legal team was officially established, and the work on the campaign began in earnest.

Following their success in having the Hamilton Inquiry altered to allow the possibility of a public inquiry, the families now needed to decide what exactly they needed from a public inquiry. They began to agitate for a cross-jurisdictional tribunal of inquiry. Any tribunal of inquiry based only in the Republic of Ireland would not be able to compel the relevant people to give evidence. In the case of the Dublin and Monaghan bombings, given the nature of the allegations relating to collaboration between elements of the British security forces and loyalist paramilitaries, this was the only way to get to the truth.

The effectiveness of the campaign up to this point had been enormous. The families had succeeded in getting a commission of inquiry established and this, it was hoped, would lead to a public tribunal of inquiry and, eventually, justice. The profile of the Dublin and Monaghan bombings had never been higher, and the government was now not only taking notice of it, but acting upon the requests of the families. However, the campaign was about to encounter a stumbling block.

Towards the end of 2000, Chief Justice Hamilton became seriously ill and had to resign from the inquiry; Mr Justice Barron was to replace him. It was a serious blow — it would slow the whole process down significantly. Chief Justice Hamilton had been involved with the investigation for almost a year now, and had already gone over the expected duration of the inquiry. He would also have been following a direct line of inquiry and had become familiar with the subject. Mr Justice Barron had none of Hamilton's knowledge. He needed to bring himself up to speed on the inquiry as it had been conducted under Chief Justice Hamilton, meet with the families and begin his own inquiry. In the preface to his report, he acknowledges that he even had to re-interview some of the people who had given evidence to the inquiry in order to ask his own questions and form his own opinion. Without doubt, the inquiry had been set back enormously.

Meanwhile, as part of ongoing efforts to organise Justice for the Forgotten, it was decided that at the next AGM (in 2000) the outgoing executive would step down to allow for the election of a new executive. Members could nominate themselves and they should be seconded by one other person, in accordance with company law. The executive would consist of eight people. Every person present on the day would be entitled to vote. Families of the bereaved and the injured of the Dublin bombings of 1972 and 1973 would also be entitled to vote and stand for election, as they too were members of Justice for the Forgotten.

At a meeting in September, the O'Neills had the first of many clashes with the other members of the executive of Justice for the Forgotten. At that meeting, the issue of funding for the planned Family Support Centre was discussed. The post of secretary in the centre arose. Denise, with her legal background and knowledge of the campaign, decided that she would apply for the job. The minutes record the discussion at the meeting:

> Margaret said everyone had been notified about the options [the method of selecting the candidate was to be discussed and then voted upon] for discussion. At that point Frank Massey stated that a family member should be given the job and he proposed Denise O'Neill. This proposal was seconded by Edward O'Neill. Edward said Denise had been in the campaign from the very start and had a great knowledge of the bombings ... Greg said that everyone should express his or her opinion and that it was not the business of the meeting to give a job to any person. There would have to be an interview process. As their legal advisor he said he would advise that it

be given to an agency to sift out the job applicants … When the vote was taken a clear majority voted in favour of option (b), that the post be publicly advertised and available to all applicants irrespective of whether they are campaign members or not. The post will now be given to an agency to sift out job applicants.

Denise was stunned by the reaction. At the meeting, she had not asked for the job and she intended to apply for it through the proper channels. She says:

I've worked for solicitors for 22 years, and there was a job for a secretary in the centre and I thought I'd go for it. I know the history of the campaign, I know everyone involved in the campaign and I've got the legal background.

The night that I said it at the executive meeting I was totally shocked by the reaction. You'd think I was committing murder by even suggesting I could apply for the job. [The reaction] was unbelievable.

Denise tried to explain that as secretary she wouldn't have access to anyone's files.

People shouldn't have had concerns about whether or not I was going to see their personal files regarding insurance claims and compensation. Because that should have been dealt with through the offices of Greg O'Neill. I presumed that wouldn't have been done through the resource centre…. The centre wasn't there to do that sort of thing. The centre was there for the work of the campaign in supporting the families.

We [the O'Neills] had certain ideas about what we thought the resource centre should be. It should be a place for people to meet; it was an ideal location in town — people could drop in, have a cup of tea; we thought there were going to be certain facilities there for them. The first counsellor who was there was Áine Grealy — she was very much involved in asking the families to be involved in what they would like to see being offered in the centre. There would have been counselling, but of course that would be done by a professional counsellor and that would have been completely private and of a confidential nature. If people wanted to go in for counselling, that would be on a one-to-one with the counsellor, and no one in the centre would have any access to any of that kind of information.

It was clear, though, that other people on the executive had different ideas about what the function of the centre would be. Denise says:

That's why I was so taken aback by the reaction to the job. I didn't see anything wrong with me typing up the minutes of meetings, typing up press releases and work involved in the campaign. That's what I was putting myself forward for. I wasn't putting myself forward as somebody who would be involved in the counselling or dealing with anyone's personal issues.

In the end, because of the furore, Denise did not apply for the job.

Meanwhile, the legal team and Margaret Urwin had met with both Mr Justice Barron and Chief Justice Hamilton. The minutes of the October meeting of Justice for the Forgotten record it as follows:

Greg said he is taking a very different approach from his predecessor. He has decided he has certain issues he needs to look at, which is quite different from Judge Hamilton. His priority is, effectively, to find evidence of those who carried out the bombings and those who controlled them. He feels the police inquiries were secondary although, of course, very important. Judge Hamilton's approach had been that we look at everything we have.

While Chief Justice Hamilton's approach was described as 'we look at everything we have', Mr Justice Barron was delving deeper into the matters relating to the bombings. This approach would, and did, take much longer.

The legal team continued to aid the inquiry under Mr Justice Barron. In attempting to establish a link between elements of the security forces in Northern Ireland and certain sectarian crimes both north and south, Barron asked the legal team to investigate a number of incidents both before and after the Dublin and Monaghan bombings and report back to him.

While all this was going on, Justice for the Forgotten was made a limited company. The families also re-focused on some of John Wilson's other recommendations. It had been almost a year since the Wilson Report had been issued, and the matter of the official inquiry into the bombings had taken up most of the families' time. They now began to examine more closely some of the other matters he had raised, chief among them the suggestion that all victims of Troubles-related violence in Ireland should be given some form of compensation.

There were other recommendations, too, that had not been implemented. The former Tánaiste had said that there should be financial assistance for ongoing medical problems and expenses; a one-off acknowledgement payment to all families of victims; and a victims' pension. He had also suggested that a high-ranking civil servant, preferably from the Department of the Taoiseach, should be appointed to take responsibility for the recommendations. Instead, the job had been given to the Department of Justice. The Minister for Justice, John O'Donoghue, had said that there would then be a consultation process and an implementation process and that, after three years, there would be a review of the implementation process. None of this had happened.

There were further delays in the inquiry process when, in December, the families were informed that it would be April 2001 before Barron would get a chance to write his report. This would take the duration of the whole process to, at the very least, a year-and-a-half. It was supposed to have been less than a year in length. They were also told that the judge had not yet asked the British authorities for assistance. Some of the family members were beginning to wonder what the legal team was doing. They felt a need to know how things were progressing. However, the legal team argued that the information being passed on to Chief Justice Hamilton and later Mr Justice Barron was too sensitive to be made public.

None of the O'Neills were happy with this. They felt that the families were, in effect, being told what to do by the people they had hired to perform the administrative functions of Justice for the Forgotten. According to Angela:

Margaret, Cormac and Greg were [supposed to be] working for us. We appointed them … but they didn't deem it necessary to give us any information … Denise and I got more and more frustrated and so did a number of other members. I suppose people were frustrated and angry at the lack of information.

In order to show the families what information they were uncovering, the legal team organised a workshop at the Writers' Museum, Parnell Square, Dublin, in March 2001. It was described as a 'Comprehensive Report of the Legal Team on their work on the Independent Commission of Inquiry: June 2000 to March 2001'. The following is an extract from the minutes:

A comprehensive oral and visual presentation was made by Greg, Margaret and Cormac in relation to their work, on behalf of the families of the victims and the wounded, with the Independent Commission of Inquiry.

Greg reviewed their entire involvement with the Commission, the work done to date and the reports submitted in respect of all aspects of the terms of reference.

Margaret presented a series of profiles of those regarded by the legal team as the main known suspects.

Cormac raised a series of questions that demand answers, focusing, in particular, on the Garda Inquiry.

Finally, Margaret delivered a paper on the Dublin bombings of December 1, 1972.

Although, Denise was happy that information was finally being handed out, she wanted people to be constantly reminded what had been done, so that they would be motivated to continue to fight. For her, this simply didn't happen often enough. She also felt that, while it was good to have the information kept in front of them, there was nothing that the families hadn't already been told by either the 'Hidden Hand' documentary or Don Mullan's book. Bernie Bergin, who had been injured in the South Leinster Street explosion, felt the same way. Nothing new had been produced — nothing that the families hadn't already known.

⌘  ⌘  ⌘

Don Mullan had finished his book and was still a part of the campaign. At a meeting in December 2000, he had asked the families to decide on what his future role within the campaign would be. In early 2001, it was decided that he would be part of a publicity team, the aim of which would be the raising of the campaign's profile. As a journalist, Mullan had numerous contacts within the industry which could be put to good use. However, the publicity team and Don Mullan's future in the campaign were to be very short-lived.

Mullan had been of great assistance to the campaign in managing to get for them certain documents through his journalistic connections. For example, while writing his book, he had come across a statement by John Weir who had alleged British security force collusion in the bombings. Realising the importance to the campaign of this document, he got his hands on a copy and asked Tim Pat Coogan, who had the original statement, if he could pass it on to the legal team in order to build up the team's various pictures and arguments. Coogan agreed, and Mullan met Greg O'Neill in a Dublin hotel and passed over the statement. Greg O'Neill would later pass the document on to the Department of the Taoiseach and the Garda Síochána.

Mullan had also come in contact with a number of eyewitnesses who claimed to have seen the bombers on 17 May 1974. On the twenty-fifth anniversary, a man approached him and told him that he had encountered the Parnell Street bomber. Mullan, of course, was intrigued and asked the man to write a statement for him. He says:

> One of the things I have learned is that if you get someone to write something down for you, it makes more sense. They have to think it through and they have to be careful.

Two days later, the statement arrived. Knowing the importance of what he was reading, Mullan rang the man immediately and asked if he could pass the statement on to Greg O'Neill in Justice for the Forgotten. The man gave permission, and Mullan passed the statement on.

On another occasion, Mullan learned of a man who had reported a suspicious vehicle parked outside his chemist shop in Marlborough Street on the morning of the bombings to the Gardai. The chemist's name was John Burke. Mullan had learned of the man's existence from Ken Whelan, the news editor in *Ireland on Sunday*. Mullan visited the man, interviewed him and wrote an article about him for *Ireland on Sunday*. Burke claimed that it had taken the gardaí two hours to respond to his 999 call on the day of the bombings and, having inspected the suspicious vehicle and expressed concern about its contents, they left the scene and didn't return until after the three bombs had exploded that evening.

Mullan discovered that this had not been an isolated incident. He learned of a second man, Roger Keane, who worked for the Department of Posts and Telegraphs in Marlborough House. On the afternoon of the bombings, Keane noticed a white van with British registration plates parked outside his workplace. He immediately telephoned the gardaí. He had to call several times before he got a response. When he did get a response, it took the gardaí a couple of hours to arrive. By then, the van had gone. He had seen the driver – a tall, athletic man – drive it in the direction of Dublin Port and he passed this information to the gardaí, who found the van, its occupant and a suitcase with the uniform of a British Army officer inside.

Mullan felt that the experience of both men was significant and was given the go-ahead by TV3 to make a *20/20* documentary about what he had discovered. Because of the possible ramifications for the campaign he rang Greg O'Neill and made him aware that he was about to interview these two men. Like the John Weir statement, Mullan felt that these were two very important interviews for Justice for the Forgotten to have. However, he was surprised to find that Greg O'Neill was less than enthusiastic about his interviewing the two men. Mullan was not deterred though.

> I had a journalist's role in all of this ... I felt it was important to get both of those men in the can ... On the morning of the interviews I went out with a cameraman and I told him that if a solicitor turned up to stop the interviews, that he wasn't to stop filming, that he was to film everything. So I did the interviews ... with Roger Keane and John Burke, which I believe were two important interviews.

No one turned up to stop the interviews, but Mullan's hunch was proved right shortly afterwards.

> I remember, a day or two later, while I was working on the Bloody Sunday film I was walking along the Strand Road [in Derry] with Paul Greengrass and Mark Redhead [the director and producer of the film] when my mobile went off. I got two phone calls within an hour of each other. One of them was from Roger Keane and the other from John Burke. Both had received telephone calls from Greg O'Neill in which he was distancing himself from the interviews I had done. He seemed to be stressing the idea that the campaign was engaged in a confidential process with Mr Justice Barron and therefore he couldn't approve of their interviews. He followed these phone calls with letters to both men which, from my perspective, were calling into question my journalistic integrity. I went and spoke to a solicitor and had a letter sent to him because I wasn't prepared to compromise myself. I spoke to a number of the families to inform them I was having difficulties.

Mullan was truly nonplussed by the actions of Greg O'Neill. As a journalist, he couldn't understand why anyone working for a campaign which was trying to blow the lid off one of the biggest scandals in the history of the state would object to such interviews. In an interesting postscript Mullan has this to say:

> Shortly before the broadcast of the interviews on TV3's *20/20*, I went with my solicitor to meet Mr Justice Barron, at his office in the Department of the Taoiseach. The solicitor to the Commission of Inquiry was with Mr Justice Barron. I asked him if it would cause him any difficulties if I broadcast the interviews with Mr Burke and Mr Keane. He said absolutely not and his solicitor said that the more information that was brought into the public domain the better.

If Mr Justice Barron had no problem with the information being in the public domain, it seemed to Mullan that there was no reason why Greg O'Neill should have had a problem with it. This experience with the JFF solicitor played a major role in his decision to eventually resign from the campaign. However, it was the publicity team that finally made up his mind for him.

Mullan had always tried to shy away from taking any role in the campaign more active than that of a journalist, but some of the family members had put him forward and he decided to help out. He made time in his busy schedule working on the Bloody Sunday film to work with the families. He travelled from Derry to Dublin for the only meeting of the publicity team.

Rather than work on his own, Mullan called for volunteers from among the families. He reasoned that if they worked on their own publicity, they would be induced to take more responsibility for the campaign, and thereby give it a stronger base to work from. Cormac Ó Dulacháin had already drawn up a publicity strategy, but Mullan decided that rather than working from this, they would assimilate it into a strategy of the families' own creation.

The meeting of the publicity team took place in Denise O'Neill's house. Present at the meeting were Don Mullan, Michelle O'Brien, Denise and Angela O'Neill, Alice O'Brien, Bernie and John McNally, Bernie and John Bergin, Garrett Mussen and Monica Campbell.

Bernie Bergin would later describe it as a 'brainstorming session' and a successful one at that. Many good ideas were proposed for further discussion: the setting up of an email campaign which was to be styled on a similar campaign begun by another group; the idea of having a website for the campaign; and the presentation of a copy of Don Mullan's book to the Garda Commissioner.

Also proposed was the idea of lobbying at both Westminster and 10 Downing Street. The members of the team hoped to arrange it so that any proposed visit to London would coincide with a visit by the Taoiseach, so that maximum publicity could be gained from the event. The idea of sponsorship from Irish Ferries and CIÉ to fund the trip was also suggested.

An information notice was written up and circulated to all members of the campaign. It was dated 6 March 2001.

On 8 March 2001 Bernie Bergin received a phone call from Justice for the Forgotten's barrister, Cormac Ó Dulacháin. The barrister told her that, following a meeting of the executive committee the previous night, he had the impression that the publicity team was deciding to do things that were already being done: in fact, a trip to London had been decided upon by the executive already.

When Bernie asked Ó Dulacháin why the members of the executive who had been present at the meeting had not informed anyone of this, he told her that they did not know this had been arranged and were only informed of the decision at the executive meeting. The meeting of the publicity team had taken place on 2 March 2001. Ó Dulacháin found out about their proposal to go to London at the executive meeting on 7 March. He rang Bernie Bergin to tell her that their decision clashed with a decision that had already been made to go to London. However, the decision had not been made by the executive committee: the key problem was that the members of the executive committee had been informed of the decision after it had already been made. This did not sit well with Bernie Bergin: 'I could not see why we had an executive committee if they did not know anything. As far as I could see the legal team and Margaret seemed to be the only ones who knew and I did not find this acceptable. I told him that we as members need to take charge. After all, the legal team are working for us, not the other way around.'

At a meeting on 10 March 2001 (incidentally, the same meeting at which the legal team and Margaret Urwin presented their 'Comprehensive Report of the Legal Team on their work on the Independent Commission of Inquiry: June 2000 to March 2001'), the issue of the publicity team was discussed. Bernie Bergin, it is reported in the minutes, asked if there was any need for the publicity team. She had asked the question facetiously, but the remarks had been taken at face value and were reported in the minutes as such. Interestingly, at the end of the discussion on the publicity team, it is noted that 'the future of the publicity sub-committee would be discussed at the next executive meeting'. It was not, according to these minutes, a matter to be discussed in front of the general assembly.

After the meeting on 10 March 2001, Bernie Bergin resigned from the team. She wrote a letter to the chairman of Justice for the Forgotten outlining her difficulties with the way the publicity team had been dealt with. She felt that she could not work under these conditions and was therefore resigning from the team.

The next meeting of JFF was held on 31 March. In the minutes of that meeting, following discussions between Bernie Bergin and Margaret Urwin, the minutes of the 10 March meeting were amended to include an addition to what Bernie Bergin had said. The addition was to read:

> During the same discussions where Bernie Bergin asked if there was any need for a publicity sub-committee she went on to say, 'bearing in mind the problems some members of the Executive had with it.'

The problems the executive had with the publicity team are not mentioned in the minutes, but it is recorded that the executive felt that the publicity team had discussed matters outside its remit. At the end of the minutes of that meeting, the publicity team is noted as having 'disintegrated', with Denise suggesting that publicity be co-ordinated from the office by Margaret.

It was the final straw for Don Mullan. He'd had enough of the internal politics of the campaign, and he wrote, telling the members that he had resigned, and noting that the publicity team had not 'disintegrated', as had been recorded in the minutes, but had been, in his words, 'culled by people who saw it as a threat'. However, although he had left Justice for the Forgotten, he had not abandoned the cause of the Dublin and Monaghan bombings;

> I was maintaining the moral right to speak and write about the Dublin and Monaghan bombings, which I have continued to do. It's not as if I've abandoned the issue. Those families have the right to justice. I will, in whatever small way I can, continue to support that.

At the next meeting, 28 April 2001, it was noted that Don Mullan had resigned. Certain, unspecified difficulties are mentioned in the minutes relating to Mullan's resignation, but nothing definite is said. In fact, there is nothing except their proximity on the page to suggest that the resignation of Don Mullan and the difficulties the minutes describe are connected. It is described thus:

It was noted with great regret that Don had resigned and his contribution to the campaign was acknowledged. The efforts of the Executive to resolve issues of the previous four months, through numerous lengthy meetings and discussions, were outlined. The view was expressed that difficulties should have been brought to the attention of the general membership at an earlier date. As against that, the Executive indicated that they had hoped to resolve the differences and that was their belief until about two weeks ago. At the end of the discussion, Phil proposed a vote of confidence in the lawyers and in Margaret. This was seconded by Martha and passed unanimously.

⌘　⌘　⌘

In 2001, Áine Grealy was hired by Justice for the Forgotten. Her experience would not be a pleasant one and she would remain quite disturbed by it for some time afterwards.

She had got in contact with Justice for the Forgotten through Don Mullan when he had gone to New York to promote his book on the bombings. Áine had been familiar with the Bloody Sunday campaign and the centre that had been set up to help the victims and those suffering from Post Traumatic Stress Disorder (PTSD) from the events of that day.

She had worked 'for years in both Ireland and New York with people traumatised by the ongoing political conflict in Ireland'. The opportunity presented itself to work with the JFF and she was employed in the position of Director of the Family Support Programme which was to be operated through the Family Support Services Centre. She proposed a programme for the victims based on her experience of dealing with post and ongoing traumatic stress and also the success of another family support programme which she had created directed in New York city.

Her understanding was that the Family Support Programme would be separate from campaign activities and that its purpose was to provide, and her function to create, a safe environment in which individual and family members who chose to do so could deal with whatever issues they considered necessary for their own, and the group's, progress.

She arrived in the campaign after Don Mullan's resignation and realised that his departure had left a lot of bad feeling within the ranks of the families.

Practically everyone was upset that Don had gone – many believed that his book had brought the campaign into prominence and he had made a very valuable contribution to its progress.

Though Don had departed by the time I arrived on the scene and it was suggested that this was all past history and the group were moving forward, it became very apparent to me that this was clearly not the case. From a campaign perspective they may have decided to move forward, but from an emotional perspective it was obvious that this was yet another deep painful loss some members were experiencing and my efforts to facilitate the processing of this loss, which I felt to be my professional duty and responsibility, was perceived as an attempt on my part to have Don Mullan re-instated.

Áine felt that, because of this misconception, everything she attempted to do for the families was undermined. There was ongoing dissension on the executive. As a result of this, she feels, an atmosphere of ill will, distrust and hostility permeated all things related to JFF and greatly compromised the effectiveness of her attempts to structure a program. Even the facility itself could no longer be regarded as a safe environment for some of the families who needed and wanted help.

After the World Trade Centre tragedy on 11 September 2001, Áine took pre-planned leave to return to her family, which was based in New York. Meanwhile, in her absence, complaints were made by a member of the executive about her perceived lack of performance. Her contract had been signed during the summer of 2001 and she had been having on-going meetings with some of the members of Justice for the Forgotten, as well as outside consultants, when she had to go back to New York.

After the Justice for the Forgotten AGM in 2001 she received word that certain remarks had been made about her by Margaret Urwin during the meeting and that Urwin had read from a prepared text. She instructed her solicitor to write to JFF and demand a copy of the prepared text together with a copy of the minutes from the meeting. Her solicitor's requests were not dealt with.

She was very distressed by her treatment at the hands of those who were in control of Justice for the Forgotten. However, she has no ill-feeling towards the families she met with. She kept in touch with the O'Neills for some time after her departure and she says that Tim Grace, who was president of the executive at the time Áine started with JFF 'and some of the other family members were as helpful as they could be.'

*AGM October 2001*

For her part, Angela O'Neill was becoming sick of all the turmoil:

> We were battle weary by the time we got to the AGM [in 2001]. We had been raising serious questions about matters that were important to us. They were broadening the whole JFF remit. We got involved in JFF to deal with the Dublin and Monaghan bombings. We'd battled long and hard to get to where we were. They wanted '72 and '73 to be brought in. I thought we were having enough of a job getting the Irish public interested without bringing in two other bombings.

Angela worried about the effect the widening of the remit would have on the Dublin and Monaghan campaign.

> ... at no stage did we sign up to be civil rights activists. We were fighting for Dublin and Monaghan. We would help out any other group as much as we could but ... the whole terms of reference for JFF had been broadened. It had now become diluted and sidetracked — it was now for people who were involved in the Troubles. In our opinion, this meant that JFF was going to go on forever. We began to wonder where '74 was in all this.

By the time the AGM had come around, Denise too was ready to give up. Although Angela had put herself forward for re-election to the executive, Denise decided she'd had enough. She did not want to be on the executive any longer. However, she was convinced by Frank Massey and Tim Grace to go again and, reluctantly, she did.

Before the AGM was convened, Tim Grace announced that Angela O'Neill wanted the AGM postponed for a month. In the minutes of the meeting it is recorded as follows:

Before opening the meeting Tim Grace the Chairperson announced that there was a proposal from some members of the Executive to postpone the AGM for one month. Angela O'Neill read out a statement prepared at the Executive meeting on Tuesday 2 October. After heated debate on the matters raised in the statement the issue was put to the vote.

In his chairperson's report, Tim Grace is reported in the minutes as having said that there were 'serious problems' with the executive committee and that he felt there should be no AGM at this stage.

No explanation of the 'serious problems' with the executive, the content of Angela O'Neill's statement or the issues mentioned in the 'heated debate' is made in the minutes. According to Angela O'Neill, Justice for the Forgotten was drawing up a constitution at the time, and they wanted to delay the process so that matters could be debated further — one of the main bones of contention for them was the matter of the criteria for membership of the campaign. It is quite probable that the phrase 'heated debate' is a highly creative euphemism for the argument that ensued. In any case, a vote was held to decide whether the AGM should be postponed. Sixteen voted in favour, with twenty-three voting against.

Yet another argument, this time described as an 'extremely heated' debate followed the Secretrary's Report delivered by Margaret Urwin. Bizarrely, no report whatsoever of what Urwin said is made at all in the minutes. The Secretary's Report for the whole year is summed up in the following brief manner:

Secretary's Report
Extremely heated debate followed. Greg O'Neill stepped in to assist the chair and the meeting moved on to the election of the executive committee.

This two-line brushing-over of the most fraught part of the meeting is highly unusual. No mention of the contents of the report or the matters arising from the debate which ensued is mentioned anywhere. According to the O'Neills, Urwin, reading from a prepared text, proceeded to make certain remarks regarding the recently departed counsellor, Áine Grealy. In any case, whatever was said in the report, it was quickly glossed over by whoever prepared the minutes. The next item on the agenda was the election of the new Executive.

According to the minutes of the AGM, there were fifty people in attendance. There is certainly a strange discrepancy in the number of people who are noted as having attended and the number of people who voted. This could be as a result of faulty minute taking, or perhaps because some people abstained. In any case Denise believes there were many more in attendance, most of whom she had never seen before, either at meetings or at commemorative ceremonies. She says:

> I can't tell you who these people were — I'd never seen them before; they'd never stepped foot inside a meeting or gone to a church service. But they came and were given voting privileges and we were voted out.

The new members' lack of familiarity with the campaign meant that they could not have been fully informed of the pros and cons of each candidate; they could not have known whom best to vote for and whom not to vote for. However, according to Justice for the Forgotten regulations at the time, they were all entitled to vote on the election of a new executive. Denise says:

> There were people there on the day that didn't know us and that I didn't know, so how could they have had the information to vote us off?

In addition to this, some members had not received notice of the AGM at all. Bernie Bergin and her husband John lived not in Dublin but in Kilkenny. They didn't go to every meeting of JFF for obvious reasons; it simply would have been too difficult for them to regularly attend. However, they attended whenever they could. They received no notification, however, that the meeting was being held. It seemed to be another example of the difficulty Justice for the Forgotten had in co-ordinating a campaign which had members spread all over the country.

The vote was held with Angela, Denise and their brother Niall going forward for election. After a secret ballot, none of them was elected. The new executive was: Monica Duffy, Pat Fay, Tim Grace, Phil Lawlor-Watson, Bernie McNally, Garrett Mussen, Alice O'Brien and Jackie Wade.

An interesting aside is that in the minutes of the AGM, under the heading 'Minutes/Matters Arising', it is recorded that Denise O'Neill objected to the minutes of the meeting from the previous month, saying that they were selective and did not record certain remarks that had been made about her in her absence.

At the time, Denise's young son was seriously ill in hospital. On the night of one of the meetings, she left his bedside in hospital to attend a Justice for the Forgotten meeting. When she arrived, a heated debate was already taking place. It seemed that nothing could be proposed without an argument of some sort. Denise gave her opinion during the meeting, as she usually did, but her participation was cut short when she received a call from her husband in the hospital, telling her that their son had taken a turn for the worse, and if the doctors didn't operate, he would surely die. Denise left immediately and made for the hospital as quickly as she could. The operation was a success.

In the minutes of the meeting, which she later read, she was described as having 'stormed out'. A 'get-well-soon' card was later sent to Denise's son from all the members of Justice for the Forgotten. But no mention of Denise's sick son was made in the minutes of the meeting.

More 'heated debate' is reported in the minutes after Denise raised the issue. Greg O'Neill cut it short by suggesting that the matter would be better conducted under Any Other Business. However, if the matter *was* discussed in Any Other Business, it is not reported in the minutes.

Although they were no longer on the committee, the O'Neills were still members of the JFF. However, while they were still loyal to the cause of justice for the forgotten, they were no longer loyal to the organisation. They decided to change solicitor. They hired Des Doherty, a lawyer for some of the Bloody Sunday families. It was, Angela believes, one of the best moves they ever made.

We no longer wanted the Justice for the Forgotten legal team working on behalf of our family. And we also felt that one person should not have a monopoly on the whole thing. It might be good from a political point of view not to have all our eggs in one basket. It also troubled us that they were doing so much work for Barron ... all the time they were meant to be acting for us and point blank refusing to give us information.

Angela recalls the constant turmoil of weekly executive meetings with Justice for the Forgotten:

Those weekly meetings were the most stressful times of my life. Denise and I were seen as the people who were asking too many questions. We weren't prepared to just sit back and accept that we weren't going to be given answers and accept that they were going to go ahead and make funding proposals without any consultation, or accept that we didn't know what the administrators were being paid. There was huge conflict.

No one outside the executive committee was aware of the turmoil and trouble at each meeting. Very little information filtered out to the general body of Justice for the Forgotten and many decisions were made on their behalf. According to Denise: 'Everything should have gone to the main body of JFF in a very impartial way so that they could make the decision.'

Although still technically members of Justice for the Forgotten, the O'Neills began to work on their own again. Justice for the Forgotten continued its work with the new executive, trying to raise awareness of the bombings and continually trying to push the authorities into acknowledging the tragedy that had occurred not just by their words, but by their actions too.

However, by the end of 2001, the families were still waiting. Not only were they waiting to see when Barron would publish his report, but they were waiting also to find out if he had been given any help from the British authorities. The whole process had, at that stage, taken almost two years.

In January 2002 a new secretary was hired in Justice for the Forgotten. A new counsellor was also appointed. Kevin Walsh had to retire from any activities within Justice for the Forgotten because of ill-health. (He had been taken on as a member in 2000 due to his work in health. (He had been taken on as a member in 2000 due to his work in getting some form of official monument to the victims of the bombings in Dublin city at the same time that the O'Neills had been working on their burgeoning campaign for justice.) A reception was held at which there was a formal presentation of a gift from the campaign, to acknowledge his part in beginning it.

In March, the families were told that Mr Justice Barron had indeed received a response from the British government. It was, inevitably, in the negative. Apart from a letter from Secretary of State for Northern Ireland, Dr John Reid, which contained a fifteen page letter summarising all of the British government's files relating to the bombings, no help was offered by the British authorities. This was a major blow for the inquiry and for the families. Without the aid of the British government, the inquiry would be missing key elements in its investigation. Barron would be left to put together a jigsaw with half the pieces missing.

Although the O'Neills were still members of Justice for the Forgotten and were still entitled to attend meetings, they were continuing to forge ahead on their own. They had been informed by the government, however, that there would be no funding available for their new solicitor. All of the funding was going to the solicitors for Justice for the Forgotten. One of their attempts to secure funding for their own legal representation was to precipitate their dismissal from JFF.

At the memorial service for the twenty-eighth anniversary, Angela handed a letter to Taoiseach Bertie Ahern, who was the elected representative for Martha's constituency, regarding their lack of funding.

Secondly, some other members of Justice for the Forgotten had followed the O'Neills in hiring Des Doherty as their new solicitor while remaining members of JFF. Around the time of the twenty-eighth anniversary a press release was issued by Des Doherty on behalf of the O'Neill family, the O'Brien family (of which Linda Sutherland was a member) and Bernie Bergin. The press release contained notification that some of the families of the bereaved of Dublin and Monaghan intended to attend the Bloody Sunday Inquiry and meet with some of the Bloody Sunday families. It also contained a message to Mr Justice Barron, urging him 'to release his report forthwith'.

A third incident occurred when, on 18 May 2002, Edward O'Neill gave an interview to the *Irish Mirror* in which he had indicated that the families now being represented by Des Doherty felt betrayed by the Taoiseach.

Also on 15 April 2002, Edward wrote a letter to the Department of the Taoiseach regarding what he believed was questionable behaviour by Justice for the Forgotten. Although he signed the letter on behalf of the O'Neill family, the O'Brien family and Bernie Bergin, he actually sent it without Bernie Bergin's permission. As it would later be part of the evidence that was used to eject Bernie Bergin from Justice for the Forgotten, he offered to go and tell the executive of the organisation that she had not authorised it. However, Bernie Bergin felt that her cards were already marked and there was no point in Ed taking it any further.

Edward's letter to the Department of the Taoiseach had clearly irritated Justice for the Forgotten. In it, he said the following:

... We believe that JFF Ltd may have unwittingly committed serious breaches of Irish Company and Employment Law which we feel obliged to bring to your attention.

We have ascertained the following points which we have written to JFF Ltd but to date the undernoted have been ignored.

1) As JFF Ltd is a limited company, it is subject to Irish Company law regardless of its legal stature. With this regard, we must note that to date we have been unable to ascertain if JFF Ltd has filed any annual return since its incorporation in October 2000. To my knowledge this is a serious breach of Irish Company law and is liable to penalties or fines or imprisonment of directors or both. The Companies Office in Dublin have also advised that under the relevant legislation, they have the power to de-list JFF Ltd from the register of companies for failure to file proper accounts.

2) A prerequisite of any Limited Company under Irish Company law is the appointment of auditors. Despite repeated requests which to date have gone unanswered we have been unable to ascertain if indeed any firm of auditors have ever been appointed. Again we feel that this is a serious breach of the relevant legislations and requires clarification.

3) At the last AGM of JFF Ltd, which was attended by two signatories of this notification, no secretary's report was filed in

accounts were filed on the day, which to my knowledge makes the previous AGM invalid. Perhaps you can clarify this situation for me.

4) As the Departments of Justice and An Taoiseach have provided large amounts of funding to JFF Ltd, both Departments have both a legal and moral obligation to ensure the proper administration of said funds to the parties which they were originally allocated to i.e. the relatives and victims of the Dublin and Monaghan bombings. As both the Departments of Justice and An Taoiseach have failed to oversee the administration of funding, we believe that this places both Departments within the reach of any possible legal action which may occur as direct result of this negligence …

The letter continued, suggesting that funds which the Departments of Justice and the Taoiseach had allocated to Justice for the Forgotten were not being used for the purpose they were intended.

> … JFF Ltd amongst other things was set up to:
> 'To provide Aid and Assistance to the relatives and dependants of those who were killed and injured as a direct result of the Dublin and Monaghan bombings of 17th May 1974.'
> Recently I made a direct application to JFF Ltd for funds to seek out my own psychological counselling support only to be told that no funds exist for such an exercise. This is despite the fact that public knowledge indicates that over 668,000 Euro has been allocated by Justice and Taoiseach's Departments to JFF Ltd. I may be incorrect when I say that as funds were solicited by JFF Ltd in the names of my father Edward O'Neill Snr (Deceased) and Mr John O'Brien and family (Deceased) and others killed and injured that these funds are to be used for the benefit of the relatives, survivors and dependants of those killed and injured. The point of my question is, therefore, why are the relatives, survivors and dependants being denied access to funds which were supposedly allocated for our benefit?

He also made reference to an attempt that he and his sisters made to see the employment contract of Margaret Urwin, only to be rebuffed:

Despite repeated requests which also to date have gone unanswered, I personally and other members of JFF Ltd have requested copies of the employment contract of Mrs Margaret Urwin and other staff employed at a resource centre which is supposedly for our benefit only to be denied such information.

The letter handed to Bertie Ahern, the press release urging Judge Barron to 'issue his report forthwith', the interview Ed gave to the *Irish Mirror* and the letter he wrote to the Department of the Taoiseach regarding JFF were to form the basis on which the O'Neills, Bernie Bergin and Linda Sutherland were to be expelled from Justice for the Forgotten.

Ed is not someone who keeps his opinion to himself, nor is he one to couch his statements in vague terms. His opinions were forthright and to the point. In a democracy, of course, this is the right of every citizen. In Justice for the Forgotten, it was prohibited by Article 13 of its constitution, which prevented any member from making any statement which was seen to bring Justice for the Forgotten into disrepute. While his remarks regarding Bertie Ahern's betrayal may have been quite strong, it was his right to make them. In a democracy, it is every citizen's right to say what he or she feels. That right and Article 13 of the constitution of Justice for the Forgotten were not compatible.

In May 2002, at a general meeting of Justice for the Forgotten which Edward O'Neill attended, Cormac Ó Dulacháin said that he would have difficulty giving a legal report in the presence of those who had instructed another solicitor to act for them. He told the meeting that the members of his legal team could report to and take instructions from their own clients only. In the minutes of that meeting the question of whether another member (the member is never named but is clearly Edward O'Neill as he was the only person listed as having attended the meeting who was not represented by the legal team of Justice for the Forgotten) should be asked to leave the meeting for the duration of the legal report. The other members who attended that meeting decided not to hold the vote.

On 20 May 2002, three days after the twenty-eighth anniversary of the bombings, Bernie Bergin, the O'Neills and Linda Sutherland were all sent letters, signed by the chairperson, Bernie McNally, stating that their membership had been suspended. They were asked to refrain from membership had been suspended. They were asked to refrain from attending personally at the Family Service Support Centre. In October 2002, having been suspended since May, they were all expelled from Justice for the Forgotten. The reasons, according to Justice for the Forgotten were:

A letter sent to the Department of the Taoiseach seeking 'that an immediate block be placed on any further funding to be given to JFF Ltd.'; a press release issued by Desmond J. Doherty Solicitors calling upon Judge Barron 'to release his report forthwith' and a newspaper article in the *Irish Mirror* accusing the Taoiseach of betrayal.

Bernie Bergin felt particularly aggrieved by her dismissal. She had not been aware that Edward O'Neill had sent the letter to the Department of the Taoiseach regarding the funding to JFF. She says: 'At no stage have I made any submissions to anyone to have the funding for the Resource Centre blocked or stopped.'

In relation to attacking the Taoiseach publicly, this too was to do with a statement made by Edward O'Neill – a statement he was absolutely entitled to make in any democracy. Bernie makes the point that, although Edward's interview did make strong comments about the Taoiseach, it was no stronger than what had already been said by Greg O'Neill when he told journalist Frank Connolly that the Taoiseach had misled the Dáil.

As for calling for the publication of the Barron Report, Bernie states that, 'this is an interesting accusation, which can only have validity if it is the belief of the executive and its advisors that publication of the report at this stage would be premature. It implies that the executive believes that the report is not yet overdue or that the deadline for production in their eyes is nowhere near.' At the time Desmond J. Doherty issued the statement calling for the publication of the Barron Report, it was already more than a year late.

In spite of all this, the O'Neills, Bernie Bergin and Linda Sutherland were all expelled from JFF. Article 13 of the constitution of Justice for the Forgotten states:

A member who brings Justice for the Forgotten into disrepute and, or who fails to abide by decisions of the organisation, may be removed from membership by the Executive Committee. A member may appeal any such decision to the General Meeting.

None of the members who had been expelled chose to appeal.

*Conclusion*

According to Don Mullan, the strength of the Bloody Sunday campaign was the solidarity of the families at the heart of it. Justice for the Forgotten had just weakened itself by ejecting family members and, indeed, whole families from the campaign. In the Bloody Sunday campaign, the solicitors — and there were many solicitors, not just one legal team — were there to assist families rather than direct families. Mullan's experience with Bloody Sunday and Omagh reminded him that, aside from the families, no one, including journalists, was actually a member of the campaign. He was always aware that he was there as a guest.

For the O'Neills, Justice for the Forgotten seems to have been a mixed blessing. The organisation was a good one. It contained many capable people such as Margaret Urwin, Greg O'Neill, Cormac Ó Dulacháin, Nora Comiskey and Don Mullan, all of whom were committed to seeing justice done for the bereaved and the survivors of Dublin and Monaghan. And they were, initially, happy to be part of the group again. The campaign had organisation and focus. According to Angela:

> It was fine. It was great to have a solicitor and a barrister and some sort of legal background. We felt that we could take this campaign places. Where it needed to go.

However, the campaign was beset by problems. It appeared to the O'Neills that the secretary and legal team were in control and directing the families, rather than the families taking control and receiving help and support from them. Although Denise and Angela were on the first executive (comprising Greg O'Neill, Cormac Ó Dulacháin, Margaret Urwin, Don Mullan, Tim Grace, Pat Fay, Bernie McNally, Michelle Byrne, and Angela and Denise), neither of the two sisters felt that they had sufficient say in the decision-making processes. This ran completely contrary to the way previous campaigns of this nature had successfully

I remember asking Greg [O'Neill] from where did he get his directions and he told me, 'I receive them from you.' But you would go into meetings and you would [not know] what you are going to do, what you are going to say and how you are going to react when something is said to you.

During the Barron Inquiry, the legal team told the families that, because of the sensitivity of the information they were coming across, they couldn't share any of it with the families. According to Denise:

> They couldn't see the irony in that. All these families had come to get information and that the people who were being paid to assist us were the very ones keeping the information from us.

For example, none of the O'Neills knew the exact manner in which Edward Senior had died. This was to cause Denise great distress at the launch of Don Mullan's book at Dublin's Civic Offices. In the course of the launch, a man approached Denise, claiming to have been an ambulance driver on the day of the bombings.

> I asked him if he'd talked to him [her father]. He said, 'Yeah, he wanted to know if the boys were all right.' And I asked, 'Was he bad?' and he told me he'd lost both of his legs. I just burst into tears and I went outside and a couple of people went outside with me. I thought, 'Jesus, I never knew that, I never knew he lost his legs, I never knew he was mutilated like that.' My mother told me he died of a heart attack. I remember being absolutely gutted. Thinking about him lying there — his legs had been blown off and he was worried about the boys. I sobbed uncontrollably outside the Civic Offices that night.
>
> Greg O'Neill came outside the Civic Offices that night and put his arms around me. It was a very distressing night.

As Denise had never known how her father had died, the ambulance driver's account was the only one she had. While she was in Justice for the Forgotten, she never found out about her father's last minutes, and the belief that he had died on the street in agony tortured her. It wasn't until their new legal representative was hired that Denise found out that, in fact, when her father had been caught in the explosion, the lock of the boot from the bomb-car had lodged in his chest, piercing his heart and killing him instantly and mercifully.

Edward O'Neill recalls an occasion when he tried to press Greg O'Neill for more information about the bombings. The solicitor turned to him and told him that he was deliberately not telling him anything so that he would retain a sense of shock and outrage when the inquiry finally made its report. Edward, never a man to mince his words, said, 'Greg, I was with my father on the day he was killed — how much more outraged do you want me to be?'

The campaign was no longer the forum for healing that Martha O'Neill had found with the first coming together of the families. The problem was not the members of Justice for the Forgotten but those who now ran the campaign. But Denise bears the other families no ill-will:

> People who were involved in the campaign saw Margaret and Greg and Cormac as the professionals. The ones that could do something. They [the other families] probably thought that they were the ones that should be listened to. If you've never been involved in something like this and you don't go out and speak publicly at events, then you [would]. I can understand that. I'd never blame the general body of JFF.

Nora Comiskey, who had introduced Margaret Urwin to the campaign, also had her own ideas on the way the campaign should have been run. She is a founder member of the Irish National Congress which is, and always was, run on a voluntary basis. She left Justice for the Forgotten in 1999 for personal reasons. She believes that as soon as the campaign began to employ people, it became a job and not a cause.

According to both Denise and Angela, the quest for justice for those who had been killed was sidetracked by internal struggling and infighting. Justice for the Forgotten, of course, has done some excellent work on the campaign for justice. Progress has been made, and the families are certainly closer to justice now than they were in 1990 when the whole campaign was set in motion by the O'Neills. However, along the way, the campaign was set in motion by the O'Neills. However, along the way, the families gradually became less central to the process. It is vital — not just necessary, but vital — to have the families of the bereaved at the centre of any fight. They must be the people running the campaign, as opposed to sitting back and having a legal team run it for them.

# THE BARRON INQUIRY

The road to the Barron Inquiry was an arduous one. After twenty-four years, it was the first time that any real steps had been taken by the government to bring a satisfactory conclusion to the whole affair. As has been mentioned in previous chapters, the Belfast Agreement contained the seed from which the current movement towards justice began. The Victims' Commission that was established under the terms of the Agreement provided a chance for the families to meet with the Victims' Commissioner, John Wilson, and put to him their desire to have a public tribunal of inquiry established to resolve finally the issue of the hurt that had been caused by the continued neglect of the subject of the Dublin and Monaghan bombings. They were bitterly disappointed when Wilson gave his report recommending a private inquiry.

In October of the same year, the families met with senior officials from the Department of the Taoiseach who told them that John Wilson had, informally, said that the families never used the word 'public' in any of their submissions. However, Cormac Ó Dulacháin produced a copy of the statement he had submitted to Wilson, which clearly and explicitly stated the need for a public inquiry. The minutes of a meeting the families had had with Bertie Ahern the previous April showed that Ó Dulacháin had clearly told the Taoiseach that a public inquiry was what Justice for the Forgotten was seeking.  .

Having negotiated with the families, the government eventually agreed to change the nature of the inquiry, and in February 2000, Chief

Justice Liam Hamilton was handed his terms of reference. They were:

> To undertake a thorough examination, involving fact finding and
> assessment, of all aspects of the Dublin/Monaghan bombings and
> their sequel, including:
> — the facts, circumstances, causes and perpetrators of the bombings;
> — the nature, extent and adequacy of the Garda Investigation,
>   including the co-operation with and from the relevant authorities
>   in Northern Ireland and the handling of evidence, including the
>   scientific analyses of forensic evidence;
> — the reasons why no prosecution took place, including whether and
>   if so, by whom and to what extent the investigations were
>   impeded; and
> — the issues raised by the Hidden Hand T.V. documentary
>   broadcast in 1993.

> 'The Dublin and Monaghan bombings' refer to
> — the bomb explosions that took place in Parnell Street, Talbot
>   Street and South Leinster Street, Dublin, on 17 May 1974
> — the bomb explosion that took place in North Street, Monaghan,
>   on 17 May 1974.

⌘  ⌘  ⌘

During his Commission of Inquiry into the bombings of 1974 and their
aftermath, Mr Justice Barron spoke with almost everyone still alive who
had had any connection with the bombings, whether they had been in
government, or had been members of the Garda Síochána or journalists
who had investigated the bombings.

In weighing the evidence, the judge, as one would expect, discounted
what could not be proven beyond doubt. Because of the time elapsed
since the bombings had taken place, his ability to question people was
limited. Some people had died, some people refused to talk about the
bombings, and some people's memories simply weren't what they had
been thirty years before. Key information had been lost, probably forever,
and there was simply nothing that could be done about it.

## *Who Carried Out the Dublin and Monaghan Bombings?*

Mr Justice Barron started his inquiry assuming that he knew nothing. By starting from this point, he would not be prejudiced in favour of one opinion or the other. He began his investigation with a clean slate, suspecting nothing but what could be proven by the information he could collect.

One of the main allegations that is regularly made about the Dublin and Monaghan bombings is that they involved security-force collusion. It has repeatedly been suggested that the UVF could not have carried out the bombings alone and that, in fact, they did so with the approval and assistance of certain sections of the British security forces in Northern Ireland. The allegation of collusion comes in many forms and has been around since before the bombs exploded.

In assessing this theory, Mr Justice Barron first had to dispense with it entirely and begin at the beginning.

### LOYALIST GUILT

Loyalist paramilitaries were always suspected of having carried out the bombings. Through examination of later admissions by the UVF, statements from politicians close to the UVF (David Ervine, leader of the PUP, said in 1998 that the UVF had indeed carried out the bombings in Dublin — he did not, however, refer to the bombing of Monaghan), and from intelligence information gathered by the Garda Síochána, the RUC and the British army and intelligence services, Mr Justice Barron came to the conclusion that the UVF had indeed been responsible for the Dublin and Monaghan bombings.

Once that had been established, the next step for Mr Justice Barron was to investigate whether, and if so, to what extent, the UVF had been helped by elements within the British security forces. To this end, he was much less successful and his decision can, at best, be described as open-ended.

Barron makes the following very important note before he begins any discussion of the possibility of complicity by members of the British army, the RUC or the intelligence services:

> … such evidence as might confirm or refute the allegations is most likely to be in the possession of the security forces themselves — that is to say, the very groups which are being accused of illegal behaviour.

It is an inherent difficulty with any inquiry into the bombings. However, such evidence should not deter anyone from attempting to investigate such allegations. Mr Justice Barron is hampered in his ability to state something as fact by a necessity, borne out of his judicial appointment, to attain a certain level of proof. However, this is a limitation which applies only to a judge. For any journalist who has investigated these allegations, no such limitation applies. Provided that journalists can provide adequate back-up for the statements they make, they can create a theory based on the facts they have gathered, and put it forward. In other words, journalists can speculate. A journalist whose speculation is incorrect can be sued by those who have been defamed — provided, of course, that it emerges in court that the journalist was indeed incorrect. A judge simply cannot make such a speculation.

Many of the previous theories floated by journalists were the basis of Mr Justice Barron's investigation. People like Don Mullan and Joe Tiernan have written extensively on the bombings and on their extensive investigations. While Joe Tiernan did not speak directly with the inquiry, his writings were referred to often by Mr Justice Barron. Don Mullan did agree to speak to the inquiry and also made the inquiry aware of certain other people to whom it could speak.

Barron states:

[T]hough some claim to have specific evidence of the security forces protecting the perpetrators of the Dublin/Monaghan bombings, others have concentrated on accumulating evidence from other incidents which they believe establishes a pattern of such protection. One is then invited to assume that this pattern applied in the case of the Dublin and Monaghan bombings.

Roughly speaking, Joe Tiernan falls into the former category, while Don Mullan falls into the latter.

Barron goes on:

Those who seek to establish a pattern of ongoing, illegal collaboration between elements of the security forces and loyalist extremists have based their claims on the following points:

(1) The adoption of a policy of counter-intelligence which advocated the use of 'friendly guerrillas' (in this case, loyalist paramilitaries) as allies in the war against the 'real' enemy (in this case, the PIRA);

(2) The cultivation of agents and informers within loyalist paramilitary groups, resulting in a refusal to act on information received for fear of compromising the information source;

(3) A widespread sympathy amongst army and police officers towards loyalist aims and objectives, combined with a general anti-nationalist bias;

(4) The existence of a group of loyalist 'untouchables', deduced from a pattern of failure to prosecute known paramilitaries; and finally

(5) Evidence of the involvement of members of the security forces in specific paramilitary attacks.

Barron did not include, but perhaps should have, a belief in the inability of loyalist paramilitaries to carry out the bombings without outside help. While all of the above provides precedent for the crime, only that key point actually provides specific motive for security-force involvement in the Dublin and Monaghan bombings. It is a key element and to omit it would make the foregoing entirely irrelevant in any journalistic investigation. For example, in Don Mullan's investigation into the Dublin and Monaghan bombings, not only does he establish many of the points which Barron lists above, but he also examines in detail the ability of the bombers to do what they did, and to do it alone.

In his examination of the allegations of security-force collusion, Barron examines the long-standing belief in the British army's use of 'friendly forces' in Northern Ireland. In order to combat the Provisional IRA, the British army adhered to the principle that 'my enemy's enemy is my friend'. It was a technique that was brought to Northern Ireland by Brigadier General Frank Kitson.

Brigadier General Frank Kitson took control of 39 Infantry Brigade of the British army in April 1970. This would, in essence, give him complete control of the British army in Belfast. He would be gone by April 1972, but his impact on the conflict was incalculable.

Kitson had been at Oxford for a year and, by the time he was posted to Northern Ireland, was the author of two books on counter-insurgency.

The second, *Gangs and Counter-Gangs*, was based on his experiences of fighting the Mau Mau in Kenya. In the book, Kitson, who was an intelligence officer during the war in Kenya, tells how he devised a method of setting up counter-gangs and having them commit atrocities which would then be blamed on the enemy. In this case, the enemy was the Mau Mau.

While Martin Dillon, author of *The Dirty War*, suggests that Kitson was not the figure who would later be mythologised and demonised by republican paramilitaries, he accepts that Kitson was responsible for putting in place the structures which would facilitate the Dirty War. In his book, Dillon describes in detail the case of the Four-Square Laundry. This was a delivery-laundry service which operated in West Belfast towards the end of 1972. It was run by two people, a young man and a young woman. Both had Belfast accents and looked enough alike for the housewives of the estates in which the Four-Square Laundry service operated to assume that they were brother and sister. They had Belfast accents and were cheaper and more efficient than the other services which were available, and they were quite successful, earning themselves a niche in the market.

One morning, the van arrived, as usual, in Juniper Park in the Twinbrook housing estate. As was usually the case, the man stayed in the van while the woman got out to collect the laundry from the houses, and put it in the back of the van. The woman chatted with a housewife at one of the houses for a while. As the two women talked, gunfire erupted all around them. The woman from the laundry service pushed the housewife back into the house and followed her. She told her that it was probably a loyalist hit-squad. Meanwhile, a local man had driven the van to hospital to save the life of the young driver who was slumped over the wheel. The van was riddled with bullets — in the roof, in the side and in the front where the young man sat at the steering wheel. The young man died in hospital and the van was transferred to the local RUC station as evidence of a suspected paramilitary attack.

The IRA later claimed to have shot five British spies that morning. The British army claimed that only one had been shot. The IRA released a statement saying:

The Republican movement has been aware for a number of months of a Special British Army Intelligence Unit, code-named MRF. This Unit, comprising picked men, has been operating in the guise of civilians. The Unit was run by a Captain McGregor who used flats and offices in Belfast and ran a laundry service.

The IRA claim was that the Four-Square Laundry service was, in fact, one part of an elaborate British army spy network which they had discovered and attempted to eradicate. In fact, the Military Reconnaissance Force (MRF) had been established in 1971, when Frank Kitson was stationed in Northern Ireland, and attached to Kitson's 39 Infantry Brigade. Although Kitson was gone, his fingerprints were all over the operation. Four-Square Laundry had collected clothes from the houses of those known to be linked to republican paramilitaries, and had had the clothes forensically tested before washing them and returning them, all at a competitive price. In the roof of the van were hidden two other soldiers, who used special surveillance equipment to take pictures and communicate with the MRF base. The IRA had discovered only the tip of the iceberg, however. The organisation itself had been quite effectively infiltrated by the British army in Northern Ireland, using the techniques of Brigadier General Frank Kitson.

Along with the surveillance afforded by the Four-Square Laundry, the British army had also managed to 'turn' a few IRA volunteers, forcing them to report back on IRA operations and potential IRA operations. It was through these 'turned' men that the IRA first discovered the extent to which the British army had infiltrated its operations.

The key to unlocking the whole affair was a young republican named Seamus Wright. Wright, like many republicans, had been arrested and taken in for questioning. When he was released, he returned to his IRA company, Company D, and gave an account of his interrogation. He told of how he had been asked about guns and weapons and about the republican leaders in his area. It all seemed fairly standard. But his Information Officer (IO) decided to keep a closer eye on him. Wright went to England for a while, ostensibly in order to find work. The IO kept a watchful eye on the matter and noted that Wright's wife followed him there, only to return after a short while. Wright soon returned himself and resumed his old life.

The IO noticed that things were going wrong for D Company. Volunteers were being called in for questioning more regularly, and the army was finding it increasingly easier to pick up stashed weapons. Seamus Wright was the obvious leak. He was taken in by D Company and he confessed his story almost immediately. He explained that, after his arrest, he had been held in Castlereagh RUC station and had been told that he would be charged with a murder which had occurred in his area and to which he could be linked. He had named every man in D Company and had continued to give his interrogators information at regular intervals. Wright told them all about the degree to which the army had infiltrated the republican movement. In England, a compound had been set up, in which 'turned' men were housed and trained and sent back to republican areas to spy on known republican paramilitaries.

Operating without referring to their superiors, the IO and Officer Commanding (OC) of D Company decided to turn Wright and use him, instead of having him shot and his body dumped. It was reasoned that he would be much more valuable as a source of information and a channel through which misinformation could be passed. Wright's superiors made it clear to him, however, that they could kill him at any moment.

D Company began its plans by planting ammunition in houses or dumps for Wright to tell the army about. Every time he returned, he would give his superiors more information about the compound in Holywood Palace Barracks. D Company soon knew the make-up of the Military Reconnaissance Force. It was composed of a number of elements: there was a group of regular soldiers divided into four-man units comprising a junior officer, a sergeant and two privates; another group was the turned men, known as 'Freds', from both loyalist and republican backgrounds.

Within weeks, Wright told D Company that something big was about to happen and that he had heard only coded reference to it. He also gave the information that another republican Fred had been working with the MRF and that he had a much higher status that Wright did within the walls of the compound. The man, Kevin McKee, came from a very well-known republican family and was very well connected within the movement. It came as a shock to the IO and the OC of D Company. They brought McKee in for questioning and collected even more information on the whole operation.

At that point, they realised that they would have to refer upwards. They spoke to the Belfast Brigade Staff and it was decided that, until further information could be found, the two Freds would be held. The compound at Holywood Palace Barracks was put under observation, and the Four-Square Laundry was watched. Also watched was a brothel in which a local woman performed sexual services for local men who were encouraged to divulge information about republican activities.

The IRA moved against the MRF and claimed it as a massive victory. In fact, it had not been. The soldiers in the roof of the Four-Square van had not been shot, only the driver. In the brothel, because of an accident with the safety catch on a weapon, a man in the waiting-room had been shot, and the operation had been abandoned. Nevertheless, the IRA had blown the cover on the MRF's operations. McKee and Wright were shot and secretly buried.

The Four-Square laundry was simply a method for keeping surveillance on suspected republican militants. It was not a project through which loyalist paramilitaries could be helped in their fight against the IRA. However, it does illustrate clearly the extent to which the British intelligence services could infiltrate organisations on either side of the divide.

At present, the extent of links between loyalist paramilitaries and British security forces is unknown. While the operations of the Four-Square Laundry service and the spy-ring that operated underneath its surface were discovered, the rest of the allegations were more difficult to prove. On the surface, the perfectly legitimate military actions of the British army in using the front of the Four-Square Laundry to spy on republican paramilitaries seems to be the extent of Kitson's impact in Northern Ireland. However, many more allegations have been made, although none have been proven. Those allegations deal with the suggestion that the British security and intelligence services may have been operating a 'friendly forces' policy in Northern Ireland. As Mr Justice Barron points out, this was a policy advocated by Brigadier General Frank Kitson. It was a policy he had implemented elsewhere with the full approval of his superiors in the British army.

There have been several high-profile incidents involving members of the RUC, British army or British intelligence services acting outside their remit and illegally to assist loyalist paramilitaries. Whether or not such actions were sanctioned — officially or unofficially — by the superiors of the perpetrators, Barron quotes two separate sources in his report which back up the fact that they occurred. He quotes from former Army Chief of General Staff Michael Carver's autobiography in which he refers to 'the suspicion, more than once proved, that some of its [the RUC] members had close links with Protestant extremists'. In 2002, in a letter to the inquiry, Secretary of State for Northern Ireland, John Reid, told Mr Justice Barron that in the early 1970s some RUC and UDR officers had already been convicted of collusion with loyalist paramilitaries. Although all of this was known and convictions had been secured, it does not preclude the possibility of the same happening again or of the links remaining intact between the paramilitaries and those tasked with maintaining law and order.

UVF ADMISSION OF GUILT
The UVF did not actually accept responsibility for the Dublin bombings for almost twenty years, and only then when it had been claimed that the organisation could not have carried them out without the aid of certain elements of the British security forces. The UVF statement read:

Following the sinister allegations of collusion mischievously constructed by presenters of the recent *First Tuesday* programme which supposedly investigated the 1974 Dublin and Monaghan bombings, the UVF avails itself of this opportunity to state clearly and without reservation that the entire operation was from its conception to its successful conclusion, planned and carried out by our volunteers aided by no outside bodies.

In contrast to the scenario painted by the programme, it would have been unnecessary and indeed undesirable to compromise our volunteers anonimity [sic] by using clandestine Security Force personnel, British or otherwise, to achieve [an] objective well within our capabilities.

The operation whilst requiring a fair degree of preparation and not a little courage did not as was suggested by the so called experts require a great deal of technical expertise.

The comments made by some of those interviewed were at best naïve if not deliberately misleading.

Given the back-drop of what was taking place in Northern Ireland when the UVF were bombing republican targets at will, either the researchers decided to take poetic licence to the limit or the truth was being twisted by knaves to make [a] trap for the fools.

The minimum of scrutiny should have revealed that the structure of the bombs placed in Dublin and Monaghan were [sic] similar if not identical to those being placed in Northern Ireland on an almost daily basis.

The type of explosives, timing and detonation methods all bore the hallmark of the UVF.

It is incredulous [sic] that these points were lost on the Walter Mittys who conjured up this programme.

To suggest the UVF were not, or are not, capable of operation in the manner outlined in the programme is tempting fate to a dangerous degree.

This does not prove that the UVF was involved, however. During the course of the Troubles, certain incidents were, from time to time, claimed by organisations that hadn't carried them out, or denied by organisations that had. This statement does not necessarily refer to the true course of events. Nor does it prove that, if UVF members did carry out the bombings, they did so without help. In his book on the bombings in Dublin between 1972 and 1974, *In Dubious Battle*, John Bowyer Bell points out that armies, whether British or Irish, have a tendency to overestimate the skill levels required to carry out an attack like this. In many cases, common sense and everyday intelligence will do. In proving that this is the case, he refers to the IRA as an example of a paramilitary organisation that, without military aid and through practice, managed to achieve a high level of sophistication in its bombing.

Barron concludes that loyalist paramilitaries were capable of carrying out the bombings on 17 May 1974. This, of course, does not rule out the possibility that they had assistance in carrying out the bombings. That they did not have the capacity to do it alone was just one piece of evidence in a large argument about whether or not they did do it. It has also been argued in the past that the bombings seem to have been military in nature. Barron does not fully comply with this, and agrees with Bowyer Bell that there is a tendency in military circles to overestimate the difficulty in carrying out certain operations.

There is, however, much more compelling evidence that the UVF had assistance with the Dublin and Monaghan bombings.

### Wallace, Weir and Holroyd

During his inquiry, Mr Justice Barron interviewed Fred Holroyd, John Weir and Colin Wallace. These three men had been key elements of the British security set-up in Northern Ireland in the 1970s, and all of them would have had access to confidential documents from the time. It is significant that in his appraisal of the information they provided, Barron finds no grounds to dismiss any of the key allegations these men made.

All three men made suggestions of improper relations between the British security forces in Northern Ireland and loyalist paramilitaries, and said that these links might in some way have facilitated the Dublin and Monaghan bombings.

### JOHN WEIR

John Weir, a native of Co. Monaghan, joined the RUC in 1970. Having spent three years as a beat constable in East Belfast, he was transferred to a Special Patrol Group (SPG) which dealt with an area described by Mr Justice Barron as 'roughly covered by County Armagh'. The purpose of SPGs was to deal with subversive crime. They were made up of uniformed policemen.

According to Weir, however, his unit was very active during the Sunningdale process in actually fomenting further unrest and sectarian violence. In his allegations, he suggests that they would tour the barricades, encouraging the strikers and attempting to sabotage any attempts to quell the protest.

Through a number of transfers and a promotion, Weir stayed with the SPG, and his final posting was in 1978 in Magherafelt, Co. Derry. In that year, an RUC sergeant named William McCaughey was arrested in connection with a kidnapping in the area. While under questioning,

McCaughey confessed to the murder of a man by the name of William Strathearn. In his confession, he also implicated Weir and two other men, Robin Jackson and R. J. Kerr. Weir was charged with the murder and convicted; Jackson and Kerr were not. Weir was sent to prison in 1980, and remained there until 1990.

During his time in prison, John Weir began to make the allegations which would be dealt with by Mr Justice Barron in his report. These allegations had been sent by Weir to a number of journalists while he was in prison.

Weir alleged that a group of men within the RUC had come to the conclusion that in order to defeat the IRA, they had to target the Catholic population of Northern Ireland. Weir joined the group and claims that senior members of the RUC, although they were not involved and had not sanctioned the actions officially, were aware of what was going on, and, by not stopping those actions, were unofficially sanctioning them. A farm in Glennane, owned by a man called James Mitchell, was being used by this group to plan their attacks and store explosives, weapons and ammunition.

According to Weir, the group, which used cover names such as the Protestant Action Force, the Red Hand Commandos or the Red Hand Brigade, was responsible for the Dublin and Monaghan bombings, as well as a number of other high-profile sectarian attacks on both sides of the border. The attacks were never claimed by the UVF or UDA.

In the case of the Dublin and Monaghan bombings, Weir claimed that Billy Hanna had been the main organiser. He also implicated Robin Jackson, David Payne, Stewart Young, and John and Wesley Sommerville. A suggestion that two other men — Ivor Dean Knox Young and Joe Bennett — had prepared the bombs was initially discounted by the inquiry on the basis that both were in prison at the time. However, later evidence showed that an earlier attempt to carry out the bombings had been thwarted, and that it was quite possible that a bomb made by Bennett could indeed have been used.

Weir backed up his claims that the RUC was aware of the Glennane group's actions. He claimed that on one occasion he and another RUC officer had been driving with Robin Jackson, a very well-known UVF member at the time, when they were stopped at a roadblock and just waved through. On another occasion, he was offered weapons by a colleague in the RUC who had received the weapons from a loyalist paramilitary group.

The RUC discounted Weir's evidence completely. According to the RUC, Weir was a convicted murder and therefore his credibility was in doubt. The RUC also raised questions about his evidence on the grounds of his failure to bring it up before — for example in 1978 when he had the chance to do so at his trial. Moreover, the RUC argued that Weir had made the allegations when Robin Jackson and Robert Kerr were dead and therefore unable to deny them; that he had a relationship with a journalist called Sean McPhelimy, and that there was 'animus between McPhelimy and the RUC'; and that he could have obtained information about the crimes he claimed to have committed from prisoners with whom he was incarcerated.

In the course of his investigations, Mr Justice Barron found that there was no basis for this suspicion relating to Weir's statements. There had been some irregularities in RUC files relating to Weir which were found by Mr Justice Barron during his investigations. According to him:

> Not only was the RUC report inaccurate in many of its attempts to adduce evidence contradicting Weir's allegations, but it also failed to draw sufficient attention to evidence uncovered by the RUC which supported Weir's stories.

He also rubbishes any suggestion that Weir's connection to Sean McPhelimy should be a reason for dismissing his claims. Weir, he says, 'never claimed to support those of McPhelimy's claims which fall outside the boundaries of his own allegations'.

The Garda Síochána had been more inclined to believe Weir, saying that he 'comes across as an intelligent and discerning man who is a very convincing witness. He is highly credible and has very comprehensive details about the crimes he purports to have knowledge of.'

Mr Justice Barron interviewed the following people who had been mentioned by John Weir: an unnamed UDR man who Weir claimed had prepared the explosives; Lily Shields, the housekeeper at James Mitchell's Glennane farm; James Mitchell; Lawrence McClure, an RUC officer Weir claimed was involved in carrying out attacks with the Glennane group; Gary Armstrong, an RUC officer who Weir claimed was also involved in the attacks. The inquiry also had the Garda Síochána ask the RUC to carry out interviews with two other men whose names were brought up in the course of the aforementioned interviews. The Garda Síochána, having read the text of the interviews, believed that nothing significant came out of them.

Barron notes that a number of discrepancies arise in many of the interviews mentioned above. For example, James Mitchell's interview with the RUC in 1978 and his interview with the RUC in 2000 gave vastly different accounts of the extent of his knowledge of when and where arms and ammunition were left on his land. The judge also notes that the RUC did not seem to think it necessary to follow this up. Moreover, Gary Armstrong's statement, in which he said that he considered what happened in the mid-1970s to be a 'closed-book', indicated that perhaps he had been involved in much more nefarious activities than he would like to admit.

In his assessment of the claims made by Weir, Barron is unequivocal. In spite of Weir's own less-than-spotless record (he is a convicted murderer; he was involved in illegal activities during his time as an RUC officer; he, in Barron's opinion, is prejudiced against the nationalist community), Barron says:

> ... the Inquiry believes that his evidence overall is credible ... [Weir] came across as someone with considerable knowledge of the events which were taking place in the areas where he was stationed ... the Inquiry agrees with the views of An Garda Síochána that Weir's allegations regarding the Dublin and Monaghan bombings must be treated with the utmost seriousness.

COLIN WALLACE

Having previously been a member of the territorial army, in 1966, Colin Wallace joined the Ulster Special Constabulary, known as the B-Specials. Both of those positions were on a part-time basis. In 1968, he was asked by the army to apply for a job as deputy public relations officer. He became a civil servant with a rank equivalent to that of a major in the army.

Wallace's role was to change dramatically with the outbreak of the

Troubles. For two years, 1973–75, he was a senior information officer in the Army Information Services Department. While working in Northern Ireland in this capacity, he was also working for what Barron describes as 'a covert psychological operations (psy-ops) unit embedded within the Information Services Department'. This was known as the Information Policy Unit, and its purpose was the dissemination of propaganda, and misinformation, and the use of news manipulation by the security forces.

Wallace claims to have been unjustly dismissed from the army and then framed for manslaughter (he served five years between 1981 and 1986). As soon as he was released from prison, Wallace began to publicise his allegations regarding the work he had done in Northern Ireland. On radio, television and in the press, he claimed that there were attempts made by elements within the intelligence services to destabilise the political process in Northern Ireland, and that members of the security forces were collaborating with loyalist paramilitaries to this end.

According to Wallace, a project entitled 'Clockwork Orange', which had initially been intended as a disinformation campaign aimed at the IRA and later loyalist paramilitaries, began also to target left-wing organisations and people who had nothing to do with the violence in Northern Ireland. According to Wallace, he refused to work on 'Clockwork Orange' when this started to happen.

In 1973, a prominent loyalist extremist was implicated in sexual abuse taking place in Kincora Boys' Home. Wallace had been informed of this by a social worker, and passed the information on to his superiors. When nothing was done about it, he began to suspect that the information was being used to blackmail the loyalist extremist in question. In a memo to his superiors, Wallace made known his feelings of disgust at the lack of action in relation to the continuing abuse.

In late 1974, he was told that he was going to be transferred because his life was in danger. He was offered the choice of two posts, of the same rank, in England. Wallace believed that his life was not in danger, and that he was being moved because of his dissension. Before his transfer, he was in contact with journalist Robert Fisk, who was writing an article on so-called black propaganda. Wallace agreed to show him a report he was writing which denied the existence of such propaganda. He delivered it to Fisk's house but it was intercepted by the army, and Wallace was suspended from duty and later dismissed. On appeal, he was given the option of resigning.

In 1976, Colin Wallace was convicted of the manslaughter of the husband of a former work colleague with whom he was having an affair. He received ten years and was released after five.

Later, the circumstances of Wallace's dismissal from the civil service were reviewed, and his treatment was judged to have been harsh. Then, Wallace's conviction was quashed after a review of the forensic evidence on which he had been convicted was found to have serious flaws. Chief among these flaws was the claim that the deceased man had died from 'a karate-type' blow to the nose, in spite of the fact that the man's nose was not seriously damaged.

Wallace's claims centre around the intelligence network in Northern Ireland, and he points out that there were rivalries between MI5 and MI6. Barron reports that Wallace claimed:

> Whereas MI6 was inclined towards a political, peaceful solution to the Troubles, MI5 saw itself as defending the realm from subversion, and preferred military over political means. Between 1973 and 1975, the militant approach won out, as MI5 gradually gained overall control of intelligence operations in the North.

Wallace claims that the MI5 had forged close links with RUC Special Branch. MI5, according to Wallace's evidence, was dominated by right-wing officers, who were opposed to the Labour government's attempts to bring about a power-sharing assembly in Northern Ireland and wanted to crush the Sunningdale Agreement. He claimed that, to this end, MI5 assisted and encouraged the Ulster Workers' Council Strike in 1974.

Wallace claimed that the system operated as follows:

> We usually had desk officers, who were people who were handling particular groups of the IRA or the loyalist paramilitaries, and so, every operation we did had to be cleared in case it compromised something else ... [if Wallace had got news of something regarding some paramilitary group in particular] I've got a story that can really cause friction within this group. I would write it up as a project and

then I would put it into the main Intelligence system to make sure that it was cleared, that it wasn't impacting on another operation and so on, because on a need-to-know basis, I wouldn't know what you're doing or what you're doing. And then eventually, someone will come and see you from the system and maybe just say, 'Thanks for the note. Go ahead ...' but what often usually happened was, that person might come back and say, 'We'd just rather you didn't touch that.'

According to Wallace, this is exactly what was happening in relation to key members of the mid-Ulster UVF during 1973–74. In that period, Wallace had made an attempt to target some members of that grouping and was told that these people were on the 'excluded' list. The people he couldn't touch were Harris Boyle, Robert Kerry, Billy Hanna, Robin Jackson, Billy Mitchell, Stewart Young and Robert McConnell. All of these men were alleged to have been involved in the Dublin and Monaghan bombings.

Mr Justice Barron quotes a letter Wallace wrote to a colleague more than a year after the bombings (14 August 1974):

> ... there is good evidence that the Dublin bombings in May last year were a reprisal for the Irish Government's role in bringing about the Executive. According to one of Craig's [Craig Smellie, the senior MI6 officer in Northern Ireland] people, some of those involved, the Youngs, the Jacksons, Mulholland, Hanna, Kerr and McConnell were working closely with SB [Special Branch] and Int. [Intelligence] at that time.

Mr Justice Barron warns, however, that nowhere in the letter does Wallace actually suggest what that 'good evidence' might be.

Wallace also claimed that because of the level of infiltration of loyalist paramilitaries in the mid-1970s, there was no way the security forces could not have known about the plans to carry out the Dublin and Monaghan bombings.

While Mr Justice Barron interviewed Wallace on a number of occasions and received written submissions from him, and in spite of the detail into which he goes in his examination of Wallace's claims, he concludes that 'the covert nature of Wallace's work, and his experience in manipulating truth and untruth to serve particular ends make it especially difficult to assess the worth of his allegations'. It must be assumed, therefore, that anything Barron puts forward without explicitly contradicting by reference to his own findings is, as with the allegations of John Weir, 'credible … and must be treated with the utmost seriousness'.

FRED HOLROYD

Fred Holroyd is a former military intelligence officer in Northern Ireland. He was stationed there in January 1974, but spent only a year there before being removed from his position at the end of May 1975, on medical grounds.

Since his retirement from the army the year after his removal from his position, Holroyd has made serious allegations regarding the British army. He has claimed that the army was engaged in kidnapping, assisting loyalist paramilitaries, and recruiting agents from security forces in this state. He has further claimed that the army was culpable of acts of gross incompetence which resulted in the loss of life.

Holroyd claimed that, during his time in Northern Ireland, he collected key information regarding the perpetrators of the Dublin and Monaghan bombings, and information which showed that the bombings were part of a pattern of collusion between the security forces in Northern Ireland and loyalist paramilitaries.

During Holroyd's time in Northern Ireland, a series of family tragedies had put a serious strain on his marriage. His superiors were aware of this. In May 1975, he went to Garda HQ in Dublin with an RUC officer to view the results of a recent arms find. His superiors were furious, as the visit was in direct contravention of an instruction that no officer from the unit should operate outside Northern Ireland. Then, days later, he had a row with his wife, and she went, while he was sleeping, to one of his superiors, and allegedly complained that he had a weapon in the house and had threatened to shoot her and his children. She denies making those claims.

Holroyd was asked to go and see a psychiatrist at the Royal Victoria Hospital in Netley, Southampton. He initially refused, stating that the stigma of such a visit would damage his career. He eventually went and he was assessed and found to be without psychiatric problems. He was not allowed return to Northern Ireland, however, and soon afterwards, he and his wife were divorced. Less than a year later, he had resigned from the army. He went to serve with the Rhodesian army, where he attained the rank of major, and served for three years.

It was on his initial return to the UK that Holroyd had begun to pursue complaints about the manner of his treatment in the British army. First, he had complained to his superior officers, then to the police. He had then left for Rhodesia and returned to continue his campaign. In 1984, he began to make his complaints to the media. It was then that his statements began to widen from a complaint about his treatment at the hands of the army to allegations of wrongdoing in Northern Ireland.

In his report, Barron treats the allegations of Fred Holroyd with extreme care. He notes that some of Holroyd's claims have changed over time, and he believes it is significant that he did not decide to make any of these claims until after he left the army. In his observations on Holroyd, however, Barron makes clear that the fact that his allegations have multiplied over time does not necessarily mean that they are untrue. He also points out that many of the people who claim that Holroyd is lying have themselves given misleading statements or statements that have been found to have been inaccurate in some way.

Barron also points out — almost as a corollary to the theory that all of Holroyd's claims are borne out of his sense of grievance with the British army — that the eagerness of both the Garda Síochána and the RUC to discredit him are a result of the capacity of his allegations to embarrass them. This does not, however, mean that Holroyd's testimony is to be completely believed. There are some glaring inaccuracies. For example, his allegations about Garda/RUC collusion are hamstrung by his inability to remember what the gardaí he dealt with actually looked like — some of them were quite distinctive in appearance; for example, one was unusually tall with a full beard and moustache.

Holroyd's allegations regarding the bombings are quite vague. Barron believes this to be because he was not part of the loop in which intelligence information regarding the bombings was circulated. It is his claims regarding the extent to which elements within the British security forces operated in the Republic of Ireland that Mr Justice Barron believes are most significant.

Holroyd alleged that he had an extensive contact network within the Garda Síochána and that, at meetings with gardaí, information was exchanged between the forces. Mr Justice Barron also accepts as true that 'there was at least one Garda Officer supplying information to the security forces in Northern Ireland over and above what was officially expected from RUC/Garda co-operation'. Mr Justice Barron concludes that the evidence points to this as being a 'relationship of mutual exchange of information, rather than one of Garda "agent" and British Army "handler".'

Journalist Don Mullan, in his book on the Dublin and Monaghan bombings, also deals with the claims of Fred Holroyd. Having studied Holroyd's police notebooks in detail (the same source from which Mr Justice Barron derived some of his information), Mullan comes to slightly stronger conclusions. Included in Mullan's book is a transcript of a section of an interview with Holroyd that he and one of the solicitors from Justice for the Forgotten conducted. In it, Holroyd tells the two men about other encounters between the Garda Síochána and the RUC and British army, which are not dealt with at all by Mr Justice Barron. Holroyd describes 'porno parties' in which gardaí were brought in minibuses to the army camps and plied with drink by their Northern counterparts, who then showed them pornographic films, which were illegal in the Republic at the time. Holroyd skirts around the issue of whether or not these parties were for the purposes of gathering information — he claims that they were simply a 'smoothing of the waters' and that 'if anyone was ever caught over the other side, these guys would be more amenable'.

It is somewhat embarrassing to think that RUC officers thought so little of the gardaí that they felt they could be bought so easily — pornographic films and free alcohol on a trip to Northern Ireland, like a group of naughty schoolboys — but, according to Holroyd, this was the case. To what extent the links between the two forces were actually exploited remains, in Mr Justice Barron's opinion, unproven.

### The Dirty War and the Clonagh Allegations

Mr Justice Barron's report has been variously criticised and praised. It is a very important document in the history of the campaign for justice for the dead of the Dublin and Monaghan bombings. Of this there is no doubt, and Mr Justice Barron is thorough in his analysis of the information he presents. However, there are several glaring omissions from the report. Although he deals in detail with the nature of the explosives used by the UVF in the Dublin and Monaghan bombings, Barron is somewhat sketchy when it comes to actually discussing the provenance of the bombs. This is strange because allegations had already been made regarding the origins of the bomb-making material, and it might have been expected that these would have made the issue a key one in the judge's inquiries into alleged security-force assistance in the Dublin and Monaghan bombings.

In February 2003, an article by journalist Don Mullan was published in the now-defunct *Magill* magazine. In one of the last genuinely investigative articles in that magazine, Mullan put forward a theory regarding the origins of the explosive materials that were used in the Dublin and Monaghan bombings. Mullan alleged that the materials in question came from inside the Irish state. The theory was chilling, yet it was ignored completely by Mr Justice Barron in his inquiry.

Mullan had been investigating the circumstances surrounding the 'retirement' from the Irish army of Lieutenant Dónal de Róiste. In the course of his investigations, he found that a good friend of de Róiste's, a Commandant Patrick Walshe, had been assigned to the Irish Industrial Explosives Factory at Clonagh in April 1974, which, because of the nature of the business being undertaken there, was under military guard.

According to Mullan, Walshe was shocked by the lack of security he found at the factory. He compiled thirty-two reports on the Clonagh plant, and handed them over to his superiors who, in turn, informed their political masters. Mullan quotes from the autobiography of former Taoiseach Garret FitzGerald, who in 1974 was Minister for Foreign Affairs. FitzGerald wrote of his fury when he heard that the 'British Army in Northern Ireland had known for 18 months that explosives being used by the IRA were being stolen from a particular explosives factory in our state but had not told us because apparently they preferred to use this leakage as a propaganda weapon against us than to save lives in Northern Ireland by stopping it.' In an interview with FitzGerald, Mullan confirmed that the factory in question was the Irish Industrial Explosives Factory at Clonagh.

When informed that the Taoiseach of the day, Liam Cosgrave, had known about the situation at Clonagh since 9 September 1974, but apparently had done nothing about it, FitzGerald replied that the fact that there were security problems at an explosives factory in Ireland did not necessarily mean that the explosives were being given to subversives in the state. He puts forward the suggestion that the lack of action on the part of a government who normally had a rather more hardline stance on republican paramilitaries was proof that Liam Cosgrave did not believe or had not been informed that the security difficulties would manifest themselves in such a way.

Colonel James K. Cogan, in an affidavit relating to the precise nature of the problems with security at the Clonagh factory, claims that, in October 1974, he told a cabinet minister the following:

> ... the very extensive factory premises were unfenced in any meaningful sense; fully prepared explosives and raw materials were being left in the open within sight and easy reach of the public road; there was an almost incredible laxity in storage and accountancy, the manner of which would defy accurate tally; there was little or no supervision of the comings and goings of employees; there was a military guard on the factory. Its duties were confined to protection of the premises against external aggression; it had no powers in relation to the internal workings; the installation was such a maze of stories, offices, mixing bays and blast walls that it would be easy for an employee to dump a quantity of explosive outside the immediate perimeter without detection.

Mullan suggests that the explosives which were being left outside the factory for republican paramilitaries were used in the Dublin and Monaghan bombings. It is possible that, at some stage prior to the bombings, material intended for use by the IRA could have been seized by British security forces and passed on to loyalist paramilitary groups. Indeed, allegations made by John Weir suggest that this sort of activity was taking place and that certain elements within the RUC were assisting loyalist paramilitaries to construct bombs. The journalist had previously quoted David Ervine of the PUP and former member of the UVF who said that the Dublin and Monaghan bombings were a case of returning the serve. He, of course, meant it metaphorically, but according to Mullan, it was in fact more literal than anyone could have guessed. The explosives were being sent straight back to wreak havoc on the citizens of the state that had made them and allowed them be used across the border in the first place.

Mullan refers to an interview he conducted with Dr James Donovan of the Irish State Laboratory who was given only a small amount of forensic material to examine in the aftermath of the bombings, while the rest was driven to Northern Ireland to be examined. No reason for this was ever given, and it seems bizarre considering that the laboratory in Dublin was perfectly adequate for the purpose. What is even more strange is that experienced ballistics officers kept the forensic material for over a week before they handed it over to any lab. It is widely known that any chemical residues last for only six to eight hours before they disappear. Dr Donovan could only draw vague conclusions, as the material he received was days old. Even then, he had filed all of his reports before Dr R. A. Hall in Belfast even got to see the material. No firm conclusions could be drawn from any of the debris given to either scientist. However, Dr Donovan did tell Mullan the following:

> I feel that the ovide prills of ammonium nitrate, blackened though they were, must have had some significance or else somebody would have come and talked to me. But when my own authorities did not do so, I find that strange.

Ovide Prills of ammonium nitrate were made in the factory in Clonagh.

Garret FitzGerald accepted, in his interview with Don Mullan, that it was possible that the material used to bomb Dublin had come from the Clonagh factory. Mullan also told him that Commandant Walshe, who had amassed so much evidence about the security problems at the factory, was speaking to Mr Justice Barron. Yet no mention of any of Walshe's findings, whether to confirm or debunk the theory, is made in the final report.

While Mullan provides no solid proof that the material used in the bombings was in fact taken from Clonagh, there is plenty of evidence to suggest that it is, as FitzGerald put it, 'a thesis to be explored'. Yet Mr Justice Barron never did explore it. It is one of many weaknesses within the report. Mr Justice Barron went out of his way to explore many other, rather more outlandish theses, yet this one was ignored.

*Conclusion*

Regarding the Garda investigation, Barron concludes thus:

> ... the following conclusions may be drawn.
>
> 1. The Garda investigation failed to make full use of the information it obtained. Certain lines of inquiry that could have been pursued further in this jurisdiction were not pursued. There were other matters, including the questioning of suspects, in which the assistance of the RUC should have been requested, but was not.
>
> 2. The State was not equipped to conduct an adequate forensic analysis of the explosions. This was because the importance of preservation, prompt collection and analysis was not appreciated. The effect of this was that potentially vital clues were lost. For instance, if it could have been definitively established that the Dublin bombs were made purely from commercial explosives, that would have not been typical of a loyalist paramilitary bomb.
>
> 3. Even if further evidence had become available, the ability to mount a successful prosecution would have been hampered. No proper chain of evidence exists either in respect of the forensic samples or in respect of the photographs. This is because records have been lost. It cannot be known at what point the chain was broken, but that in itself is indicative of a carelessness which reflected a belief that no one was ever likely to be brought to account for the bombings. This loss is all the more disappointing when one considers some of the other, much less important material, which still exists.
>
> 4. There is evidence now which shows that the informal exchange of information between Gardaí on the border and their RUC counterparts was extensive. There is some evidence to suggest that some Garda officers, unwittingly or otherwise, may have been giving information to members of the British Army or Intelligence Services. The Inquiry has found no evidence to support the proposition that such exchanges in some way facilitated the passage of the Dublin and Monaghan bombers across the border. Similarly, no basis has been found for concluding that the Garda investigation was in any way inhibited because of a fear of exposing such links.

5. Although the investigation teams had in their opinion no evidence upon which to found a prosecution, there is no evidence that they sought the advice of the Attorney General, in whose name criminal prosecutions were at that time still being brought. Had the Attorney General reviewed the file, it is likely that advice would have been given as to what further direction the investigation might take.

6. The Inquiry has examined allegations that the Garda investigation was wound down as a result of political interference. No evidence was found to support that proposition.

7. However, the Government of the day failed to show the concern expected of it. The fact that this report is looking at the issue with the knowledge of 2003, rather than that of 1974, affords some explanation for this failure.

The government of the day showed little interest in the bombings. When information was given to that government, suggesting that the British authorities had intelligence naming the bombers, this was not followed up. Any follow-up was limited to complaints by the Minister for Foreign Affairs that those involved had been released from internment.

In the preface to his report, Mr Justice Barron says the following:

On 25 November, 1999, the Oireachtas Joint Committee on Justice, Equality and Women's Rights met a delegation from Justice for the Forgotten. Following that meeting the Government decided to set up a private inquiry along the lines of that suggested by the Victims' Commission. The report of that inquiry would then be referred to the Joint Committee, who would advise the Oireachtas as to what further action, if any, should be taken.

The Hon. Liam Hamilton, then Chief Justice of Ireland, was asked to undertake the task of conducting the inquiry. He agreed to do so following his retirement as Chief Justice on 31 January 2000. Sadly, due to ill-health, Mr Hamilton was forced to resign on 2 October 2000. The Government appointed former Supreme Court Judge, the Hon. Henry Barron, in his place.

The most notable thing about this statement is the manner in which Mr Justice Barron refers to his Commission of Inquiry. He says, ' ... the Government decided to set up a private inquiry along the lines of that suggested by the Victims' Commission ...' Barron was clearly under the impression, when he took over the inquiry from Mr Justice Liam Hamilton, that he was being tasked with carrying out a private inquiry.

Where he got this impression is not clear. However, what is certain is that when the idea of a private inquiry was proposed to the families in 1999, they had rejected it entirely, eventually managing to secure not a private inquiry, but a slightly altered version of the Victims' Commission recommendation. Instead of a private inquiry, Liam Hamilton was to review the information to hand and report back to the government on the need for a public inquiry. The process was to take six to nine months only. If Mr Justice Barron was under the impression that this was a private inquiry into the bombings, then it perhaps explains why the whole thing took so long to complete.

The length of time the whole process took had raised the expectations of the families to inordinate levels. There was bound to be disappointment. And, when Mr Justice Barron's report was finally presented to them, there was. However Mr Justice Barron had come to the conclusion that he was working on a private inquiry — whether he was improperly briefed on his remit when he took over from the late Chief Justice Hamilton or whether he simply decided to broaden his remit of his own accord — the government seems to have got its way in the end.

Many of the families were disheartened by the lack of new information presented. Of the information presented, nothing new was uncovered, and it had all been made public years before through investigative works such as Don Mullan's *The Dublin and Monaghan Bombings* and Yorkshire Television's 'Hidden Hand' documentary. Indeed, such was the level of evidence being sought by the judge that much of what had already been presented through journalistic investigation was effectively discounted by Barron because it could not, in the end, be proven.

Other difficulties with the report and the inquiry were less obvious. The inquiry did not have the power to compel anyone in this state or from Britain to give evidence in front of it. The only assistance the judge got from the British authorities was a letter from the Secretary of State for

Northern Ireland, Dr John Reid. Without key information from British files and former British intelligence officers, politicians and civil servants, the inquiry was missing many key pieces of evidence which might have proven many of the assertions he mentions in his files.

Also significant was the issue of the files relating to the Garda investigation that took place in 1974. There are sinister undertones relating to the manner in which these files 'vanished' some time after the journalists from Yorkshire Television had gained limited access to them to make their documentary in 1993. This issue is not broached in any meaningful manner by Mr Justice Barron, who says:

> Firstly, some relevant security files that should have been retained at Garda Headquarters were missing. The Inquiry was furnished with the Monaghan security file, but not with that for Dublin. In relation to loyalist paramilitary organisations, the general file started in 1966 contains no information proper to the early 1980s. While there are annual files relating to the UVF/UDA, none are available for the years 1974 and 1975. The Special Detective Unit kept files on these bodies, and those have been made available to the Inquiry. But the files kept by Security and Intelligence (C3) at Garda Headquarters would have included more than just the files kept by the Security and Intelligence (C3) division, of which SDU was merely a part. These have not been seen by the Inquiry. Secondly, annual files relating to payments were not available. Of particular interest to the Inquiry were payments made to confidential sources, but full information on this matter no longer exists.

He goes on to say:

> The Department of Justice, Equality and Law Reform has found that the files are missing from its archives. A copy of the investigation report into the Monaghan bombing is the only contemporary document relating to the Dublin and Monaghan bombings of May 17, 1974. It is not only the Dublin investigation report that is missing, but also what must have been a considerable amount of security information. Extensive files have been provided relating to matters

arising after the Hidden Hand programme in 1993. This emphasises the extent of the documentation no longer available.

*Phoenix* magazine of 19 December 2003 draws its own conclusions from this:

> Barron doesn't spell it out, but it's clear that this was not a loss of files. RIC intelligence files going back to Fenian times are extant — and there are C3 and Justice Department records relating to matters before and after the event. So the disappearance of this large quantity of documents is not attributable to poor administration. All the signs are that this was a cull of records at four different locations (Dublin Castle, Stephen's Green, C3 at Garda HQ and Dundalk Special Branch Offices) which ensured that there was no trail for Barron to follow.

Whether or not the assertions made by *Phoenix* are accurate, the missing files present a real problem for the government. There is no doubt that they provided a problem for Mr Justice Barron too. With so little assistance coming from the British authorities (in the end, the entire body of files contained in the Northern Ireland office was distilled to a ten-page letter with a six-page addendum, much of which Mr Justice Barron says contained information already given to him by other sources), it was vital that information regarding the investigation be given to him by the relevant departments in this state. This wasn't provided and, for this reason, Mr Justice Barron was forced to write his report based on very little evidence. In his conclusions to the report, Barron repeatedly writes that there is insufficient evidence to prove certain theses. Without doubt, his inability to draw definite conclusions stems directly from the lack of information he encountered during his inquiry. It is clear that, should a public inquiry be recommended in the future, it will have to be cross-jurisdictional in nature and be granted the power to compel witnesses to appear before it.

If the Report of the Independent Commission of Inquiry into the Dublin and Monaghan bombings under Mr Justice Henry Barron has proven anything, it is that from all the information and evidence available in this state, no clear conclusions can be drawn.

# AFTERMATH OF THE BARRON REPORT

*'She must have thought she was going to be in government forever.'*
Martha O'Neill on Nora Owen

On Thursday afternoon, 10 December 2003, Denise O'Neill just wanted to give up. Thirty years previously, her father had been killed.

Almost fifteen years previously, she and Angela had started to draw the families together in order to fight for justice for the murdered.

Seven years previously, they had finally got the government to listen and had gone in front of the Victims' Commission chaired by former Tánaiste John Wilson.

Two years later, he had given his verdict: a private inquiry.

And almost four years after that, they had moved on by only one tiny step.

Having the Barron Report state officially what it did state was significant, but it was far too late to be useful.

Denise O'Neill was frustrated. That night, at a press conference held to launch the Report, she and her family staged a walkout. They were followed by several other families. Outside, the O'Neills spoke to the media of their bitter disappointment with yet another pulled punch. Thirty years on, and they had moved only one square further in this game. The wheels of justice grind exceedingly slowly indeed.

⌘ ⌘ ⌘

It must be remembered that Hamilton's (later Barron's) Commission of Inquiry was supposed to be only a stepping stone — a means to an end. It was never either a public or a private tribunal of inquiry. Initially intended to last only six to nine months, it ran for more than three years. It was indicative, in one sense, of the size of the task facing anyone who wanted to tackle seriously the years of cover-up and conspiracy surrounding the Dublin and Monaghan bombings.

In another, more real, sense, it was a further sign of the continual procrastination of those with the power to establish a properly constituted inquiry into the bombings. In the past thirty years, there has been ample opportunity to investigate the bombings properly. However, right from the beginning, with the initial Garda investigation, every chance has been spurned.

The investigation lay dormant for many years after the official investigation was wound down, with only a small handful of people interested enough actually to look into it for themselves. With the dawn of the 1990s, a number of these people, as if by chance, came together to bring about the current campaign. Kevin Walsh had been lobbying for some sort of memorial to commemorate the terrible tragedy he had witnessed on that day in May; Denise and Angela O'Neill were bringing the families together to try to begin a campaign to see justice done for their loved ones; Joe Tiernan had been investigating the bombings and interviewing loyalist paramilitaries who claimed to have information on them; and in England, Yorkshire Television was beginning the first organised investigation into both the bombings and their aftermath.

The revelations in the 'Hidden Hand' documentary were shocking. It seemed that the government could not ignore them. But ignore them it did. Minister for Justice Nora Owen told the two groups of families that no new information had been produced, and that the investigation could not be reactivated. She told them that if they produced any new information themselves, they could pass it on to the Department of Justice and it would be considered. The families were furious.

However, they were undaunted and continued to fight the government. Three years later, when the Belfast (Good Friday) Agreement was signed and required that the government establish a victims' commission to deal with all the victims, bereaved and survivors of

Troubles-related violence, the families seized upon the opportunity.

John Wilson, the Victims' Commissioner, listened to their calls for a public inquiry but did not recommend that this be implemented. They fought against the idea of a private inquiry, earning a compromise process which would, they believed, start with a short review of the information to hand, before going on to deal with the issue of whether or not there was cause for a public inquiry. Instead of taking less than a year to complete its report, the Independent Commission of Inquiry took almost four.

The families had been more than hopeful about the contents of Mr Justice Barron's report. They were to be disappointed.

Initially, Denise O'Neill, like the rest of the O'Neill family, wasn't very happy with the conclusions. She felt that the report had provided nothing new and that the whole thing had been a waste of time for all the families who had been led to believe that the Barron Report would bring them some closure.

She didn't entirely blame Mr Justice Barron, who had inherited the Inquiry from the late Chief Justice Hamilton, but she was unequivocal in her assessment of the Report. When she went back to analyse it coldly, she conceded that it was an important step finally to have everything in the Report actually stated officially, and finally, for the first time in thirty years, to have the government acknowledge the information that Mr Justice Barron included.

However, Denise felt, it was a step that should have been taken years ago. None of the information, apart from the admission that important files had gone missing from the Department of Justice, was news to the O'Neills, and the whole process had taken far too long. She says:

> When we entered this process, we didn't think for a minute that it was going to take four years. We entered into it thinking it would be finished within a matter of a year. We were then led to believe that Barron was in receipt of very sensitive information and the whole time we were being boosted up and we were thinking that this was it and something was going to come of it and it turned out like this.

Mr Justice Barron's condemnation of the government was another important step, but again it came too late.

We'd already known that they had been uncaring and unwilling to investigate properly. We had hoped for more detail, more information. We had hoped the government would fully participate and that included the Department of Justice

In Denise's words, 'Barron was very thorough; he just didn't go far enough.'

Nevertheless, the O'Neills are now part of the process, and Denise realises that they have to follow it through, however frustrating it might be to have had four years wasted on a report that produced no new information. The next step is an Oireachtas Committee hearing, headed by Seán Ardagh. Denise has guarded hopes of this.

I feel that the Oireachtas Committee hearings have no alternative but to call for a full public inquiry. But I don't know whether they will or not.

She remembers a time, in 1999, when John Wilson seemed to have no option but to call for a public tribunal of inquiry. But he didn't. Instead he recommended a private inquiry. She remembers her hopes, only a few days before it was due to be published, that Justice Barron's report would finally contain the truth and pave the way for justice. But it didn't. She is prepared for disappointment when the Oireachtas Committee makes its recommendations.

Denise believes that, in the end, it is a lack of co-operation in key areas that is holding the process up:

We're here four years later and we're still as frustrated as we were then. And it's because of the blatant lack of co-operation by the Department of Justice, lack of co-operation by the British authorities. That's the frustrating part.

Angela too was disappointed by the content of the report:

We expected some kind of closure but there was no new information in that report and we're bitterly disappointed.

She was also annoyed that so many in the media jumped to the defence of the Fine Gael/Labour coalition of the day. She recalls reading an article in the *Sunday Independent* which credited that government with having averted a civil war.

Like Denise, Angela is less than hopeful about the future of the campaign:

> I don't think we'll ever get a public inquiry. I want the British held accountable for their actions, and the Irish held accountable for their inactions.

It is a hope that has already been delayed thirty years and may yet be another thirty years coming.

⌘   ⌘   ⌘

*'Whatever it is about the Dublin and Monaghan bombings, they seem to hate them.'*
Martha O'Neill on thirty years of having politicians ignore the
Dublin and Monaghan bombings

The surviving members of the 1974 Security Committee were very vocal regarding their opinions on the Barron Report. Conor Cruise O'Brien was on the Security Committee in 1974 and has been one of the strongest voices heard whenever there has been any criticism of the government of which he was a member at the time of the Dublin and Monaghan bombings. Following the Yorkshire Television 'Hidden Hand' documentary, he launched a vitriolic attack on the journalists who had made the programme. Saying that the programme had 'scraped up a few … inconsequential makeweights, like the stuff about the anonymous "Jackal"', he went on to say:

> The clear implication is that the Coalition Government of 1974 knew from the Gardaí who the perpetrators of those bombings were, but failed to take any action to bring them to justice, thereby acquiescing in the murder of some of those citizens whose protection is the first

duty of any Government. As a member of that Government, I was outraged by that monstrous and utterly unfounded innuendo.

His reaction to the Barron Report was somewhat less furious, but he was, nonetheless, dismissive of the findings that the government had not acted sufficiently quickly or strongly to bring to justice the perpetrators or those who had assisted them. He said:

By and large, everything that could have been done at the Garda level and at Government level was done to bring the bombers to justice.

While admitting that there had been 'slip-ups', Conor Cruise O'Brien went on to say that he believed 'that both police forces, the RUC and the Garda, hated the paramilitaries who were murdering them all the time. There were bad apples in both forces who were doing things for money with both loyalist and republican paramilitaries.'

That he could pass this off as glibly as he does is amazing. There were indeed 'bad apples' in both polices forces and if, as the former Minister for Posts and Telegraphs asserts, some of them were colluding with loyalist or republican paramilitaries for money, surely this is a cause for much more concern than he has given it.

Garret FitzGerald was not on the Security Committee but later became Taoiseach. He too claimed that Barron had got it wrong. He did, however, accept that subsequent governments had been neglectful — his own government included. Dr FitzGerald's comments were among the most reasonable. In an article in *The Irish Times* shortly after the publication of the Barron Report, he wrote:

The relatives of the victims have been rightly anxious to have the events surrounding those terrible events thoroughly examined.

They have seen no prosecutions for these atrocities. They have seen evidence of involvement with loyalist paramilitaries by some members of the Northern Ireland security forces, including elements of the British army and they have heard media allegations of tolerance of such activities at a higher level in Britain — allegations concerning which, it now transpires, there is no evidence.

The feelings of the bereaved in this appalling tragedy had been forgotten, and their suspicions that in some way it had been 'swept under the carpet', are readily comprehensible.

In saying this, Dr FitzGerald seems to be suggesting that the fears he has just mentioned are groundless. He accepts that they are understandable, but then he dismisses them almost entirely. He goes on to say:

> Given the eventual inability of the Garda Síochána to find evidence upon which to charge any of those responsible for this massacre, it would have been better to have launched much sooner an inquiry of the kind Mr Justice Barron has now undertaken. All who subsequently held political office, myself included, must bear some of the blame for the fact that this did not happen.
>
> This lapse of time may have contributed to the disappearance of some relevant documentation, the death of some who would have been key witnesses, and the fading recollections of other participants: all these have made it much more difficult to establish the facts about how this tragedy was dealt with at the time.

In the paragraph in which he accepts that he too was to blame for the continued neglect of the Dublin and Monaghan dead, he seems to suggest that he and his predecessors and followers must share only 'some of the blame' for not bringing about the type of inquiry Justice Barron undertook. If Dr FitzGerald and the rest of the Taoisigh and cabinet members from 1973 until the present day share only some of the blame, who shares the rest? Only the government could have established a commission of inquiry of any sort, so Dr FitzGerald, on behalf of his political colleagues, should really be accepting all of the blame.

By listing the seemingly many reasons why the inquiry would be made more difficult — that is, the death of key witnesses, the loss of files and the effect of time on memory — he is also suggesting that no public inquiry could have success. The conciliatory tone throughout this article belies a concerted attempt to undermine completely any attempt to bring about a public inquiry.

In the same article, Dr FitzGerald deals with Mr Justice Barron's allegations that the Irish government of the day was told by the British government that certain of the bombers had been interned. He claims that Mr Justice Barron was

> not familiar with the different roles of the two channels through which security matters are discussed between states. Individual cases are not normally dealt with through political/diplomatic channels, lest such contact prejudice subsequent prosecutions of extradition channels.
>
> Instead contacts relating to individual cases are carried on between the police forces of states and also, when security matters are involved, between their intelligence agencies which, at least after the Arms Crisis of 1970, keep the Garda Síochána fully informed of any information they obtain.
>
> The role of the political/diplomatic channel is to ensure that the processes are in place to deal with all possible security threats and situations. I understand that following the Dublin and Monaghan bombings a review of such matters took place, culminating in a meeting between the Minister for Justice and the Secretary of State for Northern Ireland at Baldonnel in September 1974.
>
> Because Justice Barron was apparently unaware of this distinction of roles, I can see how he may not have understood why at the meetings with Mr Wilson the reference to the particular case of the reported internment of people suspected of the Dublin/ Monaghan bombings was not pursued by the Irish side through this channel.

This seems to suggest that bureaucratic red tape can be blamed for the government's failure to make any moves whatsoever even to find out whether or not those people who operated in the other channel — the intelligence forces — had followed this matter up. Dr FitzGerald seems to want us to believe that the two bodies operated completely independently of each other and that the left hand did not know what the right hand was doing. This is absurd.

By suggesting that it was a lack of understanding of these matters that led to Mr Justice Barron's portrayal of his government as not having cared sufficiently about the bombings to act upon them, Dr FitzGerald seems to have undermined Mr Justice Barron's argument effectively.

However, nowhere in his article does he provide a reason for his inaction as a later Taoiseach or the 1974 government's inaction (Fine Gael and Labour stayed in government for three years after the bombings) in not having established any sort of inquiry into the bombings when it had become apparent that the Garda Síochána was not going to secure any convictions. In three years, there was no attempt to bring anyone to justice for the Dublin and Monaghan bombings.

If, as Dr Fitzgerald claims, it would have been better had an inquiry been held at an earlier stage — to negate the impact of faded memories, the deaths of witnesses and the loss of files — surely the best time for this would have been any time within the three years after the bombings when Fine Gael and Labour were still in government. Or is it simply a case that Mr Justice Barron was right? The government did not, in fact, care enough to follow up on the bombings.

Patrick Cooney, the Minister for Justice in 1974, was the last of the three ministers to give an opinion in the two weeks following the publication of the Barron Report. Rather than giving an interview, he issued a lengthy statement in which he attacked Mr Justice Barron for having suggested that the government did not show sufficient care about or interest in the victims of the bombings. Mr Cooney, like Dr FitzGerald, says that the lack of information available thirty years after the fact would impact greatly on any attempt to inquire into the bombings. That key personnel from the Department of Justice and the Garda Síochána are now dead, in his words, 'points up the futility of trying to inquire into events of so long ago'. Apart from the breathtaking political lassitude of his statement, in it Mr Cooney completely ignores the fact that an inquiry is taking place into the events of Bloody Sunday, and it is moving along quite successfully. There is no reason why a similar inquiry should not work for Dublin and Monaghan if the same criteria were applied.

Patrick Cooney also suggests that 'the allegation that the Government failed to apply political pressure is totally without foundation'. This, however, slightly distracts the reader from the fact that, although political pressure may have been applied, there was no attempt to exhaust every possibility open to the Fine Gael/Labour coalition at the time. Had every possibility been exhausted, a public tribunal of inquiry would have been established much earlier than it was.

Of course, these statements were to be expected from the cabinet ministers of the day. Very few men go to the gallows willingly, and these men were simply protecting their political lives and reputations. However, on 29 December, after three of his cabinet colleagues had attempted to dismiss the findings of the Barron Report, one former minister made known his opinion on Mr Justice Barron and the findings of his inquiry.

Justin Keating was the Minister for Industry and Commerce in 1974 — a fact which meant that he would not always have been party to cabinet discussions on the bombings. In fact, the only people who were party to those discussions were the Ministers for Justice, Defence, Posts and Telegraphs, Local Government and the Taoiseach — Patrick Cooney, Paddy Donegan, Conor Cruise O'Brien, Jim Tully and Liam Cosgrave, respectively. And two of those men had already given their opinions quite clearly, while Garret FitzGerald, who was Minister for Foreign Affairs at the time, and later became Taoiseach, had also made his views known. Justin Keating seemed almost embarrassed to have an opinion on the bombings even though his position in government at the time was not one which would have given him much of a view into the way the government handled the atrocity.

Justin Keating, it must also be noted, opted out of politics after twelve years. He made a decision not to run any more. Having served in both the Seanad and the Dáil, he simply quit. For almost thirty years, he held his silence on the bombings and the manner in which his cabinet colleagues had handled the investigation. It was almost twenty days after the issuing of the Barron Report before he did anything. He was finally inspired to speak out by the statements made by the other three men. Justin Keating, a man who had disagreed with Conor Cruise O'Brien over Northern Ireland on more than one occasion in cabinet, spoke out simply to balance the books.

He was unrepentant in his support of the findings of the Barron Report. He defended those findings and pointed out that Mr Justice Barron was hampered by his inability to state anything as fact unless the evidence was strong enough to stand up in a court of law:

> He makes meticulous distinction between fact on the one hand and probabilities or possibilities on the other hand.

This was the judge's remit and he could go no further than simply state what he had found. Keating, however, made the reader aware that no such limitations apply to the private citizen:

> Life is not like a court of law. We do not live and decide and act only on the basis of what we can prove to be true but on the basis of what we have strong reasons to believe to be true.
>
> Taking Mr Justice Barron's conclusions in order I offer the following comments and responses.
> — That the Garda investigation was inadequate. Yes, I believe that.
> — That they failed to involve the appropriate official, the Attorney General, in their decision on prosecution. Also true.
> — That the Government of the day (of which I was a member) showed little interest in the bombings. With great regret I have to say that this corresponds to my recollection. But as Minister for Industry and Commerce, known to disagree with Conor Cruise O'Brien about Northern Ireland, I was often excluded or bypassed on such matters.

The final of these points merits repetition here:

> That the Government of the day (of which I was a member) showed little interest in the bombings. With great regret I have to say that this corresponds to my recollection.

Thus Justin Keating punches a rather large hole in the statements made by his former cabinet colleagues, Garret FitzGerald, Conor Cruise O'Brien and Patrick Cooney. Claiming not to speak on behalf of the Security Committee set up in the aftermath of the bombings, nor even on behalf of those on the cabinet with a direct or indirect security remit, Keating had called his former colleagues' bluff. Justin Keating was Minister for

Industry and Commerce, not for Defence or for Justice, nor was he ever Taoiseach. He was simply a member of a government — indeed a member of a cabinet — that seemed to have no interest in what was and still is the greatest loss of life during the Troubles of Northern Ireland. Finally a politician from 1974 had come forward, not seeking to defend his own reputation, but to add his voice to the calls for a public tribunal of inquiry into the Dublin and Monaghan bombings.

# LIST OF THOSE KILLED IN THE BOMBINGS

Patrick Askin, Co. Monaghan
Josie Bradley, Co. Offaly
Marie Butler, Co. Waterford
Anne Byrne, Dublin
Thomas Campbell, Co. Monaghan
Simone Chetrit, France
Thomas Croarkin, Co. Monaghan
John Dargle, Dublin
Concepta Dempsey, Co. Louth
Collette and Baby Doherty, Dublin
Patrick Fay, Dublin and Co. Louth
Elizabeth Fitzgerald, Dublin
Breda Grace, Dublin and Co. Kerry
Archie Harper, Co. Monaghan
Antonio Magliocco, Dublin and Italy
May McKenna, Co. Tyrone
Anne Marren, Co. Sligo
Anna Massey, Dublin
Dorothy Morris, Dublin
John, Anna, Jacqueline and Anne-Marie O'Brien, Dublin
Christine O'Loughlin, Dublin

Edward O'Neill, Dublin
Baby Martha O'Neill, Dublin (stillborn)
Marie Phelan, Co. Waterford
Siobhán Roice, Wexford
Maureen Shields, Dublin
Jack Travers, Monaghan
Breda Turner, Co. Tipperary
John Walsh, Dublin
Peggy White, Monaghan Town
George Williamson, Co. Monaghan

# BIBLIOGRAPHY

Bowyer-Bell, J., *In Dubious Battle*, Poolbeg, 1996

Dillon, M., *The Dirty War*, Arrow, 1991

Herman and Chomsky, *Manufacturing Consent*, Vintage 1994

Mullan, D., *The Dublin and Monaghan Bombings*, Wolfhound, 2000

Rose, P., *How the Troubles Came to Northern Ireland*, Palgrave MacMillan, 2000

Tiernan, J., *The Dublin and Monaghan Bombings and the Murder Triangle*, self-published, 2002

**Newspapers**

*Belfast Telegraph*

*Evening Herald*

*Evening Press*

*Ireland on Sunday*

*Irish Independent*

*Irish Mirror*

*Irish Press*

*The Irish Times*

*Sunday Independent*

*Sunday Press*

*The Times*

**Other Publications**
*Dublin Diary*
*Magill*
*Now*
*The Phoenix*

**Documentaries**
'Hidden Hand – The Forgotten Massacre', Yorkshire Television

# INDEX

**A**

Ardagh, Sean, 207
Act of Union (1800), 13
Ackerman, Mark, 116, 121, 130
Ahern, Bertie, 142, 146, 166, 169, 175
Aid (financial), 70, 151, 168, *see also*
Compensation
Alliance Party, 19
Anglo-Irish Agreement, 124
Anniversaries, 64, 90, 91, 113
seventeenth, 106, 107, 112
twentieth, 129
twenty-eight, 166, 169
twenty-fifth, 141, 153
Arms Crisis 1970, 211
Armstrong, Gary, 189
Army Information Services
Department, 190
Arnotts, Henry Street, 100, *see also*
Henry Street
Askin, Patrick, 216

**B**

Ballagh, Robert, 138, 139
Barber shop, Parnell Street, 86, *see*
O'Sullivan, Liam
Barron, (Mr Justice Henry, Inquiry),
9, 166, 147, 148, 150, 151,
155, 166, 169, 172, 175-203,
205, *see also* Hamilton Inquiry

appointment of, 147, 148
report of, of, 62, 63, 97, 98-100,
102, 103, 127, 150, 151, 155,
165, 170, 203
aftermath of, 204-15
contents of, 130-136
Garda investigation and, 199,
200, *see* Garda Síochána
Part V, 130-136
Baxter's, 78
BBC, 114
Belfast (Good Friday) Agreement,
126, 142, 175, 205
*Belfast Telegraph*, 27
Bergin, Bernie, 152, 156-158, 163,
166, 167, 169, 170
Bergin, John, 156, 163
Big Tree Pub, 75
Birmingham Six, 114
Blaney, Neil, 17
Bennett, Joe, 187
Bloody Friday, 27, 52, 60
*Bloody Sunday* (Film), 139, 155, 156
Bloody Sunday (January 1972), 18,
59, 60, 139-141, 144, 155,
156, 159, 164, 166, 171, 212
Bombings, day of, 33-48, *see also*
Dublin bombings
media reaction to, 49-65, *see*
Media

Bowyer-Bell, John, 185, 218
*Boxing News*, 78
Boyle, Harris, 26, 131, 192
Bradley, Josie, 216
Bradley, Marion, 106
Bradshaw, George, 21
British Army, 14, 18, 24, 58, 60, 98,
    130, 131, 138, 154, 177, 179-
    184, 193-196, 199, 209
  aid of, 17
  allegations against, 193-195
  Bloody Sunday and, *see* Bloody
    Sunday
  collusion with paramilitaries, 49,
    132, 135
  Four-Square Laundry, *see* Four-
    Square Laundry
  infiltration of IRA by, 181, *see*
    IRA
  intelligence units, 177, 181, 184
  NCOs, 98, 101
  subversives within, 132
  use of friendly forces by, 132, 179
British Embassy, 59, 60
British Government, 11, 143, 166,
    211, *see also* Irish Government
    and RUC
  Bloody Sunday inquiry and, 139,
    *see also* Bloody Sunday
  compensation and, 124, *see also*
    Compensation
  complicity of, 177
  cover up by, 49
  files of, 166
  Home Rule and, 14
  Irish Question, 15
  response of to Barron inquiry,
    166, *see also* Barron
  responsibility of, 12
  revelations of, 24
  White Paper of, 18
Bruton, John, 129
B-Specials, 189
Burke, John, 154, 155
Burlington Hotel, Dublin, 23
Buswell's Hotel, Dublin, 124
Butler, Marie, 216

Butt, Isaac, 14
Byrne, Anne, 216, 106
Byrne, Derek, 87
Byrne, John, 116
Byrne, Michelle, 106, 124, 171

**C**
Cabinet Security Committee, 29, *see
    also* Irish Government
Cabra Garda Station, 124
Caffrey, Peter, 43
Caffrey's Sweets, 78
Campbell, Monica, 156
Campbell, Thomas, 216
Capel Street Library, 108
Caraher, Fergal, 129
Carlton Cinema, 28
Carruthers, James, 116
Carson, William, 15
Carver, Michael, 184
Catholics, 13-20, 24, 187, *see*
  Protestants
  Northern Irish, 15, 16, 19, 20
Cavendish Row, 100
Chetrit, Simone, 216
Chichester-Clarke, Major James, 17
Church Street martial arts club, 85
Civil rights, 16-18, 20, 60, 109, 129,
    161, *see also* Human Rights
    and NICRA
  marches, 16-18, 60
Clockwork Orange project, 190
Clonagh Allegations, 195-198
Coen, Martin, 37, 38
Cogan, James K., 197
Collin JT and Company, 90
Collins, Michael, 15, 60
Comiskey, Nora, 50, 108, 109, 129,
    138, 139, 171, 173
Commemorative masses, 106, 109
Commission of Inquiry into Dublin
    and Monaghan Bombings, *see*
    Barron and Hamilton
Compensation, 70, 151, *see* Aid,
    British Government and Irish
    Government
  joint compensation fund, 124

Condon, John, 114
Connolly, Frank, 170
Connolly, James, 14
Coogan, Tim Pat, 64, 153
Cooney, Paddy, 29, 212, 213, 214
Cooney, Patrick, 212
Coras Iompair Éireann (CIE), 25, 156
Cosgrave, Liam, 20, 21, 28, 29, 58, 196, 197, 213
Costello, Declan, Attorney General, 28, 60
Council of Ireland, 18, 19
Counter-insurgency, 179, 180
Craig, James, 15
Craig, William, 24
Crinnion, Patrick, 23
Croarkin, Thomas, 216
Cruise O'Brien, Conor, 26, 29, 110, 127, 208, 209, 213, 214
Cullen, Thomas, 138
Cullyhanna Inquiry, 129
Curragh Camp Military Prison, 29
Currie, Austin, 16

**D**

D'Arcy, Mrs, 35
Dargle, John, 216
De Róiste, Dónal, 196
De Valera, Eamon, 15
Dean Knox Young, Ivor, 187
Dempsey, Concepta, 216
Department of Industrial and Forensic Science, Belfast, 102
Department of Justice, 67, 117, 145, 151, 202, 205-207, 212
Department of Justice, Equality and Law Reform, 202
Department of Posts and Telegraphs, 26, 101, 154
Department of the Taoiseach, 146, 151, 153, 155, 167-170, 175
Dillon, Martin, 22, 23, 180, 218
Doherty, Collette and Baby, 137, 216
Doherty, Des, 164, 166, 167
Doherty, Eamon, 130
Doherty, Frank, 116

Dominic Street, 34, 38, 43, 66-75, 79, 81
Donegan, Paddy, 29, 213
Donnelley, Michael, 106
Donovan, Dr James, 102, 147, 198
Downing Street, No. 10, lobbying at, 156
Doyle, Paddy, 124
Doyle's Corner, Phibsboro, 121
Dublin bombings, 9-12, 22, 24, 49-54, 58, 63, 73, 96-98, 104, 109, 112, 114-118, 121, 124, 127-130, 134, 135, 138, 140-147, 158, 161, 175-179, 184, 192, 193-197, 201-208, *see also* Monaghan bombings
*Dublin Diary*, 116, 218
Duffy, Monica, 164
Duffy, Thomas, 21
Dundalk, 23
    bombings, 9
    Special Branch office in, 203

**E**

Easter Rising, 1916, 14, 15
Economy (1970s), 67
Éire, 15
Elisabeth I, 13
Enniskillen Remembrance Day bombing, 109
Ervine, David, 177, 197
European Commission, 138, 139, 142, 143
*Evening Herald*, 42, 43, 124
*Evening Press*, 43, 44
Explosions, 25-27, *see also* Bombings and Dublin bombings aftermath, 28-32
Extradition, 22, 23,124

**F**

Family Service Support Centre, 148, 159, 169, 170
Family Support programme, Director of, 159, *see also* Grealy, Aine
Faul, Fr Denis, 106
Faulkner, Brian, 19

Fay, Mrs, 113
Fay, Patrick, 216, 164, 171
Fay, Patrick, 26, 111
Fianna Fáil, 12, 20, 21, 30, 128, 130
Fine Gael, 15, 20, 21, 58, 62, 128, 129, 212
Fine Gael/Labour coalition, 21, 128, 208, 213
Finucane, Pat, 145
*First Tuesday* programme, 114, 117, 126, 184
Fisk, Robert, 24, 54, 190
Fitt, Gerry, 17, 19
Fitzgerald, Elizabeth, 216
FitzGerald, Garrett, 25, 117, 196-198, 209-212, 214
Flannagan, Ronnie, 147
Four-Square Laundry, 180-183
Forensics, 101-104
    investigation of, 102-104

**G**
Garda Commissioner, 124, 126, 130, 147, 156
Gardaí Síochána, 56, 57
    bizarre behaviour of, 97
    evidence of, 31, 53, 63, 101, 102, 210
    files of, 133, 134, 142
    headquarters, 101, 102, 112
    intelligence information and, 177
    interviews by, 188, 189
    investigation by, 10, 11, 29, 31, 52, 53, 58, 97, 98, 131, 135, 139, 142, 143, 153, 199, 200, 202, 205, *see also* RUC
    knowledge of, 29, 31, 53, 56, 63
    negligence of, 100
    Security and Intelligence (C3), 202
    Special Branch, 23
    Special Detective Unit, 202
Garden of Remembrance, 92, 106, 112
Geoghegan-Quinn, Marie, 128
Glasnevin Cemetery, 79
Glennane group, 187, 188

Good Friday Agreement, 32, 126, 142, 205
GPO, 59, 110, 127
Grace, Breda, 142, 216
Grace, Tim, 113, 142, 161, 162, 164, 171
Grealy, Áine, 89, 149, 159, 163
Greengrass, Paul, 155
Gregory, Tony, 112
Guildford Four, 114
Guiney's, Talbot Street, 26, 27
Gun running, 17, 18

**H**
Hamilton, Chief Justice Liam, Inquiry, 9, 97, 146-148, 150, 176, 200, 201, *see also* Barron
Hanna, Billy, 26, 98, 131, 187, 192
Hall, Dr HA, 102, 147, 198
Harper, Archie, 216
Haughey, Charles, 17, 107, 112
Haughey, Sean, 112
Herman and Chomsky, 218
Henry Street, 100
Healy, John (Backbencher), 59, 60
Herman, Edward, 50
'Hidden Hand, the Forgotten Massacre', 61-63, 114-136, 137, 152, 201, 205, 208, 218, *see* Yorkshire television and Middleton, Glyn
    aftermath of, 128-136, 141
High Court, 124, 139, 147
Holroyd, Fred, 130, 135, 136, 186, 193-915
Home Rule, 13, 14
Human Rights, 109, 138, *see also* Civil rights

**I**
Illac Centre Library, 111
Information Policy Unit, 190
Insurance, 71, 72
IRA, 15, 18, 22, 29, 38, 54, 56, 62, 109, 110, 187, 190, 191
    Anglo Irish Agreement and, 15, *see* Anglo-Irish Agreement

blaming, 21, 28-30, 54-56, 58-60
border campaign by, 17
campaign of terror by, 111
Company D, 181, 182
condemnation of, 58
explosives used by, 196, 197
killings by, 131, 180
lead up to bombings and, 24
Official IRA, *see* Official IRA
official targets of, 24
operations, 181
Provisional IRA, *see* Provisional
    IRA
spies and, 180, 181
split of, 17
volunteers for, 181
*Ireland on Sunday*, 154, 218
Irish Army Explosive Ordnance
    Disposal team, 103
Irish Ferries, 156
Irish Free State, 15
Irish Government, 11, 131, 143, 192,
    204, 205, *see also* British
    Government and Cabinet
    Security Committee
aid, 70, 71, 88, *see also* Aid and
    Compensation
condemnation of, 206
cover up by, 49
inquiry and, 134, 136-139, 141-
    147, 175, 176, 192, 200, 201,
    203, 206, 207-215, *see also*
    Barron and Hamilton
inaction of, 138, 200
reaction of, 28-30, 56, 200
victims commission and, 142, *see*
    Victims' Commission
*Irish Independent*, 51, 52, 54, 61, 218
    *see also* Media
Irish Industrial Explosives factory,
    196, *see* Clonagh allegations
*Irish Mirror*, 166, 167, 170
Irish National Congress (INC), 108,
    109, 129, 137-138, 173
*Irish Press*, 51-54, 57, 60-64, 218, *see*
    *also* Media
Irish Question, 15

Irish State laboratory, 102, 198
*Irish Times*, 26, 27, 51-54, 59, 61-63,
    209, 2178, *see also* Media
ITV, 62, 114, *see also* Media

**J**
Jackson, Robin (the Jackal), 26, 97,
    131, 187, 188, 192, 208
James I, 13
Jervis Street Hospital, 40, 42, 44, 46
'Jock-Clock,' 103
Joint Oireachtas Committee on
    Justice, Equality, Defence and
    Women's Rights, 9, 10, 146,
    200
remit of, 9, 10
Report of, 10
Justice for the Forgotten(JFF), 49, 89,
    134, 137-174, 175
administrative functions of, 151
AGMs, 148, 160-163, 167, 168
constitution of, 169, 170
funding, 138
legal team of, 138, 143, 146, 147,
    150-153, 157, 164, 169, 171,
    172, 174, *see also* O'Neill, Greg
    and Ó Dulacháin, Cormac
limited company as, 151, 167
workshop, Writers' Museum, 152
Joy, Suprinitendnet John, 99

**K**
Keane, Roger, 154, 155
Keating, Justin, 213, 214
Kerr, RJ, 187, 188
Kerry, Robert, 192
Kevin Street, 59
Kildare Street bombing (1972), 30
Kilkenny Incest case, 145
Kincora Boys' Home, 190
King's Inn Street Convent, 43
Kitson, Frank, 179, 180, 183
Komac, Ed, 102, 103

**L**
Labour Party (England) 17, 19, 191
Labour Party (Ireland), 21, 58, 128,

208, 212
Lawlor-Watson, Phil, 164
Leinster House, 21, 26
Lemass, Sean, 15
Liffey Pub, Eden Quay, Dublin, 21
Littlejohn, Keith, 22, 23, 116
Littlejohn, Kenneth, 22, 23, 116
Londonderry Development
    Commission, 16
Loyalist Paramilitaries, 20, 22, 26, 29,
    36, 49, 53, 177, 179, 183-186,
    190-193, 197, 205, 206, see
    also Paramilitaries
    guilt of, 177-183
Lynch, Jack, 17, 20

**M**
*Magill*, 196, 218
Magliocco, Antonio, 216
Magliocco, Mrs, 40
Mallon, Seamus, 142
Marchant William 'Frenchie,' 116
Marlborough House, 154
Marlborough Street, 154
Marren, Anne, 26, 111, 216
Massey, Anna, 216
Massey, Frank, 124, 140, 161
Mater Hospital, 93
McCaughey, William, 186, 187
McClure, Lawrence, 188
McConnell, Robert, 131, 192
McDowell, Michael, 146
McGregor, Captain, 181
McKee, Kevin, 182, 183
McKenna, May, 216
McNally, Bernie, 156, 164, 169, 171
McNally, John, 156
McPhelimy, Sean, 188
Media,
    coverage of day of bombings by,
        52, see also bombings
    family reaction to, 63-65
    radio, influence of, 50, 51
    reaction, 49-65
    responsibility to inform public, 51
    TV, influence of, 50, 51

Yorkshire television, see Hidden
    Hand and Yorkshire Television
Memorial Stone, 106, 107
MI5, 20, 30, 191
MI6, 22, 23, 191, 192
Miami Showband, 26
Middleton, Glyn, 99, 104, 114-136,
    146, 147, see also Hidden Hand
Mitchell, Billy, 192
Mitchell, Gay, Lord Mayor, 62
Mitchell, James, 188, 189
Monaghan Bombings (North Street),
    9-12, 22, 24, 49-54, 58, 63,
    73, 96-98, 104, 109, 112, 114-
    118, 121, 124, 127-130, 134,
    135, 138, 140-147, 158, 161,
    175-179, 184, 192, 193-197,
    201-208, see also Dublin
    bombings
Morgan, John, 103, 116, 117, 130
Morris, Dorothy, 216
Mulholland, David Alexander, 99,
    100, 134
Mullan, Don, 22, 30, 99, 102, 103,
    139-141, 143, 146, 147, 152-
    160, 171, 178, 179, 195-198,
    201, 218
Mussen, Garrett, 156, 164

**N**
Nairac, Robert, 98, 132
Nassau Street, 100
Nationalist Party, 14
Nesbitt, James
Newtownards bombing, 62
Nixon, President Richard, 49, 50
North Bull Island, 77
North Strand, German raid on, 29,
    53
Northern Catholics, 15, see Catholics
Northern Ireland Civil Rights
    Association (NICRA), 16, see
    Civil rights and Human rights
Northern Ireland, creation of, 15
Northern Ireland, status of in UK, 18
*Now* magazine, 116, 218

**O**

Ó Dulacháin, Cormac, 138, 144, 145, 156, 157, 169, 171, 175, *see also* Justice for the Forgotten (JFF) and O'Neill, Greg

O'Brien, Alice, 137, 156, 164

O'Brien, Anna, 137, 216

O'Brien, Anne-Marie, 216

O'Brien, Jacqueline, 216

O'Brien, John, 216

O'Brien, Michelle, 156

O'Connell Street, 28

O'Donoghue, John, 139, 151

O'Leary, Olivia, 127

O'Loughlin, Christine, 216

O'Malley, Des, 20

O'Neill (née Caffrey), Martha, 38, 41-48, 64, 67-74, 77-80, 82, 104, 113, 118, 125, 140, 166, 173, 208

O'Neill, Angela, 33, 34, 38, 39, 43, 44, 61, 70, 71, 74, 83-85, 96, 104-106, 108, 110-113, 118, 121, 124, 125, 140, 141, 156, 161, 162, 164, 165, 171, 205, 208

O'Neill, baby Martha, 46, 47, 69, 77, 140, 217

O'Neill, Billy, 11, 33-48, 68, 69, 71, 73, 80, 82, 84, 91, 92, 104

O'Neill, Denise, 34, 35, 38, 40-42, 44-48, 61, 66-70, 80-83, 96, 104-108, 111-113, 118-122, 140, 149, 150, 156, 161, 163-165, 171, 172, 173, 204-207

O'Neill, Edward, 11, 33-48, 68, 69, 71, 73, 74, 80, 90, 90-95, 97, 104, 108, 124, 166-170, 173

O'Neill, Edward, Senior (Eddie), 11, 33-48, 66-70, 76-95, 100, 172, 204, 217

O'Neill, Greg, 138, 149, 153-155, 162, 164, 170-173, *see also* Justice for the Forgotten(JFF) and Ó Dulacháin, Cormac

O'Neill, Niall, 34, 35, 38, 70, 104, 164

O'Neill, Patrick (Whacker), 48

O'Neill, Terence, 15-17

O'Sullivan, Liam, 35, 36, 85-90

O'Toole, Mavis, 40, 108

Offences Against the State, 20, 21

Official IRA, 24, *see* IRA

Official Sinn Féin, 17, *see* Sinn Féin

Omagh bomb 1998, 140, 171

Our Lady's Hospital, 72

Owen, Nora, 129, 205

**P**

Paramilitaries, 17, 20, 22, 26, 29, 32, 36, 49, 53, 55, 58, 98, 104, 132, 136, 147, 177, 179-186, 190-193, 197, 205, 209, *see also* IRA, Loyalists, UDA and UVF

Parnell Mooney Pub, 94

Parnell Street, 11, 26, 27, 35, 38, 39, 43, 44, 51-53, 67, 69, 74, 79, 86, 99, 100, 102, 111, 137, 153, 176

Parnell, Charles Stewart, 14

Payne, David, 187

Pearse, Pádraig, 14

Phelan, Marie, 217

*Phoenix* magazine, 203, 218

Portland Court, 75, 96

Portlaoise Prison, 29, 138

Post-traumatic stress disorder (PTSD), 91, 159

Powderface, Miss, 93, 94

Pringle, Peter, 138

Protestant Action Force, 187

Protestants, 13, 15, 16, 19, 53-56, 184, 187, *see* Catholics

Provisional IRA, 18, 24, 110, *see also* IRA

Provisional Sinn Fein, 17, *see* Sinn Féin

Public Accounts Committee Inquiry, 146

PUP, 177, 197

**R**

Red hand Brigade, 187
Red hand Commandos, 187
Redhead, Mark, 155
Redmond, John, 14
Rees, Merlyn, 19, 24, 25, 130, 132
Reid, John, 166, 184, 202
Relatives for Justice, 106, 124
Reynolds, Albert, 128
Rhodesia, 194
Robinson, President Mary, 112
Roice, Siobhán, 217
Rose, P, 218
Rotunda Hospital, 42
Royal Dublin Hotel, 121
Royal Victoria Hospital,
    Southampton, 193
RTÉ, 63, 103, 116, 119
RUC(Royal Ulster Constabulary), *see
    also* British Army
    access to records of, 134
    Barron Inquiry and, 199
    British army and, 17
    Castlereagh Station, 182
    complicity of, 177
    files of, 188
    forensics lab, 30, see also Forensics
    interviews by, 30, 189
    investigation, 16, 17, 31, 52, 53,
        56-58, 61, 97, 98, 103, 135,
        143, *see also* Garda Síochána
    links with Protestant extremists,
        184,
    links with MI5, 191, *see* MI5
    sectarianism in, 31
    paramilitaries and, 197, *see also*
        Paramilitaries
    reform of, 19
    Special branch officers, 131, 191,
        192

**S**

Sackville Place, 21
SAS, 24, 30, 112
Scott, William, 36
*Schindler's List*, 76
Sectarianism, 31, *see also* RUC

Security Committee (1974), 29, 208,
    209, 214
Shields, Lily, 188
Shields, Maureen, 217
Sinn Féin, 17, 22, *see* Official Sinn
    Féin and Provisional Sinn Féin
    Ard Fheis, 1972, 22
    lifting of ban on, 24
    Office, Kevin Street, 59, 60
    split of, 17
Smellie, Craig, 192
Social Democratic Labour Party
    (SDLP), 17, 19
Somerville, John, 187
Sommerville, Wesley, 26, 187
South Leinster Street, 26, 29, 51,
    111, 152, 176
Special Patrol Group (SPG), 186
Special powers (Northern Ireland, 16
St Anne's Park, 77
St Mary's Christian Brothers School,
    73
St Saviour's Church, Dublin, 44
St Vincent's School, Glasnevin, 108
Stack, Dr, 73
Stalker affair, 114, 125
Stormont Assembly, 16
Strathearn, William, 187
Styles, Colonel George, 130
*Sunday Independent*, 31, 55, 56, 57,
    62, 121, 122, 218
*Sunday Press*, 57, 62, 218
Sunningdale Agreement, 19, 20, 32,
    132, 191
Supreme Court, 139, 143, 147, 200
Sutherland, Linda, 166, 169, 170

**T**

*The Times*, 24
Trinity College, Dublin, 26
Tiernan, Joe, 98, 99, 103, 116, 119-
    125, 130, 137, 178, 205, 218
Talbot Street, 26, 27, 39, 51, 52, 59,
    137, 142, 176
Tara Street, 44
Troubles (Northern Ireland), 18, 26,
    30, 38, 57, 58, 76, 77, 96, 103,

104, 116, 119, 151, 161, 185, 190, 191, 206, 215
Trears, Patrick, 130
Tully, Jim, 29, 213
Travers, Mick, 94
*Today Tonight*, 116, 119
Travers, Jack, 217
Turner, Breda, 217
TV3, 141, 144, 154

**U**
UFF, 31, 55, 57
Ulster Defence Association (UDA), 20, 24, 31, 55, 57, 117, 187, 202
Ulster Defence Regiment (UDR), 26, 108, 131, 184, 188
Ulster Plantation (1609), 13
Ulster Special Constabulary (B-Specials), 189
Ulster Unionist Council (UUC), 19
Ulster Unionist Party (UUP), 15, 18, 19
Ulster Volunteer Force (UVF), 20, 24-26, 29, 31, 33, 55, 57-59, 61, 62, 99, 103, 110, 117, 119, 131, 132, 177, 192, 196, 197
    admission of guilt by, 184-187
    bombings, *see* explosions
    lifting of ban on, 24
    mission of, 26
Ulster Worker's Council (UWC), 20, 24, 32
Ulster Workers' Councils strike 1974, 191
Ulster, 13, 15, 18
Unionists, 15-19, 24, 25, *see* Vanguard Unionist Party
United Ulster Unionist Council (UUUC), 19, 20
Urwin, Margaret, 129, 138, 139, 145, 157, 158, 160, 161, 168, 169, 171, 173

**V**
Vanguard Unionist Party, 18, 24, *see* Unionists
Victims' Commission, 126, 142, 144,

175, 200, 201, 204-206
Victims' Commissioner, 126, 206, *see* Wilson, John
Victims' rights, 142

**W**
Wade, Jacqueline (Jackie), 124, 137, 164
Wallace, Colin, 130, 135, 136, 186, 189-193
Walsh, John, 217
Walsh, Kevin, 103, 106, 107, 108, 165
Walshe, Patrick, 196, 198
Warrington, 112
Watson, Alan, 27, 28
Weir, John, 135, 136, 153, 154, 186-188, 193, 197
Welcome Inn, pub, 35, 36
West, Harry, 19
Westminster, lobbying at, 156
Whelan, Ken, 154
White Paper (1973), 18
White, Peggy, 217
Widgery Tribunal, 139
Williamson, George, 217
Wilson, Gordon, 109
Wilson, Harold, 17
Wilson, John, 126, 142-144, 151, 175, 204, 206, 207, 211
Wilson, Marie, 109
Woodward and Bernstein, 49
World Trade Centre tragedy, September 11, 2001, 160
World War I, 14
World War II, 29, 53
Wright, Seamus, 181-183
Wyman, John (aka Douglas Smyth), 23
Wynn's Hotel, Abbey Street, 120

**Y**
Young, Stewart, 187, 192
Yorkshire Television, 49, 63, 64, 103, *see also* Media
    Documentary by (Hidden Hand), 61-63, 114-136, *see* Hidden Hand